CHICAGO PUBLIC LIBRARY
SULZER REGIONAL
4455 N. LINCOLN AVE.   60625

D0559868

THE
WIDENING
CIRCLE

THE
WIDENING
CIRCLE

A Lyme Disease Pioneer
Tells Her Story

POLLY MURRAY

ST. MARTIN'S PRESS ✿ NEW YORK

To all who are trying to get well

THE WIDENING CIRCLE: A LYME DISEASE PIONEER
TELLS HER STORY. Copyright © 1996 by Polly Murray. All
rights reserved. Printed in the United States of America. No
part of this book may be used or reproduced in any manner
whatsoever without written permission except in the case of
brief quotations embodied in critical articles or reviews. For
information, address St. Martin's Press, 175 Fifth Avenue, New
York, N.Y. 10010.

Owing to limitations of space, permission to reprint previously
published material may be found following the Notes.

Library of Congress Cataloging-in-Publication Data

Murray, Polly.
    The widening circle : a Lyme disease pioneer tells her
story / by Polly Murray.
        p.   cm.
    ISBN 0-312-14068-1
    1. Murray, Polly—Health   2. Lyme disease—Patients—
Connecticut—Lyme—Biography.   3. Lyme disease—History.   I. Title.
RC155.5.M87   1996
362.1'9692—dc20
[B]   95-47395
                                                          CIP

First Edition: April 1996

10   9   8   7   6   5   4   3   2   1

R01088 84360

CONTENTS

PART ONE:
FOCUSING ON LYME DISEASE

CHICAGO PUBLIC LIBRARY
SULZER REGIONAL
4455 N. LINCOLN AVE. 60625

CONTENTS

PART TWO:
THE SCOPE BROADENS

ACKNOWLEDGMENTS

I could not have written this book without the help of my family and friends. I would like to thank my daughter, Wendy, for her editorial assistance and support every step of the way and my sons, Sandy, David, and Todd, who were always willing to critique the manuscript in its various stages of development. Todd and Wendy gave me great help in clarifying my writing in a number of chapters. I also value the generous cooperation of my former husband, Gil, who gave me his notes on his illness in order to aid me in the writing of the book.

I am grateful to the many wonderful people I've met since 1975 who have dedicated their lives to understanding Lyme disease. I have enjoyed working with the members of the Lyme Disease Awareness Task Force here in Connecticut.

A number of people have helped by reading and editing the manuscript or by sending me news accounts from across the country. For this invaluable advice and support, I thank my sister, Nina, and my sister-in-law, Dede; Lucinda Webb; Dr. Jenifer Nields; Dr. Brian Fallon; Ann and Dick Behrman; Tedi Cavicke; Joy Molloy; Betty Gross; Marilyn Reynolds; Michele Wyrebek; Deborah Purcell; Phyllis Schneider; Alison Ainsworth; and Kay McGrath. My Mount Holyoke friends, Pam Herrick, Liz Hall, Mary McHenry, and Jean Snyder, have all encouraged me over the years, and I am forever appreciative.

Thanks also to my agent, William Goodman, to my editor, Jennifer Weis of St. Martin's Press, and to her assistant, Tina Lee, who have all steered my course through the complicated process of putting a book together.

—POLLY LUCKETT MURRAY
Lyme, Connecticut

FOREWORD

I first met Polly Murray in the lunch line at the First Annual Yale Conference on Lyme Disease in 1988. Until reading *The Widening Circle* I had no idea of her personal medical odyssey or of the determined and protracted battle the soft-spoken Mrs. Murray had waged to marshal the resources of government and academia in her quest to identify the mystery ailment that was afflicting her, her family, and her neighbors.

To me, the title *The Widening Circle* is a triple entendre referring to the pathognomonic skin rash, erythema migrans; the ever-increasing circle of persons affected by Lyme disease; and the expanding range of manifestations associated with the illness. Mrs. Murray's experience with the World Health Organization, her ability to access medical literature, and her personal curiosity and intellectual interest in medicine made her particularly suited to transmute what might merely have been a dead end of illness and misery into a new chapter in the annals of the history of medicine.

It seems likely from her account that Polly Murray may have suffered for twenty years from the disease that was discovered (or, if you will, rediscovered) in 1975 and reported by Allen C. Steere and his colleagues. Those early heady days of multidisciplinary collaboration are summed up in a self-congratulatory preface to a Massachusetts Medical Society compilation as a "triumph for medicine and for society." In retrospect, these claims seem premature, and medical science is only just beginning to realize that the pathogen, thought to be so easily vanquished by antibiotics, is a far more formidable foe.

Lyme disease can be a kafkaesque nightmare for patients. It is still not uncommon for patients to have to hack their way through a tangle of underbrush to find the trail originally blazed by Mrs. Murray. Diagnosis can be difficult, and despite the insistence of the Centers for Disease Control that Lyme disease is a clinical diagnosis, it is not unusual for patients with unequivocal histories indicating Lyme disease to be told by physicians that they do not have the illness because tests are negative. This does not take into account the frequently desultory human immune response to the infection, or the fact that some seronegative patients, those whose immune systems may be blind-sided by the bacterium, may be most ill with Lyme disease. Should a diagnosis be made, efforts to secure adequate treatment may be stymied by a standard of care, presently upheld by the majority of the medical profession, based on obsolete concepts, out of touch with the biological reality of the disease, and scientifically, therapeutically, and morally bankrupt. Change of this standard is badly needed.

The barriers faced by patients with Lyme disease, which exist to this day, highlight Mrs. Murray's courage and tenacity. The story of Lyme disease is still unfolding. At once it is a story of triumph of the human spirit, and of scientific discovery and medical achievement—but also of ignorance, arrogance, and human folly. Polly Murray's valuable contribution documents how one person's dedication made a difference and has helped to change the course of human history.

—KENNETH B. LIEGNER, M.D.,
Armonk, New York

INTRODUCTION

People who know me would describe me as a private person; it is only after considerable deliberation that I decided to write this book about my experience with Lyme disease, and in doing so, reveal details about a difficult period in my life and the life of my family. Though the years during which my family struggled with improperly diagnosed illness were trying for us, I would like to acknowledge that many patients have had far more serious consequences of the disease than my family has experienced. For a certain number of Lyme disease patients the disease is severe and can incapacitate them for many years. Compared with these patients, we have been fortunate.

I am also compelled to tell our detailed story because the frustrating diagnostic problems that our family encountered are still being faced by many new victims of Lyme disease today, despite the nearly twenty years of medical progress since the initial investigation of Lyme disease in 1975. I receive many telephone calls from people who haven't been diagnosed swiftly enough or at all. Perhaps when doctors and health care workers are educated sufficiently about the disease, and public awareness and public health measures increase, the number of these cases will diminish, and prompt diagnosis and treatment will prevail. Too many people, even some in the scientific field, still minimize the problem of Lyme disease.

The purpose of my book is to tell the story of a disease from the viewpoint of the patient, and to emphasize that what patients tell their doctors can be important in the diagnostic procedure. The doctor who enters the examining room to see a patient is armed with knowledge. He or she has been trained to observe disease. The patient is armed with a different type of knowledge—that of experiencing the disease, of living within the disease. When these two perspectives are brought into balance, good medical caretaking ensues.

Too often physicians are unwilling or don't have time to listen carefully to the patient. Some only value what a patient says in response to a specific question. Often doctors' questions are meant to narrow down the possible diagnoses on the basis of the doctor's knowledge of the various diseases the patient may have. That many physicians lack adequate knowledge of Lyme disease means important questions may not be asked, and perhaps what the doctor sees as irrelevant information coming from the patient is in fact pertinent to diagnosis.

Moreover, the effect a disease has on a patient can also alter the patient's relationship with the physician. Lyme disease is horrible not only because of its symptoms, but also because of the effect the symptoms have on how the patient relates to the doctor. The Lyme patient may be so profoundly affected with myriad devastating symptoms—including some that affect personality, level of anxiety, and ability to express and present oneself—that he or she may come across to the physician as fixated on a diagnosis, or as having symptoms rooted in anxiety or psychiatric problems, and be dismissed. Thus one of the nightmares of Lyme disease is that the disease can make you sick in a way that makes some physicians not want to treat you as you need to be treated.

In recent years doctors have written accounts about how their attitudes changed dramatically after they themselves became patients. The frustrations and discomfort of being a patient made them realize the inadequacy of their prior simplistic view of illness as a mere collection of signs and symptoms to be identified and treated in a rote manner. They realize that being listened to and getting comfort are important parts of the healing process, and that often a patient's experience of disease may not match the textbook set of signs and symptoms.

Proliferating medical technology and tests have clouded the art of listening to patient histories for diagnostic clues. Physicians have become overreliant on tests at the expense of listening to patients' stories. Test results can sometimes be wrong, as has been found in Lyme disease.

Specialization may hinder diagnosis, because specialists have a narrowed point of view. They may not see or hear about the full range of the patient's complaints. Especially in the case of infectious disease, the patient's complete story is very important. Perhaps in the future new clinical centers comprising a broad range of doctors could evaluate difficult-to-diagnose patients. Similarities among these undiagnosables might be recognized and patterns of disease might emerge. This might foster the discovery of other new or overlooked diseases.

I feel that those doctors who practice in areas where Lyme disease is prevalent and who see cases over a long period of time, or who have had the disease themselves, may have a clearer picture of the disease than those in large medical centers. It comes down to close, hands-on experience.

Over the years some people would ask me, "What is the matter that you keep getting bitten by ticks year after year? Why can't you take more precautions? Why haven't you moved?" At times I had thought about moving away from the Lyme area; however, several considerations made me decide against it. The disease is a risk all along the coastline in the Northeast, so if I were to move to a new community, I might get bitten there just as easily. Also, I am drawn to the shore. I have a great attachment to the ocean and Long Island Sound. I love my garden, studio, and friends here in the lower Connecticut River Valley. And so I have decided to stay in Lyme and try to find ways to deal with the problems associated with Lyme disease. I have taken measures to cut down on ticks—I've used repellents, cut grass short, cleared land of brush, and worn protective clothing—but despite that I have been infected, just as many others have who live in endemic areas.

Our family story is based on medical records, personal notes, yearly calendars, telephone conversations, medical journal articles, scrapbooks containing media coverage clipped out since 1976, and the collective memories of the family. Although we have no way of knowing for certain which symptoms and illnesses we experienced during the 1960s and early 1970s were actually Lyme disease, I decided to include almost all of the unusual family ailments I had recorded. I did this because Lyme disease is a relatively new disorder, still being described by the medical profession.

Yearly more and more symptoms are being related to the illness. In retrospect, it seems clear that at least some of our early symptoms were probably attributable to Lyme disease.

During the years when I was searching for an answer to our family's mysterious symptoms, Lyme disease, of course, was an unknown. Doctors were at first stumped as to how to explain our family's ailments, but they worked to the best of their abilities to solve our health problems.

Out of a wish to protect the privacy of individuals whom I know and respect, I have given fictitious names to some of the dramatis personae, and have left other players unnamed, in instances where I deemed that the words said were more important than knowing who, precisely, spoke them. I have tried to recreate conversations to the best of my ability.

I decided to go forward with the book for all those whom I don't know as well—people who may still be in the throes of Lyme disease, with or without the comfort of a definitive diagnosis, as well as those weighed down with other illnesses that are still misunderstood. I hope that my book opens doors for others, as Henrietta Aladjem's *The Sun Is My Enemy* (an account of her search for a diagnosis of her disease, lupus) did for me.

PART ONE

FOCUSING ON LYME DISEASE

Even though what is discovered has always been there, the scientist seeing it for the first time has the sense of calling it into being, and thus of belonging not only to the moment of discovery but also to the fact discovered and even to the scientists who will study it next.

JUNE GOODFIELD, *AN IMAGINED WORLD: A STORY OF SCIENTIFIC DISCOVERY*[1]

During the 1960s and 1970s, my husband, four children, and I were periodically plagued with mysterious symptoms. In time, I came to suspect that these ailments were somehow linked.

From the earliest hints during this time that unusual physical problems were affecting some people in the area of Lyme, Connecticut, to the First International Symposium on Lyme Disease at Yale University Medical School in 1983, I chronicled the identification of this puzzling infection. After 1975, when the disease was initially reported, more and more people became involved in an intense search for answers to the puzzle of Lyme disease.

By 1983, many of the physicians (they came from the United States and Europe and represented nearly every medical specialty), microbiologists, entomologists, veterinarians, epidemiologists, and public health officials gathered to share their knowledge at Yale University Medical School.

CHAPTER ONE

"SEE WHAT YOU STARTED?"

Early in the morning of November 16, 1983, I left my rural home in a heavily wooded area of Lyme, Connecticut, and made the sixty-minute drive to New Haven. It was a drive I'd made what seems like thousands of times before; I knew every turn and dip in the road we live on, every exit on I-95. Three of my four children were born in New Haven. But that hour's drive was entirely different; even the torrential rainstorm I encountered seemed to attest to it. It wasn't the road that had changed, of course, but my destination: I was on my way to attend the First International Symposium on Lyme Disease.

Maneuvering in the rush-hour traffic, I thought back to the times a dozen years earlier when I was so terribly alone and bewildered, desperate for a diagnosis and a cure for my baffling symptoms. As I pulled out of the Branford toll booth I looked in my rearview mirror, as though to make sure those hard times were indeed behind me, as though I could somehow see them receding in the distance. I was nervous about the upcoming conference, but greatly relieved, too, by the tremendous progress that had been made in Lyme disease research. I glanced at the map of New Haven and the directions to the conference laid out on the seat next to me. I was to go to the Hope Building at the Yale University Medical School on Cedar Street. It was familiar territory. The Hope Building is just beyond the Yale Medical Library at the Yale University School of Medicine, where I had spent many hours. I remembered how I had felt like a trespasser there as I timidly walked through the rotunda and down the stately hall, studying, as much as I dared, the impressive oil portraits of eminent doctors and the display cases of antique medical instruments and journals. I had gone there in search of answers. Tucked away in the stacks of the library, poring over medical texts, I had hoped to find some overlooked clue, some disease description that would mirror the symptoms I had—the mysterious rashes, the terrible fatigue, aches, swelling, and fevers. I was so tired in those days, so tired of asking, "What is the matter with me?" only to be told again and again that my symptoms fit no known disease.

As I parked my car and entered the Hope Building for the conference, I couldn't escape the sense that I had become a part of an unbelievable saga, one that I could not possibly have foreseen during my years of despair.

Dr. Allen C. Steere, then an associate professor of medicine at Yale and the chief investigator of Lyme disease, and Elise Taylor, a clinical studies researcher at the Yale Lyme Disease Clinic, came to greet me after I registered. There was a whir of introductions and brief conversations, and people began to take their seats in the large lecture hall. I found a chair and sat down, rather exhilarated by the scope of it all. More doctors gradually took their seats as well. Some had traveled from great distances and foreign lands; others came directly from duty in nearby hospitals, and were still wearing their white coats and beepers. I scanned the room, looking for familiar faces; I had met so many doctors and researchers in the course of Lyme disease's unfolding. I was afraid I'd meet the gaze of some doctor who had previously told me, "It's all in your head." I heard someone say, "How are you, Polly?" and turned around, pleased to see Dr. Stephen Malawista coming toward me. He was then professor of medicine and chief of rheumatology at Yale. I stood up to greet him. He shook my hand, welcoming me, and quietly said, "See what you started?" breaking out into his usual big grin as he gestured at the assembled crowd. I felt overwhelmed.

To reach this point had taken a great deal of effort, and I feel that the tale of my journey is worth telling. I tread lightly, still afraid of how things will turn out in the final analysis, realizing that I am part of an unfolding story—one that began years ago in an unrecognized form. In any event, now we will learn from whatever course the story takes because we are aware and questioning and our minds are open. As is true of most events in history, it is only by knowing intimately the conditions that preceded a cultural, political, or scientific advance, that we can fully appreciate the ground gained, the knowledge found. It is not often that one can look back and point to a specific time and place that truly altered one's life. But I can honestly say there was a pivotal point for me and my family: It occurred on October 16, 1975, when I made a phone call to the State of Connecticut's Department of Health Services. I remember telling my husband, Gil, as I gathered my notes and headed for the telephone in the study, that I felt it would be a very important call. But it wasn't until I began to dial the number that it hit me what a lonely call I was about to make. Would it lead nowhere? Would I again be misunderstood?

As it turned out, the call was indeed important—well worth the trepidation—but before going further with the story, I will recount the events leading up to that call, that turning point.

CHAPTER TWO

ART AND MEDICINE

The most that the scientist and the artist accomplish is new understanding of things that have always been. They "create" a clearer perception. They are both, in this sense, observers, the obvious difference being that the scientist impersonally describes the external world, whereas the artist expresses the effects which external things exert upon his own mind and heart. In both cases, the more generally applicable the observations, the greater is the science or art.

HANS ZINSSER, *RATS, LICE, AND HISTORY*[1]

As a child I was anxious to keep up with my older brother, Bill, who was two years ahead of me. When he went off to school, I wanted to go also. So at the age of four, I started first grade at a private country day school overlooking the Hudson River, not far from New York City. I was commencing what my mother called being "a little ahead of myself." I enjoyed school, and my childhood with my brother and my younger sister, Nina, was a happy one. With the exception of a badly broken arm, my childhood medical history was uneventful, nothing more than the usual sore throats and earaches, a round of measles, an episode of chicken pox.

Like that of most children, my concept of the patient-doctor relationship was grounded upon the image of the doctor as a reliable, all-knowing father. Two incidents when I was very young may have caused me to be particularly in awe of the medical profession. The first occurred when Bill cut himself badly and blood spurted from an artery in his wrist. I was sure he was going to die, but my mother rushed him to the nearby hospital emergency room, and he came home alive, smiling—gloating, in fact, over the lollipop the doctor had given him as a part of his treatment. The second event involved my sister. Nina had acute appendicitis and went off to the hospital; her pain frightened me, but like my brother, she returned home happy and healthy after receiving a doctor's care. I learned that no matter how bad a situation might look, doctors could cure, and all would return to normal once again. Doctors were there to make you well, plain and simple.

My own first encounter with notable illness came when I was in my early teens and had a severe attack of bronchial asthma. The attacks continued into my twenties, recurring seasonally, usually during the late summer and early fall, a time when I had always been vulnerable to hay fever. Initially there was little doctors could do for me, but later, as medical knowledge grew, I was given drugs that relieved the asthma, and I eventually outgrew the condition. My improvement after so many bouts of struggling to breathe reinforced my faith in the curative powers of the medical profession. Later in life, my innocent trust was gradually to change.

Throughout my life I have been active in the art world, and have, in one way or another, been fascinated by medicine as well. As a child, I read a great many medical stories and always devoured anything to do with medical science that appeared in newspapers and magazines. Many of the research papers I wrote in high school and in college were on medical subjects. In the late 1940s I wrote a paper on the newly formed World Health Organization of the United Nations, and another on the use of cortisone and ACTH (adrenocorticotropic hormone) in treating various forms of arthritis. At the time, these were considered miracle drugs. I studied the difference between osteoarthritis, gout, and rheumatoid arthritis, as well as the arthritis caused by rheumatic fever. For part of the summer after my first year at Mount Holyoke College, I worked in a hospital in Irvington, New York, for city children with rheumatic fever, many of whom were very ill. There I learned the effects of streptococcal bacteria on the heart and joints. The advent of penicillin would make possible the prevention of this disease, making such hospitals a thing of the past.

The following summer, through a college friend of mine, Ann, I had the opportunity to work in Copenhagen for the World Health Organization of the United Nations. Ann's father, a well-

known doctor, made the arrangements. She and I worked as assist-
ants in the Tuberculosis Research Office, which was evaluating the
use of the BCG vaccine for TB. Ann had assisted her father in the
editing of his medical textbook, so she had some experience; I had
none. Little had I imagined when I wrote my school paper on the
World Health Organization that two years later I would be far
across the world working for them. Ann and I had a very stimulating summer, researching at the embassy library, tabulating information, updating mailing lists, proofreading charts for
publication, and editing medical articles for the British medical
journal *The Lancet* and other publications. Often we filled in for
people on vacation. Some days we would work on tuberculin test
charts and percent curves, other days on bacteriological experiment culture-colonization charts. We met many doctors from all
over the world.

The two of us worked hard, frequently putting in long days,
five days a week and every other Saturday morning. We felt great
excitement at having the privilege of being included in this research encompassing so many nations.

Those summers of work in Irvington and Copenhagen provided me with a reservoir of knowledge that I would call upon in
the years to come. My experience with children who had rheumatic fever taught me that a relatively common infection like strep
can develop into serious, long-lasting illness. The editing of material for medical journals gave me a glimpse into the nature of
scientific research. Had I not had that "summer romance" with
the world of medical research, I might not have persevered, years
later, to find out what was plaguing the health of my family.

As I have mentioned, I had always loved art, and as a young girl
I sketched constantly and enjoyed looking at paintings in museums with my father. He taught me a great deal about the history
of art.

During my senior year of high school, I was allowed to take a
specially designed full-year course in studio art and art history, and
I went on to major in art in college. At that point I thought of
combining my interests into one career, perhaps becoming a medical illustrator or occupational therapist, but decided against this

path because it was too confining. I like to be unrestrained in my art; what I want to put on the canvas is an expression of my emotions, not a rendering of scientific accuracy.

After I returned from Denmark, I pursued my interest in art. While at college I did a stage-set design, art-edited the yearbook, illustrated a children's book, and painted a few oil portraits of faculty children. During the summer following my junior year I studied portraiture with Jerry Farnsworth of Cape Cod, and then went on to a fellowship at the Yale–Norfolk Summer Art School in Norfolk, Connecticut. This was an intensive and stimulating six-week session taught by artists prominent in graphics, photography, painting, and drawing.

In the spring of my senior year I was awarded a Mount Holyoke Skinner Fellowship to do graduate work in painting and was elected to Phi Beta Kappa.

Since my freshman year of college I had been dating Gil, a Harvard student who shared my interest in art history and also liked to draw and paint. In June 1954 he and I were married, and after a honeymoon in Canada we settled in New York. There he started a job with Procter & Gamble, and I studied portraiture with Robert Brackman at the Art Students League.

My first year of marriage was hectic. In order to hold my fellowship and make ends meet, I got a job at F.A.O. Schwarz selling toys. I'd never spent so much time on my feet; between taking the subway at rush hour, walking long city blocks, and standing in the store waiting on customers and at art school while painting, I couldn't wait to get home and kick off my shoes. My parents were in the process of getting a divorce, and this, of course, brought many adjustments, too.

I finished up my fellowship in 1955 in Noank, Connecticut, where Robert Brackman had a summer school. At this point Gil was doing a great deal of traveling with his job. At Noank I started a commissioned portrait of a little girl from Essex, Connecticut. When working on it during August I became very sick. I had been feeling absolutely dreadful all day while lying on the beach in Old Lyme, where Gil and I had gone with family friends. I had slept off and on, not wanting to do anything but lie absolutely still, and by evening I had an excruciating headache and felt terribly ill. Back in Essex at our friends' house, I took my temperature and it was 105. It was decided that I drive with Gil to the home of my in-laws. Their doctor came to the house and gave me a shot of penicillin. I spent a week at their house, unable to return to my studies in Noank until I had recuperated.

The following fall, I visited Essex again to complete the portrait. Gil and I were captivated by this quiet village situated on the Connecticut River five miles up from the coastal town of Old Saybrook, and liked its location just about midway between New York and Boston, and within driving distance of Truro on Cape Cod, where Gil's parents had a summer house overlooking the bay. When it became definite that Gil's job would require constant traveling and we had no real reason to live in the city, we rented a small house in Essex.

The historic village near the mouth of the Connecticut River was a peaceful and fascinating place to live, and I continued my painting and became involved in learning about the field of antiques with my friend Kay, who had a shop near the harbor. Colonial history was everywhere, and we took joy in learning all about it.

Gil and I lived in a little house on South Main Street that had a spectacular view of the cove. It seemed the perfect place to settle down and raise a family.

CHAPTER THREE

GOOD TIMES, BAD TIMES

I believe that in life it is not what happens to us that makes us what we are. Over this we usually have no control. It is how we react to what happens that matters.

ROBERT MASSIE, *JOURNEY*[1]

In the spring of 1956, when everything in my life seemed to be in bloom—I was pregnant with my first child; Gil and I were fixing up our tiny house; I was even taking sailing lessons—I began having an array of inexplicable health problems.

The first episode hit when Gil and I were driving home from Bedford, New York, where we had attended the wedding of a friend of mine from art school. I ached all over and felt feverish; it seemed we'd never reach Essex. Once home, I discovered that I was bleeding vaginally; I was afraid I was having a miscarriage. I went to see my doctor first thing the next morning, and he gave me a prescription and recommended bed rest. The bleeding stopped; I was advised to stay very quiet for a month and thus I gave up my sailing lessons. (Instead, I watched the sailing school's Blue Jays from my window as they zigzagged up the Connecticut River.) By July I felt stronger, although I would often get dizzy in the sun, which wasn't like me. All my life I'd spent summers on the beach— swimming, boating, engaging in fierce, afternoon-long tennis matches beneath the hot summer sun—it had never caused the weakness I was experiencing now.

The remainder of my pregnancy was normal, and our first child—a boy we named Alexander—was born on a snowy night in January 1957. We nicknamed the baby Sandy.

When I became pregnant with our second child we decided to

move across the Connecticut River to Lyme, to a house that had more room and a bigger yard. Right after our second son, David, was born on an extremely hot night in August 1959, I developed a blotchy rash on my chest. In the months that followed, I had bouts of sore throat and then an episode of painful pleurisy.

This pattern continued with my third pregnancy. In October 1960, when I was two months pregnant, I erupted in angry red rashes that began on my hands and gradually extended up my arms to my elbows. Ointments prescribed by a dermatologist made the rashes worse. Later the dermatologist gave me several hot quartz treatments. He shielded the fetus by laying a protective apron over me before he began. Despite treatment, the rashes were to recur for many years.

After a couple of trips to the hospital with false labor, Wendy was born in the first week of May. I was thrilled to have a daughter.

Taking care of three children certainly kept me on my toes, but living in the country allowed them to spill outdoors, where there was plenty to entertain them. Gil and I built a stone terrace the summer after Wendy was born. I often worked in my rock garden, which bordered our new little terrace, while the children "swam" in a kiddie pool my mother had brought us.

Sometimes after being in the garden, I would find a tick embedded in my skin. After removing the tick (which was difficult to accomplish sometimes), I always put alcohol on the area of the bite. On several occasions the skin became bruised and sore for weeks afterward. In those days a tick was a tick to us. We didn't make the distinction between what we now know of as dog, wood, and deer ticks. Small ticks were simply thought to be baby ticks.

In the two years after Wendy was born, I would get sudden headaches, so excruciatingly painful that I would want to close my eyes and sleep. The bouts of sore throats and laryngitis continued. I had periodic shooting pains in my legs, hips, and knees. At times, my knee felt as if it were popping out of joint. Sometimes the pain would be in my buttocks, radiating down the backs of my legs. One day when I leaned over to lift Wendy out of the playpen, I couldn't straighten up without intense pain. When I consulted my doctor, he diagnosed slight scoliosis and thought I had transient nerve-root irritation.

In May 1963, when I was two months pregnant with my fourth child, my left foot became severely painful, although I hadn't wrenched it. My ailment was diagnosed as synovitis and I was given medication for the pain.

One day later during the summer, when I had come in from the garden to get some iced tea, my son David glanced at me and said, "Mom, your face looks funny." I glanced into the mirror— and saw that I looked as though someone had painted a wide red streak on my chin and neck, running toward my hairline. The area felt strange: prickly and tingly, like sandpaper, slightly raised and warm to the touch. Had I brushed against some nettle or poison ivy, or been bitten? This didn't look or feel like that at all, and it didn't itch or sting. I hadn't been near any high bushes, and I didn't remember being bitten by a bug. Within a few hours my body ached and I began to run a fever.

A local doctor diagnosed my symptoms as erysipelas, an expanding bacterial infection of the skin, and prescribed a course of penicillin. After several days of medication, I began to feel better, and gradually the rash receded.

For the remainder of my pregnancy, I felt unusually fatigued, hardly able to get through the day. It bothered me to take a deep breath. I had never felt such exhaustion, and though I didn't dwell on the thought, I knew it was due to more than just being in late pregnancy and caring for three small children. And I knew I needed help with housework and the children for at least a few months, until I felt stronger. A woman named Nellie came to our rescue, and was a godsend to me. Todd, our third son, blond and blue-eyed like his father, was born on a blustery, snowy evening in early December. I managed to regain my stamina in the months that followed.

April 1964 brought more difficulty to the family. Several of us broke out with a measleslike rash and fever, and my joints ached, especially my fingers. They were so stiff and painful that it was an ordeal just to fasten the safety pins of Todd's diapers. I consulted our doctor, who said we had German measles. The doctor suggested that I give up breastfeeding. Todd started episodes of diarrhea and broke out in the rash four days later. The diarrhea continued.

On the twentieth of May, five-month-old Todd spiked a high fever, and I took him to our doctor the following day. He diagnosed the illness as an ear infection and prescribed penicillin.

But now Todd developed an intolerance to feeding; he had diarrhea so severe that the doctor told us to keep charts of every feeding and episode of diarrhea. Gil was out of town on business during the week in those days, and so I had to keep up the around-the-clock vigil on my own. By the end of the week I was bleary-eyed, and Todd's condition was worse. He was still running a fever. On Saturday the doctor came to the house and suggested that we hospitalize him to combat worsening dehydration. Gil and I left the other children with a friend and drove to New Haven. Todd remained at Grace New Haven Hospital for several days of intravenous feeding. The doctors there were unable to pin down the cause of his sickness.

Two days after we brought him home from the hospital, he developed a pinprick rash and red welts, fevers, and a red eye. We continued to monitor him and had daily phone contact with our doctor the rest of the summer. We kept him separated from the other children as much as possible, moving his crib to a part of the house distant from his siblings.

In the weeks that followed, we were all hit with gastrointestinal problems. We were given a battery of tests; all turned out negative. The well water was tested and was all right. The doctor suspected a viral enteritis. I lost ten pounds, and the sore throats returned. In June Wendy had an expanding inflammation of her left foot caused by a bite; this was diagnosed as cellulitis. The redness moved up her leg and she was put on penicillin. It was quite a summer.

And if the summer wasn't enough to take the sheen off parenthood, in December all four children celebrated the holidays with chicken pox. It seemed as though Gil and I were heading up a medical clinic instead of a family!

Despite the physical problems, those years were in many ways the highlight of parenthood. We lived in an idyllic place that was ideal for raising children. In 1963, we had purchased an old house on several acres of land, on the same hilly, wooded road in Lyme we had lived on when we were renting. The road parallels the Connecticut River, offering spectacular views.

Gil and I both loved being parents. We never regretted getting out of New York City, and we indulged ourselves in the country life, giving our children plenty of pets over the years—from No-No the tiger cat to Charlie the gerbil to Dede the parakeet to Chipper the black-and-white rabbit. Most beloved of all was Nanny, our brown standard poodle.

The children played on our big front lawn, which for years was the scene of endless games of freeze tag, kickball, football, Frisbee, soccer, croquet, baseball, and badminton. Neighboring children would come over, too, and often these games would last until darkness forced the players inside. As all children will, they rolled in the grass, went barefoot, and traipsed through the woods.

Bicycle riding was another of their favorite pastimes. They loved to speed through the lanes of grass between my flower gardens and, with the exception of the time Wendy plowed right through my zinnias on a neighbor's minibike, they were pretty good about avoiding the blossoms, as they knew I loved my gardens. As soon as it was warm enough I would be out digging, weeding, and planting. We had a vegetable garden for several years, but my real pleasure was cultivating flowers.

Gil loved the woods and often took the children on weekend walks, so it wasn't long before they knew the woods for miles around. They would set out on their own to the various spots that Gil had endowed with names such as the Big Mountain, Indian Lookout, the Big Meadow, and the Deer Patch (a grove of soft moss and cedar trees where the deer would sleep at night). The children named every body of water for miles around. There was the Brook, and Lake Erie and Lake Superior, two tiny cow ponds where peepers always first chirped in the spring and where, in winter, the children would hold their figure-skating championships. (I remember one year David couldn't skate because of a foot injury, so he played commentator and judge. I'll never forget the sight of him on the ice, all bundled up and wearing a red slipper on his injured foot, relishing the role of deciding which one of his siblings had performed the better figure eight.) In later years they all graduated to a bigger pond down the hill.

Their favorite spots were the places that afforded beautiful views of the Connecticut River; from some perches, they could even see Long Island Sound, way in the distance. Candlestick Ledge was one such place. Not only was there a view of the Sound, but also one could see down to a nineteenth-century barn of weathered red, complete with surrounding Old World haystacks reminiscent of a Monet painting, and sloping fields curving down to sparkling Hamburg Cove, a safe haven for boats. In June the far hill beyond the barn turned pink with the blossoms of mountain laurel. Joshua Rock was another great getaway for them. Named after a local Indian named Joshua, who died in 1676 (he was the son of the sachem Uncas), the dramatic ledge overlooks a particularly scenic part of the Connecticut, where the river gently curves one last time before flowing into Long Island Sound. The children went there for picnics and loved to catch the attention of boaters by shouting and waving. They were especially thrilled when someone on the great oil barges would see them and wave in return.

When they were very young, perhaps their biggest excitement during the spring and summer months was the visits of the cows, who wandered from the farm over the hill to the edge of our front yard in the early evening. At the sound of cowbells, the children would exclaim, "The cows are here!" and jump up from the dinner table to dash outside.

Up until about fifty years ago, the wooded hills near our home had all been sheep and cow pastureland. When the children were little, the cows roamed through the relatively new woods off Joshuatown Road in search of grass; they were kept from the road by barbed wire and old stone walls.

That is, the cows were *almost* always kept from the road. One hot summer night, when Gil was away, the children were in bed, and I was sitting in the living room reading, I heard something brushing the front screen door. My heart beating fast, I went to the door—to find a jet-black cow had climbed the front steps and was staring at me through the screen! I phoned the farmer, and before too long he came with his brother, who ran the farm with him. He carried a big lantern and coaxed the cow back to the barn over the hill.

The farmer and his herd of cows are long gone now. We realize now they were the last vestiges of a bygone time in America. But back then, the cows were simply the chief joy of a summer night, and Gil and I delighted in their visits too. We would stand with the children at the stone wall, and watch them timidly pet the cows on their noses.

The woods were also home to various secret forts. To this day the children talk about them as though they were true outposts in the wild, lawless West. As the boys grew out of cavalry games and into Cold War–era fantasies, the woods became the territory of games of espionage. My daughter was not included in many of their top-secret missions, but she and the girls who lived nearby loved to use the woods as a place to play "house."

Another advantage of living in Lyme was our proximity to Long Island Sound. I don't know what we would have done without the beach each summer, where the children took swimming lessons and met up with other young people. Many summer nights we'd take a picnic supper down to the beach. Gil loved nothing more than to shed his business suit, shirt, and tie and go for a long swim in the late afternoon.

CHAPTER FOUR

IN THE THROES OF ILLNESS

The birth of an infectious disease is not as simple a matter as that of man. Gestation is not a mere matter of ten months or so, but represents complex biological interadaptations and interactions which cover thousands of years.

HANS ZINSSER, *RATS, LICE, AND HISTORY*[1]

During the summer months the children would often get fairly pronounced reactions to insect bites. At one point David's earlobe was bright red and shiny and swollen to double its normal size, until antibiotic medication countered the reaction.

In addition to coping with the various ailments of my children—from the normal colds to the more puzzling illnesses—I continued to have perplexing ailments of my own.

A sore throat returned in April 1965, accompanied by swollen glands, a dry cough, and conjunctivitis in both eyes. In the early part of the summer, the back of my hand became red and puffy and tingly. Its condition reminded me of the rash I had had that summer I was pregnant with Todd. Both outbreaks seemed to have occurred during a time of year when I had been working in the garden. Was I allergic to some plant? I vaguely remembered being nicked by a rose thorn. Could that be the cause of the reaction? Or was it due to some unseen insect that had bitten me while I gardened? As I was fixing supper on that evening when my hand was swollen, I began to feel achy and feverish. I knew then that the rash was something more than allergy, so I went to a local doctor the following morning; I was given penicillin tablets to take. Over the next few days I felt better and the rash eventually faded.

At the end of April 1965, I found a tick lightly attached to the skin behind Todd's ear. It must have gotten into the house by dropping off our dog. I removed the tick with tweezers and applied alcohol. The area wasn't red at all; in fact, you could hardly see where the bite had been. But by the following day, Todd developed a high fever. He was given penicillin for a middle-ear infection. The medication didn't seem to be effective, so on May 1 he had another checkup with his doctor and a shot of penicillin. Soon he broke out in a rash all over his body. I called the doctor, who surmised that it was an allergic reaction to the medication and advised that we discontinue it.

On May 21, 1965, Wendy awoke with a sore throat and earache; her face was swollen on one side. The doctor said that she had cellulitis and "periorbital edema"—swelling around the eye—and she was put on penicillin. We wondered again whether a bite was the cause. Later that year, in October, she had a recurrence of the periorbital rash.

One morning in the spring of 1966 I awoke with a painful headache that lasted all day. It was gone when I woke up the following morning, but when I looked in the mirror I discovered that I had a hemorrhage in the top portion of my eye. Over the next few weeks, the blood descended over the lower part of the eye, making the white bright red. It gradually faded. I thought back to the conjunctivitis of the previous spring, and wondered if it was in some way related to this.

On the twenty-ninth of April, David came down with a sore throat and cough and was given penicillin. The sore throat returned in June, along with swollen glands in his groin, and he had more penicillin.

Summer was hectic, as summers usually are with four young children, and Gil and I were looking forward to our annual family trip to Truro in early September 1966. As artists, we relished the spectacular Cape light, and the children loved everything about the place. Packing provisions for the getaway and keeping our spirited children entertained in the car for five hours was no small feat, so when we finally arrived in Truro, we were more than ready for the ocean's restorative powers. But the morning after we arrived I woke up with a high fever and an extremely sore throat. I couldn't swallow or talk without pain, and I ached from head to foot. All I could do was to stay flat in bed for three days, hoping the illness would subside. I wanted so badly to join Gil and the children at the beach, but merely swallowing a sip of water was more than I could do. And with that, I had moments of feeling blue, feeling as though I was letting Gil and the children down. One morning Wendy came into the bedroom and asked me whether I was coming to the beach with the rest of the family. I had to tell her no. She looked at me as though I had done this deliberately, as though I were choosing to be sick, and then she left the room. Through the large floor-to-ceiling windows of the bedroom, I watched the family as they scrambled through the dune grass toward the beach below. I felt utterly alone.

I continued to get worse, so I insisted on finding a doctor as soon as possible. We found a medical center in Wellfleet, and I was given a shot of penicillin. The sore throat and fever gradually subsided, but I developed laryngitis and the familiar dry, choking cough.

At about this time, Sandy suddenly had the same periorbital cellulitis that Wendy had and was given an antibiotic. In the following month, October, Sandy, then nine years old, had a bout of pharyngitis (inflamed throat) and developed a reflex dry cough, which was to become recurrent from then on.

My own sore throat came back again in December. In the middle of January 1967, Sandy's pharyngitis returned, and he was given penicillin. Toward the end of that month, David, age seven, complained of a sore jaw and earache and was given an antibiotic.

I had a sore throat again in March, along with aches and fever, and this time I had swelling in my left knee. Thinking I had a touch of rheumatic fever, my doctor put me on a course of penicillin. Several weeks later I saw "Dr. Beckland," an internist in New Haven who did an electrocardiogram. He said that although I had no heart involvement, he thought it would be a good idea for me to keep track of my symptoms. During the pelvic exam, he noted an inflammation of the cervix and suggested I see my gynecologist. Was I a living petri dish? I wondered.

On the first of May, Todd, then three and a half, was limping noticeably and was reluctant to put any weight on his right leg. He hadn't had any trauma. The doctor diagnosed a right adductor spasm and synovitis of the right hip. A few weeks later, Sandy's pharyngitis returned and he was given an antibiotic.

In October, my left heel became painful and tender for no apparent reason. I could hardly put any weight on it. After a few days, I went to a local doctor, who asked me if I had injured it. I told him I could remember doing nothing that would have brought the tenderness, but as I spoke, I remembered the weird soreness I'd had on the top of my left foot a few years earlier. I didn't mention it to the doctor; the idea that there would really be any connection seemed farfetched. The doctor thought the pain might be due to a spur and he ordered an X ray, which was negative. I was given an anti-inflammatory drug, phenylbutazone. The heel improved after a week or so.

Shortly thereafter, the sore throat returned, and once again I was put on penicillin. When the sore throat subsided, I developed an incapacitating stiff neck; it seemed that when one symptom or set of symptoms ebbed, another flared, keeping me from ever having enough of a stretch of time to regain my sense of equilibrium. My fingers became swollen and red, sometimes blotchy, ulcerated, and cracked. I continued to feel dreadfully tired all the time, and struggled to keep up with the challenge of caring for children, husband, house, yard, and pets, and endless carpooling. Just lifting up my arms bothered me. Some days it hurt to take the steps to go upstairs; even getting in and out of the car or a chair was an effort. Sometimes I would bend over and be unable to straighten up. I noticed that I was very stiff every time I changed positions.

In mid-November of 1967, Gil discovered a tick deeply embedded in the back of his shoulder. The ticks were still around on warm days at that time of the year, waiting at the edge of a blade of grass or tip of a shrub for a passing victim. Since he couldn't have spotted the tick easily without looking in the mirror, it had probably been in him awhile; the skin around where it had dug in looked red and inflamed. The bite was very tender, so he made an appointment right away with a doctor who dug out the tick and cleansed the wound.

(In the earlier years of our marriage, when Gil was bitten by a tick he would leave it in his skin, saying that it was nature's way to let the tick fall off naturally and that, after all, animals didn't get sick from ticks. I argued that ticks transmit Rocky Mountain spotted fever, relapsing fever, and other human diseases, and eventually persuaded him that his attitude was naive. From then on he did help in watching for ticks on the children and our dog.)

During December my throat condition returned and I was given more penicillin. In 1968, I had four more episodes of the extreme sore throat, two of which were treated with penicillin. At times I had pain in my lower back or in my hips; it would come on suddenly and was absolutely incapacitating, and then it would disappear as abruptly as it had started, though sometimes I would feel lame afterward. At other times my hip or knee would feel as if it was going out of joint, and would go into spasm until I could get it into proper position.

Gil's mother's health was failing that year, so he and I became involved in taking care of her and of Gil's father, whose health was also declining. His parents lived about an hour and a quarter away from Lyme, and we tried to see them as often as we could.

Early in the summer of 1969, Gil and I went out for a day trip to Block Island on a friend's boat; I was exposed to the sun for hours. By evening I had broken out into an angry raised rash over my nose and cheeks and I ached and felt very jittery. Cold sores erupted on my lips the next day. These symptoms lasted a week.

Earlier in my life I had spent summers at the Jersey shore and on Cape Cod. I had always loved the sun and had tanned easily. Now, after coming out of the sun I would feel jittery and a little dizzy, and I would get these symptoms and feel achy. Why was I suddenly reacting to the sun?

I tried to wear sunglasses more often to protect my eyes, but they seemed to aggravate the rash where they touched my skin. I had to keep wearing them, though, because the sunlight really bothered my eyes, more than it ever had in the past, and gave me a headache. I wondered if the steroid ointment I was told to use was somehow reacting with perspiration, heat, and the plastic of my glasses. (My skin had recently become very sensitive to adhesive tape, becoming red and inflamed where the tape touched.) Some mornings I would wake up with the area around my eyes swollen, or with swelling only around one eye. At times my vision would be blurry in one eye.

In July, I had a siege of gastrointestinal symptoms—severe bouts of nausea, diarrhea, and fever. I lost quite a bit of weight. My skin was slightly jaundiced for several days, and I had trouble falling asleep at night, which had never been a problem before.

We had been under a great deal of stress. Gil's mother had had surgery in Boston; his father, who was also ill, came to stay with us while she was there. Her health continued to decline following her surgery; she was rehospitalized and died several weeks later. Following her death, Gil's father was hospitalized with heart problems, and was in and out of the hospital or nursing facilities from then on. By then the emotional and physical strain of all this was affecting our marriage. In addition, Gil was working hard developing new products for the company he worked for, and he had his own stresses.

As the summer wore on, I continued to get terrible cramps in my hip and lower back, especially while driving. My hands shook. At night I'd awaken in feverish sweats and then get chills and have to sleep beneath a blanket, even on a hot August night. My circulation was affected. My legs, feet, and hands were always cold. There seemed to be a war going on inside my body, a war that moved around from place to place. What could be the cause of this?

I remember one Friday evening getting a baby-sitter so that I could meet Gil at the beach for supper. I was so exhausted that I couldn't even gather enough strength to walk across the beach to the water. I just lay down on a towel in the sand and slept.

My behavior fluctuated wildly; periods of irritability and insomnia alternated with periods of extreme drowsiness, lethargy, and fatigue. At times I felt terribly weak, as though all my energy had been drained from my body. I never seemed to dream anymore. I became more and more impatient with life's stresses. I also became more emotional.

That fall of 1969, there were times when I would wake up in the middle of the night and not be able to move. My arms seemed paralyzed, and turning over in bed was very painful. My limbs would go to sleep on me.

David, we noticed, had developed a "wandering eye," so we made an appointment for him to see an ophthalmologist. He was prescribed glasses. In September, Sandy had a round red rash diagnosed as pityriasis rosea, and in December he developed a rash diagnosed as psoriasis.

In February 1970, I made an appointment with Dr. Beckland, my internist in New Haven, for a thorough evaluation. It was important for me to know why these symptoms kept recurring, and I planned to ask a lot of questions. At that point I had lived with my illness long enough to be impatient, and therefore was a little bolder in my attempt to extract an explanation from those who were trained to know. The list of possible causes for my illness that I had compiled lay in my lap as I sat in Dr. Beckland's office. Slowly I went down the page, and asked him about each one:

A form of arthritis?

An effect of streptococcus infection?

Could it be a virus?

Early lupus erythematosus, before blood tests became positive?

Leukemia?

Allergy—to my immediate environment?
        —to food additives?

Some change in our well water?

Delayed reaction to tick bites? [I had had bites in Lyme and at the Cape.]

Some kind of pollution?

A hormone imbalance?

The doctor thought the strongest of the possibilities was that I was in an early stage of a connective-tissue disease such as lupus, but he emphasized that it was hard to tell at this point. He explained that connective tissue is the most abundant tissue in the body, binding (like glue) the body together. With diseases of connective tissue, as in lupus, many parts of the body become inflamed.

With collagen (a protein in the connective tissue) diseases the tissues of the musculoskeletal system of the body become inflamed—this group of diseases include rheumatoid arthritis (RA), systemic lupus erythematosus (SLE), scleroderma, juvenile rheumatoid arthritis (JRA), and Sjögren's syndrome.

Systemic lupus erythematosus is a disease that may affect the skin, joints, tissue linings, nervous system, and many other organs of the body. It is more common in young women, and ultraviolet light is known to cause trouble with lupus patients. Dr. Beckland felt that in my case it would be best to wait and observe the symptoms a while longer. If they became worse, then more blood tests, and perhaps even a diagnostic workup in a hospital, should be done. He ordered a number of blood tests, an electrocardiogram, and a chest X ray.

Leaving his office, I remembered that we hadn't discussed the possibility of my symptoms being a delayed reaction to the tick bites that I'd had in the past. When I brought it up with him, Dr. Beckland assured me that tick-borne rickettsial diseases like Rocky Mountain spotted fever did not cause the symptoms I had.

Late the following month the sore throat came back, accompanied by the usual aches and fatigue. It was an effort to walk; climbing the stairs became a major undertaking. I tried to cut back on my trips up and down stairs. I got in the habit of leaving a basket of folded clean laundry on the bottom step so the children could take it upstairs and put it away for me. After a visit to the doctor I was put on penicillin again.

At the same time, Sandy, then thirteen, developed a facial tic and eye twitch and was constantly clearing his throat and coughing. He became nervous, irritable, aggressive, and impulsive. He was very unhappy. He had always been a good student; now his schoolwork suffered. His teacher told me she noticed a big change in him over a period of a few months. Sandy had an unusual gait and had started to have a lot of spontaneous nosebleeds.

Gil and I had Sandy evaluated in a hospital to see if there was a physical cause for his distress. Following his hospital stay, Gil, Sandy, and I started a program of regular counseling with a specialist in adolescent medicine. The doctor felt that Sandy's behavior changes were due to a childhood depression.

I was exhausted with the stress of the additional problems, and in mid-May I lost my voice and had another sore throat, and another course of penicillin (400,000 units four times a day). I lost ten pounds between April and June, and had little appetite. My weight fluctuated between these episodes of symptoms.

In early June I suddenly developed a bad back. The pain radiated from my middle back down into my left thigh. My thighs would throb and then a few days later I'd erupt with black-and-blue marks. This same phenomenon appeared on my upper arms as well. I had been in the sun, which may have aggravated it. At the same time I had pain in the joints, and they cracked when I moved. The children would listen in amazement when I bent down to tie their shoes or pick up something. I had blood tests at a local lab; there were no abnormalities to explain the bruising.

At a follow-up appointment with Dr. Beckland on June 15, he noted the bruises on my thighs and arms, saying that I had vascular fragility. I mentioned to him that I had taken a few aspirin for the pain in my hip. He advised me to discontinue taking them, to see if perhaps aspirin was the cause of my bruising. As to the other symptoms I was having, he again said to "ride along with them a little while a longer."

Todd was having nosebleeds now. They were so frequent that he had to have his nose cauterized.

In early July, I had another episode of pressure headache, chills, cramps, and black-and-blue marks erupting on my thighs and upper arms. The headache was sometimes caplike, sometimes one-sided; at other times there was just a steady pain at the back of my lower head and neck. I had cramps in my feet. My eyes ached, and my eyelid twitched uncontrollably at times. I called the internist and he recommended a hematologist by the name of Dr. Abramaroff for further blood work.

I telephoned Dr. Abramaroff's office. The first available appointment was July 24, 1970, a full three weeks away. I knew the face rash and blossoming of black-and-blue marks would have faded by then. The doctor would not have a clear picture of what I was going through, but there was nothing I could do about that.

At my appointment with Dr. Abramaroff I was tested for lupus, rheumatoid arthritis, and abnormal clotting time, and a platelet count was done. He told me that since I had lupuslike symptoms, it would be wise to stay out of the sun and wear a hat as much as possible, as sun exposure worsened the disease. Wearing a large hat to shield me from the hot sun during the days after my appointment with the doctor did help. This improvement made the possibility of lupus seem more likely, and I tried to brace myself for such a reality.

But later in the week Dr. Abramaroff called with the good news that all tests for lupus and rheumatoid arthritis were negative. I was elated, but on another level, it was hard to go back to not knowing what on earth was happening to me. If not lupus, then what was it?

Dr. Abramaroff ventured that perhaps vascular fragility was causing the bruising, and that it was also possible that it was caused by menstruation-related changes in hormone levels. A third possibility, he continued, was that a vitamin C deficiency was to blame. He recommended that I take a hundred milligrams of the vitamin daily. I couldn't help but feel that he was grasping at straws.

In a letter to Dr. Beckland, Dr. Abramaroff noted that he had observed a fading butterfly rash on my face and several fading bruises. Because of the joint pains I described, he had wondered about early lupus or rheumatoid arthritis, but all tests were negative.

I dutifully took vitamin C supplements throughout the summer; nothing improved. Trying to forget about my illness, I became busy getting Sandy ready to go off to boarding school in September. His good friend had gone off to school the year before, and Sandy liked the idea. He had chosen a small school in northwest Connecticut.

A few days after we drove Sandy to school my father came to visit; we sat in the backyard, enjoying the late-afternoon sun. It was the only time of day I sat out in the sun without a hat. Evidently, I should have worn one even then, for a puffy, red, hot, prickly rash broke out over my nose, cheeks, and chin right before my father's astonished eyes. I could feel it coming on, as if someone had directed a high-wattage heat lamp near my face. I told Dad I thought we ought to go into the living room and sit. He said, "Gosh, sweetie, are you okay?" and then he followed me inside.

As we were sitting in the living room, and I was trying to forget about the rash, I could feel the back of my throat getting sore, and I felt achy. Here I go again, I thought.

At Truro later in the month, after a bout of insomnia that lasted for days, plus throbbing in my elbows and knees, a black-and-blue mark as wide as a tennis ball erupted on my right thigh. I was appalled at its size, and bewildered by the fact that all these black-and-blue marks cropping up were not painful to the touch the way an ordinary bruise is.

In the weeks that followed, I watched carefully to see if maybe I was just bruising more easily, but when I accidentally banged my shin or thigh, I did not tend to bruise. These bruises that I was getting over and over again weren't the result of trauma. I also noticed that they would erupt only after a period of deep throbbing within an area like my upper arm or thigh.

In October, Todd's hands, feet, and mouth were strangely swollen. In November, just about all my symptoms came back, and I was exhausted. My heart felt as if it were racing, beating very fast and hard. My pulse was very fast. I had sharp, intermittent pain in my left temple.

All my symptoms became almost continuous as the months went on. In December, my neck and shoulder became stiff and painful, making driving and moving around almost impossible. I could hardly lift my left arm. It hurt to turn over in bed, and if I woke up in the night, my legs would start twitching and jerking uncontrollably, making getting back to sleep difficult. It was frustrating just finding a comfortable position.

I noticed that even the most minimal activity—raking leaves, weeding the garden—triggered my aches, and that my symptoms were always worse from midafternoon on. My menstrual periods accentuated my symptoms, too. Penicillin always made me feel better. At one point the arthritis seemed to be across my lower chest or rib cage; a sharp pain made it hurt to take a deep breath.

I was dragging myself around, determined to keep going, but I often felt I couldn't keep up with the pace of it all, that I didn't have the stamina I had always had.

Gil was tired of dealing with my constant questioning of what was the matter with me and we fought more. He is someone who likes to shrug off troubles fast, not dwell on them. He'd rather turn his back on life's nagging concerns and go on a picnic or a walk in the woods, or jump in a car and go on a day trip. This free-spiritedness is partly what drew me to him; during our college years he would take me away from the grind of studying and exams, on weekend trips to the Cape and other places. Now he was enthusiastic about family trips.

But with so little energy and so much restoration work to do on the house, I found it harder to drop the rake, or the paintbrush, or whatever project we were working on, and while away a Saturday at the beach. I wanted to get the major work done and out of the way; Gil was apt to stretch projects out for months.

My knees felt full of fluid at times, and my hand and finger eruptions were so bad that I had to keep them bandaged. My fingernails were ridged and pitted with little holes, and they broke easily. I had blotchy redness on the palms of my hands as well; you could easily see the veins and capillaries.

We heard from Sandy's school doctor that our son developed another skin rash while he was away, early in 1971. The rash was located on his left thigh; his doctor treated it with steroid and antibiotic ointment, and slowly it improved.

Meanwhile, I had another bout of rashes, black-and-blue marks, and petechiae, which look like tiny dots of blood under the skin. I called Dr. Abramaroff to let him know of my flare-up. Considering the recurring nature of the symptoms, he felt that they might well be due to a hormone imbalance of some kind. He told me to rest, avoid heavy exercise, and refrain from taking any aspirin product.

In February, after suffering another bad stiff neck, fever, and gastrointestinal symptoms, and waking up with my right eye swollen, I made another appointment with my internist, Dr. Beckland. More tests were done; all came back negative.

March brought sore throat, rashes, laryngitis, the dry, choking cough, and blurred vision in my right eye, as well as swelling of the eyelid. I was depressed and exhausted. One day I was shopping for a birthday present in Old Saybrook, and I asked a saleswoman where I could find the board games. My voice was faint from the laryngitis, and I imagine I must have looked run-down, because she suggested that I forget trying to find the gift, and go home and take care of myself instead.

CHAPTER FIVE

"IT'S ALL IN YOUR HEAD"

Words are weapons or building blocks, especially when used by a physician. They can set the stage for auspicious treatment or they can complicate and retard it.

NORMAN COUSINS, *THE HEALING HEART*[1]

In mid-March of 1971, I entered a large medical center for tests to discover the cause of the fever of unknown origin from which I suffered. It was a teaching hospital, so I was seen by a whole battery of doctors. I was placed in a room with three other patients. In the course of interviewing me about my symptoms, several doctors detected in the way that I answered their questions that I knew a little about the medical world, and a few asked where I'd gotten my information. The doctors kept asking me when it was that I first sensed that my well-being was threatened. I told them that I felt as if something toxic were affecting my body in numerous ways; I was reacting to something, and that something was making me feel miserable. I was ready to face whatever disease I had, but in order to overcome it, I wanted a known entity. I had to know what germ I was fighting. Further blood tests were ordered, as were joint X rays, upper and lower gastrointestinal series, and a gallbladder test; all results were negative, although the X rays did show slight synovial thickening of my left knee, which had been swollen in the spring of 1967. Like my other doctors, those at the medical center had suspected connective-tissue disease. Dr. Beckland came into the hospital to discharge me; he asked me why I never smiled; he said I always looked so serious. I told him that given my chronic ailments, I didn't feel I had very much to smile about. I left the hospital late on a Saturday afternoon, still without a diagnosis. The only possible cause of my problems that the doctors could think of was some type of allergy. It wasn't much to go on. The rigorous tests and the disappointment of being no closer to a diagnosis left me exhausted and frustrated.

In the hospital I had shared a room with a woman who was convalescing from plastic surgery. As we became acquainted, she told me that she couldn't help hearing all the questions the doctors were asking me. She confessed that she had heard my entire story, and said it sounded as though I had lupus. Her teenage daughter had been diagnosed with lupus the year before, so she knew the disease firsthand. Several months later, when I was about to go to another hospital for more tests and was feeling frantic, she called me to find out how I was and to encourage me to pursue the possibility that my illness was lupus. She told me not to give up hope. Her support meant a great deal to me, and meant more and more in the weeks to come.

During this period, I kept up my outside interests as well as caring for the family. I didn't want to focus only on my problems. I made a conscious effort to not think about my symptoms. My art got me through some very difficult times. I entered juried shows whenever I was able and painted whenever I had a spare moment. The best time for me to paint was when the children were all in school. I would set up my canvas on the kitchen wall, put my palette and the sketch I was working from on the kitchen table, and paint until I heard the school bus chugging up the hill. Oil was the medium I worked with for many years, but after my hands became so cracked and swollen I decided to work with colored pencil and pastel. I was still using the cortisone ointment on my face and hands.

I studied the work of Mary Cassatt and Edgar Degas, and did a series of drawings of Wendy and David at horseback-riding lessons. My children provided an endless source of inspiration. In order to capture them in unself-conscious moments, I would sketch or photograph them without their knowing. Or occasionally I'd call out "Freeze!," which they knew meant to hold still a minute. Now my closetful of paintings and shelves of drawings serves as a family photo album of sorts: Todd learning to crack an egg; Sandy holding his paper airplane; Wendy picking Queen Anne's lace; David all decked out in riding hat and boots, holding the reins of a horse; the four children sitting on the open tailgate of the station wagon, waiting for a ride to the end of our driveway.

But no matter how hard I tried to will them away, the symptoms continued. Soon after I got home from the hospital, I noticed a dime-sized lesion on my arm. My legs and arms twitched, and a rash appeared over my nose and cheeks when I was in the sun. Later in the spring, I suffered periods of terrible insomnia, night sweats, and eye puffiness. Black-and-blue marks kept erupting; I began to have difficulty swallowing, and it hurt to touch the front of my neck. I was engulfed by an unbelievable fatigue.

Others in the family had strep throats and laryngitis, and we were all given penicillin. David broke out in a rash when he started the medication. I had thirteen days of penicillin. The others got better; I did not. It hurt to swallow and talk, and the roof of my mouth was sore. Red dots broke out on my upper chest, my low-grade fever persisted, and I ached all over.

After giving it a lot of thought, I told Gil I wanted to get another opinion, and he was all for it. I called a friend of mine who is a pathologist and talked to him about the situation. He thought it was a wise step, and recommended a specialist in connective-tissue disease at a Boston medical center.

When I called Dr. Beckland to tell him that I was seeking a second opinion in Boston, he was defensive and said that unless my symptoms were acute, he doubted the doctors would turn up any answers. He suggested that all had been done that could be done.

I tried to gather all the test results from my previous hospitalization, and asked that they be sent to the new medical center so that the specialist there could review them before seeing me.

The night before I left for the hospital, I received a phone call from a friend of mine in Lyme who had heard of my trouble. She, too, was plagued with health problems, so she knew what I was going through. She had terrible rashes and had been hospitalized many times. Countless biopsies and tests had turned up nothing. She told me that she had had to learn to be a professional patient, and she encouraged me to trust my instincts and keep pursuing a diagnosis.

One Monday in late June 1971, Gil and I made the two-and-a-half-hour drive to the medical center in Boston. By then I was feeling a little better. Perhaps the antibiotics that I had been taking were finally working.

Gil stayed a day to get me settled and then returned home. As we were saying good-bye, I noticed how tired he looked. My coughing had been keeping him awake at night; my malaise worried him, and it must have been depressing to live with.

Gil had given me a beautiful book on Mary Cassatt for our seventeenth wedding anniversary, and after he left I delved into it to keep myself from missing home. I had brought paper and a set of colored pencils with me, too.

"Dr. Ligmann," the specialist who oversaw my case, was rather dogmatic and brusque. When Gil and I met with him for the first time, I was irked to discover that the medical records we had arranged to be sent from the other medical center had not arrived. Dr. Ligmann didn't seem to share my concern. He said it was all right, that he would like to approach my case with a fresh eye. "The results of previous tests might color my thinking," he went on. From his tone, Gil and I inferred that there was a degree of rivalry between the two medical centers.

I was intimidated by the doctors' rapid-fire questions, and their style of interviewing never allowed me to communicate the chronology of my symptoms, the patterns I had noticed. As a result, they missed out on gaining a broad perspective on my illness. But despite my feeling intimidated and their tendency to want to stick to their agenda, I managed to ask them a lot of questions, and I became bolder about making sure the questions got answers. I don't think they were used to patients doing this. At times it was clear my thoroughness irked them.

One time, when several physicians were in my room, I showed them a drawing I had done of my face rash. One of the doctors glanced at it and quipped, "Why not take slides of the rash next time?" Not a bad idea, I said to myself.

Dr. Ligmann called in a dermatologist who took scrapings of

my rash and gave me an ointment that I had had before, a steroid. My degree of fever was carefully recorded night and day, and a myriad of blood tests were ordered.

In the hours between the tests and consultations, I managed to do a few drawings and some reading, which helped alleviate the loneliness I felt. How strange it was to draw children playing in the sand at the ocean, and to lie in a hospital bed while summer went on without me. I kept thinking about the children, wondering how their day was going.

The medical center was a teaching hospital, so many doctors reviewed my case. Because I was experiencing a constant lump in my throat when swallowing, they suspected a thyroid disorder. The ear, nose, and throat exam was probably the most unpleasant test for me to undergo, and after my return to my room from having the test, two doctors came to tell me that they now thought I had thyroiditis and that an endocrinologist would be in to see me the following day.

The next morning I was taken down to an examining room and tested for thyroid dysfunction. The doctor in charge said the scan showed a low-grade thyroiditis.

When Dr. Ligmann came to see me the following morning, I asked for the results and he said that when the doctors put together the thyroid results with those of all the other tests, they voted five to two that I didn't have thyroiditis. They were unable to find a physical cause for my complaints. He then looked at me and said, "You know, Mrs. Murray, sometimes people subconsciously want to be sick."

I asked him what he was implying, and he went on to say that sometimes psychiatric problems manifested themselves with physical symptoms.

"That isn't the case here," I replied. "I just know this isn't a psychosomatic illness. I have too much I want to do in my life."

I did admit that I had felt very discouraged at times because of my illness and the other problems we had encountered recently— the death of Gil's mother, and his father's hospitalizations—so that yes, tears came very easily now.

Dr. Ligmann looked down at me from the bedside. "Sit up

straight," he told me. "You don't need to lie down—you're not ill." He insisted that I was depressed, suggested that I see a psychiatrist at the hospital for an interview that afternoon, and then went on his way.

I felt very alone and defeated. I thought a lot about where I stood with the whole problem of my health, and lying there in my bed, I decided that the only chance of fighting my way out of this ongoing predicament was to exhaust all possibilities. Dr. Ligmann had backed me into a corner, and while his manner was unforgivable, at least it made me more determined than ever to find out the cause of my symptoms; if doctors were going to stand there at my bedside and call my illness psychosomatic or neurotic, the only way to cope was to see a psychiatrist, once and for all find out where I stood, and, I hoped, prove the doctors wrong. It was a scary thing to accept; the hurdle of seeing a psychiatrist was an enormous one for me. I had admitted that I was discouraged; I had admitted that I was depressed. Sure, I didn't smile much from the vantage point of a hospital bed. (How many patients do?) But I was pretty sure the tension and low spirits the doctors detected were the offspring of living with an undiagnosed ailment, not the cause of the illness, as they seemed to think. Their recommendation seemed too facile. I felt misunderstood and disregarded.

That afternoon I was escorted by an aide to the other side of the hospital, where I talked with a psychiatrist named "Dr. Havelin" for about an hour. I described the recurring symptoms and the almost-constant fatigue. He asked a lot of questions about the stresses in my life, and I explained how the demands of raising four children had not brought Gil and me closer together, but pushed us further apart.

Earlier in our marriage, at the time when I was often pregnant and caring for our small children, Gil's business had required him to be away from home during the week. We had started out trying to work together on household projects on weekends, and occasionally we succeeded.

Now that he was no longer traveling, he had more time to be a nurturing father, dedicated to stimulating the children's interests, imaginations, and creativity.

I expressed to Dr. Havelin that I am a pragmatist; Gil is a dreamer. I like a lot of order in my life, and tend to tackle a household chore or a family issue sooner than later. Gil is comfortable with disarray and tends to put things off for later.

I told Dr. Havelin that I liked to set boundaries for the children, believing that they were happier with structure, while Gil was more permissive and free with them. We seemed to disagree on most issues, and the entire family was reacting to the lack of consistency in our lives. Our differences were confusing to the children, and there was little harmony in our family, especially during those times when we were all together. It seemed that every little thing became a battleground.

My appointment with Dr. Havelin went quickly, and I found him understanding and easy to talk with.

The psychiatrist, feeling that I needed supportive psychotherapy in handling the stress of my puzzling illness and my marriage, suggested that I enter a program at the hospital of three weeks' intensive treatment, as well as undergo further physical tests and evaluations. I felt so overwhelmed by all the responsibilities that I had at home, I didn't feel I could be away for that long. Money was terribly tight, and insurance covered only part of our bills. The cost of hiring baby-sitters alone was staggering. I felt that the best thing for me to do was to get home and take it from there. Dr. Havelin said that if I needed to I could call and enter the hospital at a later date. He gave me a telephone number to call if I found that I could break away from the demands of my family.

Gil came the next day to bring me home. I was in a state of shock. We had to walk several blocks to the car in the hot sun. As we were getting on the highway headed for Connecticut, Gil glanced over me and said, "Oh, boy, here we go again." I looked in the rearview mirror. The sun rash was back. I felt very discouraged.

On the trip home Gil filled me in on the children and all that had been happening at home. He told me that the sitters who had cared for the children had done a very good job, but the disruption of their routine had been upsetting to the children nonetheless. And, he joked, they were sick and tired of eating nothing but the Waldorf salads and hot dogs that he fixed for dinner.

It was a lovely early evening when we reached our home. At the sound of the car hitting the gravel driveway, the children, barefoot and in their pajamas, came bounding out the front screen door and across the lawn to greet me. They all chattered at once, full of the news of the week I'd been away. I was glad to be home.

After getting back to the household routine, I renewed my efforts to figure out the cause of my ailments. The first thing I did was eliminate certain household products that I had been using. I switched to the mildest forms of soap and shampoo. Nevertheless, my strange symptoms persisted. The phases of jitteriness and insomnia continued. My periods became irregular, and I started to spot sporadically.

I worked on a series of drawings of children at the beach, and exhibited them in a show at a seaside gallery. Because I was losing weight, I drank milkshakes and tried to eat more, but it didn't help.

In August, I went to New York City to see my sister, Nina, and her family before they sailed for England, where they were going to live. Her husband, a doctor, was fulfilling a sabbatical year at Cambridge.

My mother came from Florida for the bon voyage, too. It was then that I realized how ill she had become. She was coughing and very short of breath, and still smoking heavily. I made her promise me that she would have a thorough checkup as soon as she returned to Florida.

I had a brief visit with my good friend Ann, with whom I had worked in Denmark years before. She was now living outside New York with her husband and children.

Sandy, now fourteen, went off for another year of boarding school in September and the other children returned to the local grade school. The children had had a good summer; Sandy had been a counselor at a local day camp, while David, now twelve, had gone off to summer camp, and Wendy, ten, and Todd, eight, kept busy with art lessons, science-center activities, and the beach.

However, I was exhausted by severe headaches and wasn't sleeping. With insomnia came depression, and I began to wonder whether I could make it on my own. I debated returning to the hospital. I was given meprobamate to help me sleep, but it seemed only to make me more agitated. I was wide awake and dreaded hearing the birds in the early morning because the sound meant I'd been up all night. I just couldn't sleep. My head ached, my hands shook, and my hands and feet were constantly cold. I couldn't function this way because the fatigue was unbearable. I knew I had to return to the hospital. I talked to friends, called our doctor, organized, and arranged for household help.

When I arrived at the hospital I was exhausted, anxious, and very thin. I was admitted and then an aide showed me to a room I would share with three other women. She recited the hospital routine to me, a jam-packed series of whats and whens and rules and regulations—and tacked on to the end of it was a question: Did I feel like hurting myself? The notion shocked me; suicide was the most farfetched thought imaginable to me. Here I was, desperately trying to make myself better! I realized what a low point I had reached—and how totally misunderstood I was. I told the aide that all I wanted to do was sleep. If I could only sleep, I'd be much better. I had gone three nights without any sleep at all.

I had an initial interview with a psychiatrist, "Dr. Rohne." (The psychiatrist I had seen and liked in June was no longer there.) Dr. Rohne asked about my childhood, my family history, and why I was there. I was so fatigued I had trouble answering his questions. At the end of the session, he assigned me to a doctor who would see me daily.

That day I was in a daze, and I had no appetite. The evening was horrendous. I still couldn't eat much, which made me feel weaker. I read for a little while, hoping this would help me to fall asleep, but again, for the fourth night in a row, I was wide awake. I was so discouraged that I couldn't stop the tears that flooded my pillow. A nurse in the hall realized I was awake and came and talked with me. She was kind. I finally fell asleep about four-thirty in the morning.

But at six forty-five, a nurse awakened me so that I would be ready for my seven-thirty appointment with my new doctor, a beginning resident in psychiatry. (I will call him "Dr. Jeffcoate.") I couldn't believe it. Was this medicine or was this torture? At the time I was too intimidated to say anything, but now I get very angry thinking about the insensitivity of their procedures. I would expect that if a patient were admitted to the hospital with a history of incapacitating insomnia—which in and of itself can produce psychiatric symptoms—the doctors would be humane enough to make sure the patient got sleep before anything else.

My first days in the hospital were the toughest. There were daily appointments with Dr. Jeffcoate and group sessions of all kinds, including physical therapy. I missed my husband and children. I missed being around people who knew me, who knew who I was. It was as though I had been dropped onto another planet, and no one knew of the place I had come from. It was frightening at times, and always bewildering.

And at times it bordered on the absurd. One arrogant psychiatrist—not Dr. Jeffcoate—led me to occupational therapy, saying, "Mrs. Murray, you ought to enjoy the next hour. You are an artist, aren't you?" Whereupon he brought me into a basement room where there were other patients and a therapist. I was given a piece of paper and a shoe box containing broken, dirty bits of crayon, and told to go to work. I felt insulted. It was as if I had taken the doctor to therapy and said, "You should enjoy the next hour, you're going to play doctor," and then handed him a black doctor bag filled with a plastic toy thermometer and stethoscope and sticky old candy pills. Most of the other patients were tranquilized and sat there doing paint-by-numbers. Memories of an abnormal-psychology class I had taken in college came back to me; we had visited facilities for the psychiatrically ill. It was horrifying to face the fact that I wasn't a spectator here in this basement room full of troubled people.

The doctors ran more tests on me during those first days, checking for hypoglycemia and thyroid trouble. I continued to lose weight. I was down to ninety-eight pounds. I was given a gynecological exam, and the gynecologist discovered I had chronic cervicitis and recommended that I have a hysterectomy on my return to Connecticut. I was given Sultrin for the inflammation, and was using steroid cream on my rashes. I refused tranquilizing drugs, but did take a relatively mild sleeping pill every night, and gradually the insomnia subsided. I questioned whether some of my problems weren't due to sensitivity to drugs that had been prescribed for me.

When I went to see Dr. Jeffcoate, he'd tell me how happy he was to talk to a patient who was normal. He told me that he thought that I had the intelligence to sort out my problems and assured me things would come out all right, although he acknowledged that it wouldn't happen overnight. We talked about my marriage to Gil, which was falling apart. Gil and I looked to each other for support, and at times we were caring and loving, but it seemed we had become polar opposites as parents, as artists, as individuals. We seemed to be less and less able to reach a compromise on any issue. On matters of health, we had very different points of view— he would delay getting medical attention until a crisis point, feeling that nature would take care of things and that time would heal all. He acted as if he was invulnerable, taking what struck me as unrealistic chances.

I confided that Gil and I fought more and more. It was as though I were oriented around a work ethic, and Gil was increasingly oriented around a play ethic. He claimed more and more time on weekends for exploring the outdoors, swimming, writing, doing artwork, and drawing cartoons.

My only way of coping with my marriage was to take on more and more responsibility where I could. There were so many things that needed attention in our lives and household, and Gil's lack of concern constantly set me on guard and upset me. Whenever I tried to reason with him about a problem, he had some excuse for not dealing with it. I wished for organization and teamwork; he was for rugged individualism and a laid-back attitude, and he always minimized my concerns. I think he was frustrated and a little frightened by my not feeling well, but despite my illness, I did not delegate more responsibility to him (except for the times I was hospitalized). I always tried to take care of the family's needs as well as the house and outdoor work.

The doctors thought that Gil also needed therapy, so he came to Boston regularly during my weeks at the hospital to see his own therapist.

Midway through my hospital stay, I learned that my mother had been diagnosed with lung cancer and had to have surgery. She knew of my hospitalization and understood why I couldn't come. My brother, Bill, and my aunt Caddie flew down to Jacksonville, Florida, to be with her. Her lung was removed, but the cancer had spread. She barely survived the operation. It had affected her voice and she couldn't speak.

Years later I found a note she had scribbled to my brother while in intensive care. In hardly legible handwriting she had written, "What is the matter with Polly? How is she?" We were both going through such hell, and not being able to help each other through the hardship was painful to both of us. For my mother, her hospitalization was the beginning of the end. She spent the rest of her life bedridden in the hospital or in a nursing home, too ill to be moved nearer her family.

After my second week at the medical center, I returned home for a weekend's visit. Back in Lyme, surrounded by children and books and shopping lists and all the color of daily life, the experience at the hospital seemed a strange dream. It was difficult getting back on the Boston-bound train on Sunday night, and positively heartbreaking to sit at the window to watch my children wave good-bye from the station platform.

One of the most excruciating experiences I had in the hospital occurred a day or two after that. That night, the occupational-therapy project was to cook a Chinese dinner for our group of patients and our doctors and therapists. I was told to go to the kitchen and start chopping celery and onions. Standing at the counter, I glanced at a white-coated woman at the end of the kitchen and recognized her as a classmate from college. She looked at me in surprise and said, "Why, Polly, what are you doing here?"

"I'm a patient," I stammered. After an awkward pause she went on to tell me that she was in charge of occupational therapy at the hospital. I remembered that she had been off during college for a couple of years studying nursing as part of a special course of combined study. I hadn't seen her since those days.

Seeing her was the realization of the biggest fear I had during my stay at the hospital: the fear that I would meet someone I knew. I was ashamed and I felt this couldn't be happening to me. My former college roommates lived just outside Boston, and as I walked through the streets of the city on group outings—often accompanied by therapists—to parks and museums and stores, I dreaded meeting up with a familiar face.

When the three weeks of diagnostic tests were over, I was more than ready to leave Boston behind, and for years afterward I didn't enjoy visiting the city. I returned home rested and got right back in the swing of things. Gil and I began our counseling with a Yale-affiliated psychiatrist named "Dr. Bolen" who had been referred to us by one of the Boston doctors.

A month later, Gil and I returned for a meeting with our therapists in Boston. I had grown fond of Dr. Jeffcoate. He was very helpful and supportive to me, and he listened. He called me several months after I had left the hospital, as he was doing a follow-up report on his patients. I wish I could locate him now and tell him how it all turned out.

The hospital's final evaluation was that I was depressed as a direct result of a chronic, debilitating health problem, as well as of the marital and family problems that were so numerous then. A diagnosis for my physical symptoms still eluded the doctors, but they did not feel that the symptoms had a psychosomatic basis. "Allergy" and "sensitivity" were the words I heard most. The doctor's suggestion: continued supportive psychotherapy.

What I wanted to get from psychotherapy was good old-fashioned reassurance; my self-confidence had been eroded. I had come to realize that I would have to believe in myself, wholly. No one, not even those who loved me, could do that for me. As a starting point, my conviction that whatever was plaguing me was not of my doing gave me courage. I would try to persevere as well as I could, to follow my gut reactions to what was going on. I had to be sure enough of my feelings and observations that no matter what others said and no matter what reasons they had for saying so, I would stick to my own hunches and try and find my own answers.

To know that something is very wrong with you, and yet continually have doctors say, "We are very happy to say that all your tests are normal," is a scary thing. It elicits a lot of complex, painful feelings and questions: "I should be happy, but I'm not." "If they can't find anything definite medically, then maybe it is all in my head." "Could the human mind affect the body that way? How? Why?" "Am I losing control of my mind?" "Is there some underlying reason for me to want to be sick, the way the doctors suggest?"

One easy way out of these difficulties is denial. How wonderfully simple it is to say, "Okay, I'm going to go home and try and forget all about it—I won't be sick." Or "I'll pretend my physical problems don't exist." I had tried this technique time and again, but learned that it was successful only until the next round of severe headache, joint pains, aches, swellings, fever, and bleeding hands. You can't just will your ailments out of existence.

The problem I faced after my stay in the hospital was that all those easy illusions were long gone, but I had yet to come up with an alternative. In time, the way became clearer. I proceeded methodically, quietly; I went underground. I decided to become my own expert, to find my own answers. And so, in the mornings when the children were at school, I haunted libraries, exhausting the resources of local and college branches before I got up enough nerve to walk into the Yale medical library pretending I belonged there. I searched for clues to explain my ailments, and on these journeys there was the ever-present fear that I would turn some corner in the stacks and come face-to-face with one of the doctors who had said, "Mrs. Murray, your tests are entirely normal, so please go home and forget about it."

CHAPTER SIX

CONFRONTATIONS

The greater the ignorance the greater the dogmatism.

SIR WILLIAM OSLER

I began my research in the autumn of 1971, reading medical texts devoted to diseases whose symptoms were similar to my own. I had been tested for many of those illnesses during my hospital visits, so I knew their basic characteristics. I studied differential diagnoses. I again investigated tick-borne illness—Rocky Mountain spotted fever, relapsing fever, and tick paralysis—but, as my internist had said in 1970, none of them quite matched the pattern of crazy symptoms that I was having.

I went at my work as if it were a college thesis, reading through texts, taking copious notes, filing them in manila folders. Despite my organization and determination, I was scared. I knew the stakes were high: I had to find the answer somehow, or suffer serious misgivings about my very being.

I read anything that I could find on connective-tissue disease. Lucinda Webb, a dear friend of mine who is a nurse and was baffled and troubled by my problems, sent me a newspaper clipping that told the story of a lupus patient. It mentioned a newly formed Manhattan chapter of the Lupus Foundation. I decided to join it. (I eventually joined Lupus Foundation branches in Connecticut and Massachusetts to be sure that I was kept abreast of new information.)

As I read about various diseases and their diagnoses, I could better see how, given the inconsistent nature of my symptoms and the lack of positive test results, as well as the intensity of my pursuit, many of the doctors I encountered would think to themselves,

"Psychosomatic." I didn't accept it, or think it was good medicine, but I understood it.

In the weeks that followed my hospitalization, even close relatives suggested that I was sick because of fatigue and depression, saying that all I needed was to pack my bags and get away for a change of scenery. "It will do you a world of good," one relative would say, as though all I needed was to kick a common cold or the February blues.

I had tried that quick-getaway approach during the period when I was really sick the year before, in 1970. On the spur of the moment, Gil and I booked a baby-sitter and hopped a train for a weekend of museums and galleries in New York City—a desperate attempt to leave it all behind. But we didn't succeed. While viewing an exhibit at the Whitney, I ached so that I had to sit down halfway up the stairs. I had very little strength. On Sunday I was so exhausted that I stayed in the hotel and slept most of the day.

In the weeks that followed, my symptoms continued, and with my physical and mental world threatened, I felt very vulnerable and washed out, and I was depressed. I had always been very motivated and active, and now, at the age of thirty-seven, I felt like an old lady. I was really very angry, too. I knew I had symptoms and yet I couldn't convince anyone to take me seriously. I was a "flighty woman" in the words of one doctor. "Do you have a lot of time on your hands?" several doctors asked. "How old are your children?" "All in school?" "What do you do all day?" "Do you think about yourself a lot?" "How do you get along with your husband?" "Why don't you find yourself a good hobby?"

In asking these questions, the doctors misread me—indeed, they misread what it's like to be a mother raising four children. This endless free time they spoke of was a mystery to me. We were busy restoring our old house. Did they think that once the kids were on the school bus, it was playtime for dear old Mom? No laundry to do, no house to clean, no yardwork, no errands, no meetings with teachers, no grocery shopping, to name only a few of the things a mother attends to during school hours?

And I did have hobbies. In addition to my painting, drawing, and gardening, I collected antiques, knitted, and did embroidery.

And yet the doctors continually insinuated that I had spare time to imagine my problems, as though I were some "housewife" suffering from ennui in front of the television.

At the time I was also coping with my mother's deteriorating health. I talked regularly with her doctors and nurses. In November Gil and I made a trip to Florida to see her after she had been moved from the hospital to a nursing care facility. My brother, Bill, and I took over her affairs, as Nina was still in England with her family.

In January, my mother's health worsened, and Bill, Nina, and I flew to Florida. We stayed a week, visiting with her, getting things in order.

I was still having trouble with the cervicitis, but my gynecologist, "Dr. Winder," wanted to postpone the hysterectomy until we had tried other methods of controlling the bleeding.

I developed a sore throat and fever and was given five more days of penicillin. As soon as I finished the medication the sore throat returned and I developed a chest cold, laryngitis, and a cough. The following week I suddenly had a lot of pain in my shoulder and arm. I had vasculitis and I had to use cortisone ointment on my hands. Some fingers were so swollen that I couldn't bend them.

My psychiatrist, Dr. Bolen, saw me at the height of my symptoms and said they were certainly real; my local doctor said that I had bursitis and an infection and gave me phenylbutazone and hetacillin, an antibacterial. The pain had been so bad that I couldn't sit up from a lying-down position without help and I needed help putting on my clothes each morning. It hurt my scalp to brush or move my hair. I was told to use heating pads and wear a sling. The phenylbutazone lessened the pain, but seven or eight black-and-blue marks soon erupted on my thighs and throbbing joints. I was told to discontinue all medication. My eyesight was blurry at times during this period. Penicillin always made me feel better while I was taking it, and for a while thereafter, but could I have developed a sensitivity to it? Could I have some kind of serum sickness? Could I have an allergy to the streptococcal bacteria? Could the cortisone ointment be affecting me adversely?

At one point, Dr. Bolen suggested that I try an antidepressant. I took one pill and slept fourteen hours, waking with an angry rash on my thighs. I felt drugged and terrible, and discontinued the medication after consulting Dr. Bolen. This kind of overreaction to drugs had happened so many times before that I was always cautious and warned doctors of my sensitivity. When I spoke of it, they often turned off, shrugging, and I always came away feeling neurotic for even entertaining the idea that I was hypersensitive to drugs. Even cold creams and some synthetic clothes have triggered allergic reactions on my skin. PHisoHex, containing hexachlorophene, gave both my daughter and me problems when used for routine skin care in the hospital at the time of her birth.

In light of the fact that the doctors seemed to emphasize the possibility that my symptoms were some kind of allergic reaction (though not one of them suggested my seeing an allergist), I began to eliminate and test certain things on my own. I had noticed during the summer that my face rash would come out only when I had been in the sun; I always wore sunglasses because I had developed photosensitivity; the sun gave me a headache and made me dizzy. The frames of my sunglasses were made of black plastic. I had noticed that my rash would come out in the area where the plastic hit my cheeks, the skin above my eyes, and the tops of my ears. Within hours I would have a bright-red, sore welt, which oozed fluid; general swelling around the eye; and blurred vision. I would also have a general systemic reaction—a feverish feeling and achiness. My fingers would react, too.

I wondered whether the steering wheel of my car, also black plastic, might be causing my hand eruptions. And could the ointment I used on my hands and face be setting off some chemical reaction with the plastic, perhaps triggered by heat, sun, or perspiration? I suspected this because the plastic did not cause a similar reaction in areas that were not treated with steroid ointment.

In my research I learned that skin sensitivity varies from one part of the body to another, and that allergic reactions are often affected by light and moisture in combination with the offending allergen. I wrote to the president of the company that manufactured the glasses, and a representative from the company that made the frames for them was very cooperative and supportive. He did some testing, and said that such cases are rare and usually due to an "idiosyncrasy of the individual." I felt like I had reached another dead end.

I was still quite thin. I tried to eat a well-balanced diet with plenty of fresh foods, and made a concerted effort to get enough sleep every night. Despite these efforts, in April of 1972, I had a cough, laryngitis, and my hand and face rash, and I ran a fever.

My aunt and I went to Florida to be with my mother, who was in the last stages of her cancer. We stayed several days; it was terribly difficult to leave knowing what her condition was and that I probably wouldn't see her again. Indeed, she died ten days later.

Bill and I began the long process of sorting out our mother's affairs. Her death and the grief I felt made me realize the unusual stress I had been under in the past year or so. Dr. Bolen had been telling me this all along, but it wasn't until my mother died that I could see how enormous the emotional strain had been. He had told me again and again that there was nothing psychologically wrong with me, only that I was under a lot of stress due to life's circumstances, and needed support in coping.

He confided, too, that had he seen me before I was hospitalized, he would not have recommended hospitalization. He thought it would have been far better to see me often on an outpatient basis, and at the same time schedule further outpatient medical tests here in Connecticut. This assessment meant a great deal to me.

In July 1972, Todd had cellulitis of the foot and was prescribed an antibiotic. Shortly thereafter, Sandy had a lump and red rash in his right armpit; this was diagnosed as ringworm. As for me, my symptoms continued throughout the summer. It hurt to raise my left arm. I chilled easily and had cramps in my feet; my thighs and upper arms throbbed. I ran a low-grade fever day after day. I had lost more weight. My hands were swollen; my limbs twitched. I had strange sensations in the skin in certain areas of my face and trunk. The local doctor was baffled, saying that he had another female patient in the area who had similar symptoms. He was almost certain she had lupus, but test results were negative.

In the fall, I made an appointment with a rheumatologist whom I will call Dr. Tellsey. This was suggested by my gynecologist, Dr. Winder, who wanted an evaluation of my problems, especially if a hysterectomy became necessary.

This time, I decided, I would be truly prepared to present my case history, so there would be less chance for me to feel intimidated, less chance that the doctor would be able to direct the presentation of my medical history in such a way that the picture was distorted. I planned to take with me notes of my symptoms and the many different diagnoses for each one that I had been given so far by so many doctors.

Behind these preparations was a very simple need: to find a doctor who was truly receptive to the untidiness of my problems, who was willing to step back and look at the full pattern of my symptoms, and from there, decide what tests might be worth running. I needed a doctor who would do blood tests when I was at the height of a flare-up to see if something could be detected when the symptoms were at their peak. So often, while I waited a few days or a week for an appointment, my symptoms had subsided, so blood tests were never done at the ideal time.

This lag between calling for an appointment and seeing the doctor also meant that I would often have to describe the joint and skin symptoms; the doctor didn't see them firsthand. I hoped to find a doctor who would see me when my symptoms flared, and who would more generally view the search for a cause as an interesting challenge, not as a threat to his competence, as so many seemed to do. So it was with high hopes—and plenty of notes—that I went to my appointment with Dr. Tellsey.

I gave him my carefully prepared medical history and my many diagnoses, and explained that I was disappointed with the lack of continuity in following my case. I told him that I was seeing a psychiatrist, who did not think my symptoms were psychosomatic. I described the family's propensity for allergies.

I thought my forthrightness and thoroughness would be met with compassion, but they were not. When I told Dr. Tellsey of my recent theory that my rashes were due to a reaction to the plastic in my sunglasses, he said, "Mrs. Murray, I admire your fortitude in writing Polaroid, but I'm afraid the sunglasses have nothing to do with your problem." He then gave me a chilly smile and said, "And how is Dr. Land?"

He carefully examined me, providing terse answers to my questions. Afterward he sat down at his desk and spoke into his dictating machine, describing that I had brought notes and a photograph of my face rash. He then went on to describe my symptoms, sometimes inaccurately rendering what I had said. I got the idea that he liked to hear himself talk. He said he was testing for psoriasis with arthritis, periarteritis nodosa, lupus, and rheumatoid arthritis, and that he wanted to see me again in several weeks. After I told him of the skepticism I had faced from other doctors, he said that he did not believe I was making up a story.

Just before my next visit with Dr. Tellsey, I wore the black plastic sunglasses—testing, I suppose, his assumption that they could have nothing to do with my rashes. Sure enough, I broke out into an angry rash; it was in full bloom when I went to see him.

The blood tests had all come back negative. Given this, and given the unequivocal presence of the rash before his eyes, he was more receptive to the idea that an allergy was the cause. In fact, he was enthusiastic. He spun on his heel and went in search of the doctor in the adjoining office, hoping to get him to come see the rash. (As it turned out, the doctor wasn't in his office.)

The week after that visit, I received a letter from Dr. Tellsey stating that my rashes were due to contact dermatitis caused by plastic. The letter also confirmed that all tests performed were negative for inflammatory disease and that my symptoms were best thought of as manifestations of allergic response. Dr. Tellsey concluded by requesting that I see him again in six months in order to repeat some of the lab tests, especially those that would indicate lupus.

The ambiguity of the letter perplexed me. On the one hand Dr. Tellsey asserted that my problems were caused by allergies (though he offered no plan to alleviate them), and then on the other hand he was suggesting that he still thought it possible that I was suffering from an inflammatory disease. And it was disheartening once again to have a doctor who seemed to be shutting the door on the idea of seeing me when I had a flare-up. I read the letter again and could only shake my head at the inconsistency of his diagnosis.

We were building an addition onto our house, and this kept my mind off my health. Gil and I, with the help of an architect, designed the addition, and there were a thousand decisions and details to attend to, from buying a few new pieces of furniture and appliances to overseeing the construction. We wanted the new kitchen and eating area to be inviting and casual, so we spent a great deal of time making every detail right. I remember spending hours mixing different stains until we got just the antique color and tone we wanted for the kitchen cabinets. We started construction in early September and moved in in early February. Life was chaotic during those months, with the house all torn up, but the result was well worth it.

Before Thanksgiving of that year I bought Henrietta Aladjem's book, *The Sun Is My Enemy,*[1] which I had learned about through the Lupus Foundation newsletter. The book opened up new doors for me. The author's poignant story of her many years of struggling to find a diagnosis and cure for her illness gave me the courage to continue in my search for understanding of my own mysterious illness. The book taught me that yes, the burden of responsibility did come back to me and me alone, and that no one else cared about finding the answer as passionately as I did.

That one should be so alone in seeking the restoration of one's health is wrong; that many of those who have been trained to heal draw such neat and tidy boundaries around their territory of duty is unfortunate. But this wasn't the time to lament the shortcomings of the medical profession. It was time to persist, just as Henrietta Aladjem had done, and maybe I would be fortunate enough to find a diagnosis for my illness as she had.

On February 1, 1973, I wrote to Henrietta Aladjem, telling her how much her book meant to me. I wrote that "over the past few years I have had varying explanations for the multitude of mysterious symptoms which have afflicted me. What a pat on the back to read your book and to know that someone else has been confused by such identical symptoms and has had differing opinions from the medical world." I went on to tell her that I was moved to read that she, too, had been told that her illness was due to nerves when the doctors either didn't know the reason for the symptom or hesitated to use the word "lupus" until they had a screaming case and all the lab tests positive to prove it.

I continued, "Whatever I have is not, so far, an acute case. . . . Doctors suspect allergy or collagen disease, but so far no positive tests. I have had varying symptoms on and off for years, have always had allergies, and my symptoms are becoming more acute each year.

"My reaction has been to find out as much as possible about the disease and this knowledge has helped me to live with my symptoms. I think the unknown can be frightening, and, like you, I keep pursuing answers.

"I have learned a great deal during the past few years. One of the most significant things I've learned is that I get worse after exposure to the sun. Also, cold and drugs affect me easily. Like you, the drugs given to me to help my symptoms made me much worse. I am much more cautious than I used to be."

I described my problems more fully, and again thanked her for the reassurance her book provided me.

Mrs. Aladjem called me from her home in Massachusetts a couple of weeks later. I remember it was the first morning we were in our new addition. We were eating a big breakfast as a kind of housewarming party, and beautiful winter sunshine reflected off the snow outside and poured into the room, making it as cheery as a greenhouse.

Hearing Henrietta Aladjem's kind and encouraging voice was comforting. She made me feel that somehow, despite how little progress I had made, I should be optimistic, that there was reason for hope. She reminded me how fortunate I was to have the ability to ask the right questions, seek out the pertinent research. Her phone call was a great inspiration to me. I felt very strongly that she believed in what I was doing. Having lived with her illness, lupus erythematosus, for so many years before diagnosis, she knew fully the anxiety I was experiencing—the self-doubt; the agony of wondering whether my mind was conjuring up this illness; the pressure to prove to doctors that something was physically wrong even if they could not easily detect and label it.

During the winter of 1973, I continued to have periods of incapacitating neck, hip, and knee pain and stiffness, and my hands were very bad. My knees felt full of fluid. (A few months back, in November 1972, both Wendy's knees had been painful and tender, and I wondered if there was a connection. There was no trauma; however, the doctor could tell that the knees were quite tender. Suspecting osteochondritis, he ordered X rays, which were normal.) I had fevers and nausea and other gastrointestinal disturbances, as well as canker sores and cold sores. My glands were swollen. In April, I developed numbness and pins-and-needles sensations in my fingers, and my hands were very shaky at times. At this time I bought a *Merck Manual* (an encyclopedia-like resource that describes diseases and their treatment.) and did further reading to try to find out what might be happening to all of us.

Despite all these problems, it became more and more important for me to keep pursuing my creative endeavors. For one thing, it made me feel better psychologically to see progress in one area of my life. So I continued to take my paintings to exhibitions around the state, and was constantly on the go to keep up with the activities of my children. Whenever I had a little spare time I worked on a new series of beach drawings.

With the advent of warm weather, I noticed that the ticks were back more than ever that year. When we first owned dogs, we would find ticks on them only when visiting Cape Cod. Over the years, however, the ticks in Lyme became more prevalent.

The increase was due largely to the changing terrain of the town. As farming decreased, the pastureland where sheep and cows grazed diminished, too, and the underbrush grew up. In 1920s photographs taken of our house the vegetation is sparse, with single trees standing in the background. By the early 1970s, the land around our house was thick with trees, wild roses, barberry, bittersweet, wild grapevines, and other vegetation.

A friend of mine with small children had also noticed the increase in ticks that year. As she put it, she "freaked out" when engorged ticks dropped off her longhaired dog and onto the kitchen floor like little gray peas.

Ticks seemed to come in waves, depending upon moisture and heat; their numbers seemed to recede in extremely hot, dry weather. They were to be found from early spring until late fall; however, they could emerge on warm winter days. Although Gil thought I was being over cautious, I taught the children to check themselves over after being in the woods. While living in Wilmington, Delaware, as a child, I had been warned of the danger of getting Rocky Mountain spotted fever from ticks. One child in my school had died. After an outbreak of the disease, our teacher had us inspect our bodies and our hair once a day.

Also, at this time I had read an account in *The New York Times* of a child from somewhere along the Connecticut shoreline being near death in a hospital with severe fever and neurological problems, with no definite diagnosis, until an alert nurse found a tick had embedded in his scalp. The tick was removed and the child's symptoms started to subside.

We had our dog, Nanny, clipped and dipped regularly in a tick repellent. (The children always laughed at Nanny when she came home from the "dog parlor" with her fur uncharacteristically cut in a "poodle pompadour" and a pom-pom tail.) That year Nanny was sick on and off, with periods of lameness, and was treated for a urinary problem. Sometimes her legs would twitch uncontrollably.

In early spring, abnormal vaginal bleeding continued to afflict me sporadically and I had a cauterization, which seemed to help for a while. My gynecologist still thought it better to avoid a hysterectomy.

My entire system was still reacting to something—but what?

In early May, I prepared to see Dr. Tellsey for my six-month follow-up appointment. I had done a lot more research in the months since I'd seen him. In addition to reading Mrs. Aladjem's book, I had ordered a textbook, Dr. Edmund L. Dubois's *Lupus Erythematosus.*[2] I had also been keeping up with the lupus newsletter and other research articles and texts on the disease, and had compiled data on differential diagnoses relevant to my group of symptoms.

I was interested to read in Mrs. Aladjem's book a quote from Professor Dr. Liuben Popoff, a dermatologist from Bulgaria, who described how very difficult it is to diagnose lupus and other connective-tissue diseases:

> *Systemic lupus erythematosus and rheumatoid arthritis have so much in common. Even great clinicians with years of experience are fooled by one of the diseases masquerading as the other. It used to be said years ago that syphilis was the great imitator. It could mimic almost all other diseases. Now, if syphilis is treated early enough with penicillin, there are fewer late complications. Today the great imitators are connective-tissue diseases— rheumatoid arthritis, lupus, and other diseases like them. They can do anything. Believe me, they can affect any part of the body. They can even make you crazy without giving obvious trouble on the skin, in the kidneys, or anywhere else. Connective-tissue disease is a very clever opponent for the clinician.[3]*

I remembered reading that the famous physician Sir William Osler had said, "Know syphilis in all its manifestations and relations, and all things clinical will be added unto you."

Dr. Dubois's textbook on lupus also spoke of lupus as a great imitator; Dubois mentioned a Dr. A. M. Harvey "who listed 24 different diagnoses made on his patients during the early stages of their diseases."[4]

Although I felt empowered by my increased knowledge and my contact with Mrs. Aladjem, I dreaded another confrontation with Dr. Tellsey. For while I am quick to learn information, I am hesitant when it comes to verbal debate. And the more heated the debate, the less I am able to spar. I freeze; I always have. In school, I was the one in the classroom who sat there positively praying that the teacher wouldn't call on me to provide an answer—even if I knew I had the right one. Still, I was determined to not let the doctor get the better of me. So I armed myself with notes and questions.

I described to Dr. Tellsey all that had been going on since I'd last seen him, telling him that I often felt cold, that it was very painful to put my feet in warm water, that I had continuing black-and-blue marks and strange rashes. And I told him of Mrs. Aladjem and the research I had done. I told him that I wanted to have a good dialogue with him, and that I thought that it would be wise to have a blood test done when I had systemic symptoms and felt ill, not after the symptoms had subsided. I asked him again if I might be predisposed to allergic responses, given that my family had a strong history of allergies. Should I be tested for allergies? Should the children be tested for their allergies? In my heart, though, I believed my symptoms were indicative of early-stage lupus.

What followed was an hour of heated discussion. Dr. Tellsey seemed threatened by my assertions, repeatedly crying, "Not true!" when I mentioned the research being done on a possible genetic predisposition to lupus, and the fact that some lupus patients reported that they overreacted to vaccines, drugs, and other toxins.

He accused me of chasing doctors about lupus, totally disregarding the fact that *he* had requested this appointment so that he could retest me for the disease. He told me I was anxious and fixated on lupus, and suggested that I see a psychiatrist. I reminded him that I had been seeing a psychiatrist, as I'd told him during the first visit, and that that psychiatrist supported my research.

"I'm shocked that he would support you in doing this research on your own," Dr. Tellsey responded. "I find it hard to fathom that he supports you as well in your questioning of the treatment you received in two fine medical centers."

I was stunned. I tried to steer the conversation toward less-explosive issues, but it seemed that even routine questions that a patient might ask incited a riot in him. For example, when I asked him whether I should avoid exposure to the sun given that it always made me feel worse, he exclaimed, "No caution is necessary for you or the children for any reactions!"

He ranted on about "triage" and told me that in the grand scheme of things, my symptoms were really of no serious consequence. At the end of our verbal battle, he had not yet examined me or taken blood for tests. Saying that I would have to return for another appointment, he walked me to the door.

When I got home I looked up "triage" in my medical dictionary, and discovered that it means "The classification of sick, wounded or injured persons in order to ensure the efficient use of medical and nursing manpower, equipment, and facilities. Classification is concerned with the casualties who would live without therapy of any kind, those who would die no matter what treatment is provided, and those who would survive if given adequate care."[5]

The next appointment, four weeks later, made the last one seem like a congenial chat. After Dr. Tellsey examined me and drew my blood for testing, I took a deep breath and said, "I am not chasing doctors." He rolled his eyes, but I continued. I told him I had never heard of lupus before I had been exhibiting symptoms for several years and the medical profession suggested it to me. Pacing the floor, he implored, "Mrs. Murray, how can I convince you to stop this anxious search? If I wake up with a backache, that doesn't mean that I should look up in the medical literature everything to do with backache and immediately jump to the conclusion that I have a serious problem! Please, please, accept the fact that everything has been done, and forget this fruitless search for a label. Nothing at all has shown up on tests. We can do no more. I personally think you are a case of wounded intellect and you are obsessed with making a case for a disease that exists most likely only in your own mind."

(I thought, but did not dare to say, "If the disease is psychosomatic, then why do my symptoms improve soon after a course of penicillin?")

Exasperated, he ended his speech thus: "Frankly, Mrs. Murray, your range of symptoms can just as easily be classified with possible tertiary syphilis as they can with lupus." With that he asked me to leave his office.

Following the appointment, I was to meet Gil for lunch at a

little pizza place in Old Saybrook, near his office. As I sat waiting for Gil to arrive, I pondered my diagnostic dilemma and said to myself, "I will be a good girl and stop thinking about it, just as the doctor says. My fingers ache and bleed; I have unexplained rashes, fever, weight loss, stiffness, and nausea; but it doesn't matter."

I was angry, and as much as I tried to put them out of my head in the days that followed, my mind kept working over my encounters with Dr. Tellsey. I recalled the way he had paced the floor while rebuffing my questions. Was he threatened by me? Why did he grow so impatient at my mention of various allergic reactions in my family? Why was he so quick to say that no precautions were necessary in regard to drugs, the sun, or reactions to insect bites?

It was clear that he considered me overly anxious—and yet hadn't his letter of the previous fall delivered ambiguous messages and encouraged me to return for further testing? Was the tension between Dr. Tellsey and me the result of my trying to converse on his level? Of my trying to have a dialogue with him? I couldn't help but wonder if he would be treating a man in the same manner he treated me. I made a list of the series of events, writing down only the bare outline of what took place, so that I could gain perspective.

1. On a referral from the medical center in Boston, I see my gynecologist about having a hysterectomy. He, in turn, refers me to a rheumatologist for an evaluation he thinks is necessary prior to possible surgery.

2. The rheumatologist sees me, thinks he has the answers, and quickly dismisses my theories as wrong.

3. He sees me again and says my theories are probably right after all; he follows up with a letter requesting that I see him again in six months for further tests for lupus.

4. Six months later, after an hour of intense discussion about the possible causes of my complaints, he doesn't have time to examine me and says I'll have to come back for another visit.

5. I go for an exam in four weeks; there is another battle of
    words, and the rheumatologist requests that I leave,
    insulting me by saying that I am chasing doctors and
    bothering the best doctors in the field of rheumatology;
    he makes comments like "Congratulations, you have
    sought out the best!"; "Oh, no, you've seen him, too?";
    and "If you are seeing a psychiatrist and he encourages
    you, *he* needs a psychiatrist!"

No matter how many times I read the list, Dr. Tellsey's sarcasm, to
say nothing of the inconsistency of his statements, was shocking.
Even if my illnesses were psychosomatic and I was chasing busy
doctors, his lack of compassion was unprofessional. And what right
did he have to say that I was chasing doctors, when the truth was
that, to a large extent, I was being bounced from doctor to doctor,
referral to referral?

In mid-June I received copies of my lab reports, along with a
letter from Dr. Tellsey stating that he was happy to report that all
my tests were normal. Receiving it brought little solace; my disappointment in him could not be assuaged by a few cordial words.

CHAPTER SEVEN

FINDING AN ALLY

Even more important, every generation of clinicians has experienced and taught what Peabody expressed in his famous remark, "The secret of the care of the patient is in caring for the patient." Whatever the system of medicine in vogue, patients want and often actually need to be treated as individual human beings; they want their physician to deal with them as if they required special attention and were entitled to it.
                    RENÉ DUBOS, *MAN ADAPTING*[1]

The summer of 1973 was busier than ever. David graduated from eighth grade. In those days the public school in Lyme put on a formal graduation. The young boys dressed in jacket and tie, the girls wore long white gowns and teetered in their new white pumps, and they marched to "Pomp and Circumstance," awkward and serious and charming as can be. David was over six feet by then, and skinny as a fence post. He wore gold wire-rimmed glasses, and his sandy-blond hair hung down to his shoulders, à la John Lennon.

Sandy was home from boarding school and working as a counselor at a day camp. His best friend, Johnny, who lived a stone's throw down the road, had just gotten his driver's license, so the two went off on escapades in Johnny's beat-up blue station wagon a good deal of the time. Johnny would pull up to the driveway, honk the horn, tip his bright red baseball cap, and smile brightly each morning; then the two of them were gone until well past sundown.

Wendy was busy baby-sitting and looking forward to a two-week trip to Maine with a friend's family. It was her second trip to Maine with them. The summer before, she and her friend had come back with suitcases full of Maine rocks and sea urchin shells, a fondness for lobster and rambling summer houses, and a crush on the dock boy who ran the launch boat at Winter Harbor.

Todd was taking swimming lessons and he and Wendy attended a recreation group at the school; I was exhibiting my paintings and beach drawings at galleries in the area.

My hands and face flared with rashes, and the abnormal bleeding still occurred despite treatment. My gynecologist, Dr. Winder, gave me another cauterization and did an endometrial biopsy, which was negative.

The cauterization hadn't worked, for I experienced intermittent bleeding in August and September. In October, my gynecologist recommended that I have a dilation and curettage.

The evening before the operation, a nurse took my temperature and discovered that I was running a slight fever, just under 100. I told her this was what I had been doing on and off for years.

Following surgery I had a reaction to the iodine antiseptic used; I had a rash for weeks afterward. I also had a sore throat, chest pain when I took a deep breath, and black-and-blue marks; I developed pain in my left hip and thigh. The insomnia and jitteriness returned. The following month my eye swelled, I developed canker sores again, gastrointestinal problems, and a terribly stiff neck. The bleeding and the slight fever continued.

I read in the Connecticut Lupus Foundation, Inc., newsletter that there was to be a lecture on lupus at the University of Connecticut Health Center in Farmington on Sunday afternoon, November 18, 1973. Henrietta Aladjem would speak, as would Dr. Peter Schur, a rheumatologist and expert on lupus at the Robert Brigham Hospital in Boston. Dr. Schur was also an associate professor of medicine at Harvard Medical School.

I really wanted to go to the lecture. The similarities between my symptoms and those of lupus were so many; I couldn't rule out the possibility that I had the early symptoms of the disease. I had to go and find out more information. Gil decided to go with me, so we arranged for someone to be home with the children.

The university's modern medical center sits on a hill in Farmington, and it was quite a crowd that gathered for the meeting that brisk November day. We found seats in the large lecture room.

The rashes shown during the first part of the slide presentation did not look like my rash, and I had a moment of feeling utterly foolish for attending the meeting, but then slides of rashes came upon the screen that looked incredibly similar to mine. Gil and I looked at each other when we saw them, and then we sat in rapt attention for the rest of the lecture.

Dr. Schur spoke of the continuing research into finding the cause of lupus and said that an open mind was very important, and that clues and answers might even come from outside the medical profession; perhaps even from a housewife suffering from the disease who might have insight that the doctors might overlook. I remember getting goose bumps when he said that.

Dr. Schur's open-mindedness gave me hope. Henrietta Aladjem gave an inspiring talk as well. After the meeting I went up and introduced myself to her. She remembered our phone conversation and was very cordial, and asked me about my health. I told her of my continuing problems, and she said that she thought another opinion would be a good idea. She gave me her card and said to call and she would help set up a meeting with Dr. Schur.

Following a telephone conversation with Mrs. Aladjem, I wrote to Dr. Schur in Boston for an appointment.

My appointment with Dr. Schur at Robert Brigham Hospital would be on Monday, December 17, at ten-thirty. I called Mrs. Aladjem to thank her and she invited Gil and me to visit her in Wellesley the night before my appointment, to talk further about my story. We had made reservations to stay at a hotel in Boston, and I said we would love to stop by briefly late in the afternoon.

I had a large painting entitled *In the Greenhouse* accepted for exhibition in the Connecticut Women Artists Show at the Slater Museum in Norwich, Connecticut. The opening reception would be on Sunday, December 16. I could go to the opening on our way to Boston.

To prepare for my interview with Dr. Schur, I wrote up a nine-page medical history covering all the episodic problems I had been having over the years to give to him for reference.

After being questioned so many times by so many doctors during my quest for a diagnosis, I had decided to actually give an up-to-date, thorough medical history to the doctor I was consulting. It helped to have it in front of me as well, since I always found medical interviews intimidating, which made it easy to lose track of the sequence of symptoms.

I'd learned, too, the importance of noting when symptoms were occurring, and whether or not they appeared in conjunction with other symptoms. I was looking for some kind of pattern to my illness, one that would give a doctor something substantial to go on, and I knew that seemingly unimportant details might well add up to one. A while back, I had begun keeping a running record of my symptoms on the calendar. (The children would often buy me calendars for Christmas and they knew that big spaces for each day were a must.) My medical history took me hours to compile, but it proved to be well worth the effort.

It was a raw, cold, wintery day, threatening snow, when we left the children with a sitter and drove to Wellesley. There we were warmly welcomed by Mr. and Mrs. Aladjem. By then it was dark, and bitter cold, and the Aladjems offered some homemade soup to warm us up while we talked. We had a lively conversation, comparing notes and discussing the possibility that allergic reactions might trigger lupus. She reminded me that some of her doctors had suspected insect bites as the possible cause of the outbreak of her lupus. She was very supportive and wished me luck in my pursuit of answers.

Gil and I found a cozy restaurant in Boston where we had a good dinner, and went to the hotel early to be rested for the appointment the following day.

We found the hospital with no trouble. Gil had grown up in Boston and knew the city well. Dr. Peter Schur greeted us kindly and then gave me a thorough examination and consultation. He ordered that X rays be taken of my neck, because I had pain when turning my head, and sent me to the lab for a series of blood tests, including a bleeding-time test whose results might explain my black-and-blue eruptions. (Bruising can be caused by low platelet counts and coagulation abnormalities.) I gave Dr. Schur my complete medical history, and we went over it together.

I told Dr. Schur that the skin rashes on my hands and arms had been diagnosed as contact dermatitis, housewife's eczema, and nerves; my face rash as seborrheic dermatitis, allergy to sun, and nerves; my black-and-blue marks were said to be caused by a hormonal problem or allergy or vascular fragility or vitamin C deficiency or idiopathic thrombocytopenia; my sore throats had been attributed to a virus, allergy, thyroiditis, or streptococcal infection.

Dr. Schur was kind, and said that I definitely had something going on, given these chronic problems; he felt that at this point in time, however, my problem simply might not be diagnosable with current medical knowledge. He said to hang on and stay in contact with him or a large medical center; someday we would have the proper clues and some answers—someday the pieces of the puzzle would all fit together. He said that he wanted me to try taking an antihistamine called Periactin regularly to cut down my allergic responses. I felt more hopeful after my meeting with him than I had in a long time.

I began by taking a dose of four antihistamines a day, but my mouth became very dry and I rapidly gained weight. Dr. Schur reduced the dosage to one a day, which I took at bedtime. To my great relief, I experienced none of the daytime drowsiness I had experienced with other antihistamines, and within a few weeks I felt remarkably better. The antihistamine brought my appetite back to a more normal level; my gastrointestinal problems and nose and throat symptoms also improved. I was sleeping more soundly as well. I was beginning to feel like a new person.

The antihistamine's immediate and substantial effect on my symptoms brought to mind my conversation with Mrs. Aladjem about the interrelatedness of allergies and lupus. I went back to *The Sun Is My Enemy* and read the passage in which she discusses the possibility that an allergic reaction caused the onset of the disease in her: "Bugs loved me. In 1951, I had something similar to lupus in Gorham, New Hampshire. It was during the month of June when the black flies were at their worst. The bites got infected and blistered and I ran a fever of 101 degrees. Luckily, I got over it quickly. In previous years, some doctors had suspected insect bites as a possible cause for the outbreak of my lupus—lupus has many ways of starting."[2]

It was hard to fathom that the bite of an insect could wreak enough havoc on the immune system to instigate so complex a disease as lupus, and yet it rang true to me. Given that I had experienced a myriad of allergic reactions in my life, could it be that one of them—or all of them—had set off lupus within me? If I didn't have lupus, might I have some other connective-tissue disease that could also be triggered by a particular allergic response?

In mid-January 1974, I received a letter from Dr. Schur describing the results of the tests. He wrote:

> Your tests for lupus were entirely negative. As for complement levels, which are indications of lupus, vasculitis or other immunological diseases, these were all normal also. Furthermore, your immunoglobulin levels, particularly IgE, which quite often indicates a propensity for allergies, were also normal. Studies regarding bleeding tendencies, abnormal clotting studies were also entirely normal.
>
> We therefore are left with an inability to explain your symptoms with our present technology and strongly recommend that you take symptomatic therapy for your various difficulties. . . .
>
> The X-ray of your cervical spine was essentially normal except for slight narrowing of the C5, C6 disc space. This may account for some of your neck symptoms. If your neck does bother you, I recommend a "Thomas" collar.

Despite my desire for a definitive diagnosis, I was relieved to once again get the news that the lupus test was negative. And the success of the antihistamine in calming my symptoms also quieted my fear that I would never feel truly well. I wasn't in perfect shape—my abnormal bleeding continued—but in comparison with the way I had felt six months earlier, I felt great.

Dr. Winder, my gynecologist, was now considering hormone treatment. Dr. Schur recommended my seeing a gynecologist in Boston in early February for a second opinion, and I had another exam and biopsy done there. The results indicated no sign of malignancy. The gynecologist recommended further cauterization of the area of inflammation, as had been done previously. Over the next few months I improved and the area healed.

In February, Sandy was confined to the infirmary of his boarding school, under siege with a rash and flu.

Life went on at a fast pace, and we did happy things. In March Todd and Wendy took ceramics classes on Saturday mornings. I met each week with the Lyme Craft Guild, which I loved. We dubbed ourselves "the crafty ladies" and threw ourselves into all sorts of endeavors. We learned a lot from each other, as we each had an area of expertise. From the ancient art of making the Ukrainian Easter eggs called *pysanky,* to pottery, silk screening, and quilt-making, we all pooled our talents. It was a productive way to get together with good friends and we always had a good gab session while we worked or took a break for tea.

I continued to paint in what little spare time I had. On the second floor of our addition we had built a wonderful studio, with lots of windows and a skylight. No more canvases propped precariously on the kitchen wall; no more taking a step back to get some perspective and ramming into the kitchen table instead!

I entered my work in various exhibitions in the lower Connecticut River Valley. In March I was thrilled to learn that my work had been accepted into the juried show of the New Haven Paint and Clay Club for the second year in a row. Later in the spring I was invited to be an artist member.

Over the years I had also exhibited in numerous banks in the area, and was invited to be an artist member of the Essex Art Gallery, the Clinton Art Society, and Connecticut Women Artists.

In April, my stretch of good health came to an end when my hands erupted again. I wondered if the sun or gardening affected them, and I wore gloves to see if this would help. Gil also had a similar rash on his hands, off and on.

My hands were very swollen and inflamed during June and July. I also had a rash around my lower legs and ankles; the tiny red dots looked like bleeding into the skin. Dr. Schur suggested I increase my dosage of antihistamine. I tried it for a few weeks, but my mouth got very dry again, so I went back to taking one at night.

In July, I started using cortisone ointment again on my hands, applying it at bedtime, and wore white cotton gloves to help the medication absorb. In early August I had a bad attack of bursitis and had to keep my arm in a sling for a while. My fingers were still swollen and sore.

My summer exhibitions kept me running around to galleries. That year I won an award and an honorable mention for my work, which gave me a boost, and I showed drawings in a new commercial gallery. The children continued to inspire many paintings.

The children's health was mostly good that summer; the exception was David, who had a very stiff neck, fever, headache, and swollen neck glands. He was given an antibiotic. Sandy was a counselor at camp again and Wendy was baby-sitting for a young family for the summer. Todd went to a recreation group and then day camp for a few weeks.

One afternoon during the summer the mother of one of the families that Wendy baby-sat for was dropping her off at the house and stopped to talk. She noticed the outbreak on my hands and said she had had very similar eruptions on her hands over the years. She told me she had had knee trouble since she was a teenager summering in Lyme. Her eyes, hip, feet, and back were also affected. She mentioned that her arthritis and skin troubles seem to flare up in tandem. I scribbled down her observations on my trusty calendar; I didn't know what was causing these symptoms, but I was baffled to learn that not only Gil and I but someone within a mile of us had what sounded like the same joint problems and strange skin condition on the hands.

Thus, during the past months, by pursuing my basic hunches about our illnesses, I had found allies in Henrietta Aladjem and Dr. Peter Schur. This inspired me to keep looking for answers, despite the roadblocks that I seemed to encounter along the way. I would continue to keep my eyes and ears open for any information that might shed light on our medical mystery.

CHAPTER EIGHT

CHAOS

Every physician must be rich in knowledge, and not only of that which is written in books: his patients should be his book, they will never mislead him.

PARACELSUS (1493?–1541)

In September 1974, with the children back in school, Gil and I felt free enough to take off for a long weekend in Nantucket. We loved the ocean at that time of year, and we had four days of bright, clear weather. I look back on that weekend as a last hurrah of sorts, an idyllic stint before things got out of hand. From then on, our mysterious symptoms were to come with increasing regularity and affect the family in more and more debilitating ways.

In October, Sandy, now seventeen years old, woke up in his room at boarding school to discover that his neck and shoulders were stiff and painful, for no apparent reason. He was captain of the soccer team that year and very athletic, and we asked him if maybe he'd wrenched the muscles during practice. He said no, he didn't remember doing anything that would have strained them. It was the height of the soccer season, and he was in excellent shape, so it was unlikely that this episode was just a matter of his overexerting himself. The stiffness lasted several days.

In early November, Sandy's left thigh suddenly became very painful—and again, he had no memory of doing anything during soccer practice to have caused such pain. He went to the infirmary, soaked in tubs of hot water, and rubbed Ben-Gay on the stiff, sore area. He couldn't lift his left leg.

The last game of the season was approaching, and it meant a lot to Sandy. It was a big, festive weekend up at his school; lots of parents and families, including ours, would be attending. When we spoke with Sandy the night before the game, he told us that the school coaches would not let him practice that afternoon on account of his stiffness. He said that he had been soaking his sore leg, but to no avail.

In the last soccer game we'd seen, Sandy was center halfback and had played very well, scoring a few goals for the team, so we knew full well how eager he was to play in this final game. The coach had instructed him to play center fullback this time, so that he wouldn't have to run as much.

Gil and I hoped to get to Sandy's school well ahead of the game so we could visit with him. But getting the three children up early on a Saturday morning always took longer than we anticipated; we arrived just minutes before the game started.

Waving to Sandy as he stood amid the other players, all decked out in their red-and-black uniforms, Gil and I couldn't help but notice how much thinner he looked. His face was pale and drawn.

When the game started, we observed that Sandy was limping and his left leg appeared to be stiff. By the end of the game he was wincing with every step, dragging his left leg. The game ended in a tie, but by then I didn't care who won or lost, I was just glad the game was over so that Sandy could get off his feet.

As Sandy came toward us, we could all see he was valiantly trying to hide his pain, but by the time he reached us, he'd changed his mind. "I don't know what is going on with me," he said on our way to the car, "but I've been having sharp pains in my groin and thigh, and the muscles keep going into spasm." When he tried to get into the car, he couldn't lift his leg; we had to help him into the backseat.

As this was the long "Fall Weekend" at school, Sandy didn't have to return until the following Wednesday. We drove home with him, stopping for dinner at a favorite German restaurant on our way. Sandy rested up for the next few days. We made an appointment for him to have a physical exam the Friday following Thanksgiving.

Back at school the following week, Sandy broke out in a rash around his shoulder and around his hip. The doctor in the infirmary diagnosed it as pityriasis rosea. I recognized the name, as Sandy had been given the same diagnosis back in 1969, and at the same time of year. Out of curiosity, I decided to look it up in the twelfth edition of *The Merck Manual,* in which the skin disease is described as *"a self-limited, mild, inflammatory skin disease characterized by scaly lesions, probably due to an unidentified infectious agent. . . .* It is a slightly erythematous, rose or fawn colored, circinate or oval patch, with a scaly, very slightly raised border resembling a superficial ringworm infection."[1]

The rash gradually cleared up.

At a dinner party the next weekend, I told a friend of mine who lives in a nearby town about Sandy's inexplicable illness. Her eyes widened and she told me that in August, her daughter had come down with a fever and a serious and puzzling joint problem. She had difficulties with her toe and ankle, and the muscles of her abdomen were stiff and sore. She had been an active young girl who loved horseback riding, and out of the blue her illness made it impossible for her to move without pain. She had been ill for months and had missed a great deal of school. She had to use crutches. I was appalled to hear the story.

Then later on in the month, after being in the sun at a family reunion at the Yale–Princeton game in New Haven, I had another episode of stiff neck, achiness, and rash. Even our poor dog, Nanny, was sick again with her recurrent urinary problem. We brought her to the veterinarian for another course of medication and told him that we were surprised to be finding ticks on her so late in the year. He said that the ticks were unusually prevalent that year.

The more I spoke to friends about my own strange symptoms, the more willing others were to share their stories. A friend's daughter recently had a weird rash appear on her hands; another friend from Old Lyme confided that several years before she suddenly developed fatigue and arthritis, for which she was taking medication.

Sandy arrived home very happy at Thanksgiving, announcing that he had won the Soccer Cup at school. He had a checkup and his doctor noted nothing unusual.

December 1974 was very busy. I was exhibiting paintings, getting ready for the fair that our craft guild organized annually, and doing my usual hundred-mile dash for Christmas gifts.

Sandy arrived home from boarding school for vacation on Friday, December 13, seeming subdued and tired. On Sunday, he awakened with aching and stiffness all over his body, especially in his neck. He was feverish, drowsy, and feeling terribly fatigued. He remained flat in bed. We consulted the doctor, who prescribed aspirin and rest. Several days later, the stiffness spread to Sandy's upper torso and he had pain and difficulty breathing, opening his mouth, or moving his jaw. He had trouble moving his left arm. His mouth area was quivering. His hands were shaking, he had swelling and drooping of his left eye, and his ear ached. He developed a pins-and-needles sensation in his fingers. Yet his legs and lower body seemed okay. David, whose bedroom is next to Sandy's, had heard him crying out during nightmares for several nights. The other children were upset to see their usually very active brother so incapacitated.

Sandy went to see the doctor the following day. By then, his fever, which had never been very high, was down. He was using a heating pad for his neck and shoulder, was eating again, and generally felt a little better, although he still couldn't lift his left arm up higher than shoulder level.

Seeing Sandy so stiff, the doctor had the impression that Sandy looked as if he had been wrenched in a car accident. It was decided that I try to reach Dr. Schur at Robert Brigham Hospital in Boston and tell him of Sandy's strange and frightening illness.

The tests from the local lab showed that the sedimentation rate in Sandy's blood was slightly elevated. (A high sedimentation rate indicates possible inflammation or infection.) His rheumatoid arthritis screen was normal, as was his ASO test to detect antibodies to streptococcal infection. When I spoke with Dr. Schur I gave him these results, and he suggested that Sandy be given an antinuclear antibody test (ANA), a blood test that is used to find antibodies to nuclei.

Sandy had another checkup at the doctor's two days before

Christmas. A second blood test showed a still-elevated sedimentation rate.

At a holiday gathering, I told a friend of mine about Sandy's illness, and how worried I was about him. She listened attentively, shaking her head. She said that there had been other baffling cases in the area, and revealed that approximately two and a half years earlier, in July 1972, there was a high incidence of meningitis at a nearby hospital: nine cases, six or seven of them from Lyme.

Her husband had been one of these cases and she related his story in detail. He had been working outdoors, spraying poison ivy at the edges of his property. Shortly thereafter, he began to feel unwell. Several days later, when he was eating lunch at the table with her, she noticed that one side of his face, especially around his mouth, was pulling to one side. Alarmed at the distortion of his face and his malaise, she called an ambulance and they went to the hospital. He was initially thought to have had a stroke. His jaw was affected and he couldn't open or close his mouth; he could swallow only after someone closed his mouth for him. The paralysis moved to the other side of his face, and to his limbs, and he had trouble closing one eye, then both eyes. After observing this, and doing blood tests and a lumbar puncture, the doctors changed their diagnosis to viral meningitis, although they couldn't be certain. He remained in the hospital for several weeks, and was treated with cortisone. At home the weakness continued and he was overcome with extreme fatigue; he relapsed and returned to the hospital.

I couldn't get the story out my head. It made me all the more upset about what was happening to Sandy.

We took Sandy for follow-up blood tests on December 31. By the end of the first week of January he was feeling well again. His blood tests were back to normal, and he returned to school.

Although I was relieved that my son was feeling better, uneasiness about his and the family's health haunted me. Even during the stretches when we were all well, I couldn't shake my worry about the debilitating episodes that would strike and then abate without reason or warning. What could be causing them? Was I doing something wrong? The symptoms were so varied and incongruous. My mind played over the same old list of possibilities: Was it some strange cyclical infection? Could it be diet? Food additives? Pollution of our well water? Some other environmental contamination? Now that Sandy had been stricken, I even wondered if I had passed some genetic weakness on to him.

I knew some of these ideas seemed outlandish, but I kept going back to Dr. Schur's words, when he spoke of the importance of being open-minded, and of how a patient living with a disease can offer insights that a doctor might miss.

In January 1975, Gil went to see a specialist, "Dr. Esbensen," about his left knee, which had been painful for several weeks and caused him to limp. He had injured his right knee a few years back in a fall while jogging. But he couldn't recall doing anything that would have traumatized his left knee. His X rays were normal. The specialist said the problem was either tendinitis or synovitis, and told him to do weight-lifting exercises to strengthen the knee, which he did.

That winter and spring I had more joint and skin problems. But I kept up with my artwork, exhibiting in numerous shows in galleries, banks, and libraries in Connecticut. I did several oil paintings of Wendy and Todd in the snow, and worked on a large oil of a band playing in the Boston Common on a hot summer's day. Todd and I worked on drawings of rabbits and made soapstone sculptures.

With the arrival of warm weather, I enjoyed working on the flower and vegetable beds. I found that I fared better if I wore a hat in the sun and protected my hands with gloves.

That spring David went to Philadelphia on a work-study project. He was a teacher's assistant in a school there and had to write a report of his experiences when he returned.

Gil's knee continued to trouble him, and he often limped. That spring he also had rashes. He was under the pressure of a job change, which added to the family tensions.

May brought shopping for Wendy's graduation dress and dance rehearsals for her spring performance, Parents' Weekend at Sandy's school, a class reunion for me, a visit from my father, and

Sandy's graduation from boarding school. With so much activity it
was tempting to forget the trials of the past year.

Then the month of June ushered in events far less pleasant
than May's. In fact, June was the beginning of a long period in
which small and large ailments hit the family with such regularity
that it seemed we were always in a state of emergency. Dealing with
crises became the norm. Emotionally, that time was incredibly tax-
ing. In telling what happened I will refer to my diary, because it is
almost impossible to relate these events in any other way.

WEDNESDAY, JUNE 4

Todd discovered a red, elliptical, angry-looking area in the
crease behind his knee. It didn't look like a reaction to any insect
bite I'd ever seen, and it wasn't itchy. The red area got larger as the
hours passed; it looked like it might be an infection that was
spreading, so I brought him to the doctor. The doctor prescribed
an ointment and after a week or two the rash faded.

THURSDAY, JUNE 19

Wendy arrived home from a rehearsal for her graduation,
which was scheduled for Monday night. She and other students
were going to read poems they had written as part of the ceremony, and she'd been practicing reciting her poem for days. She
came into the kitchen where Gil and I were fixing dinner and said,
"Something's up." Gil chuckled, thinking she was kidding, because her voice sounded comical, as if she'd sniffed helium. "My
tongue is real swollen," she went on. "Liz says it's something that
happens when you're low on vitamin C." Her speech was impaired. "I think I'll eat a few oranges quick," she joked. Gil and I
told her to tilt her head back; sure enough, her tongue was visibly
swollen, and we could see that the glands at the back of her throat
were enlarged, too. I took her temperature. She was running a
fever. "I can't be sick for graduation," she said. "This can't be
happening."

We took her to an emergency clinic for treatment because we
were worried the swelling might get worse and inhibit her breathing. The doctor at the clinic didn't know quite what to make of her

swollen tongue and altered speech. He tested for mononucleosis and strep, and gave her a prescription for erythromycin. The medication worked rapidly, and over the next few days she improved, although her throat felt odd for a few weeks.

A nurse at the Lyme school called and reported that Todd had a welt and a circular red rash on his left arm, and that his eyes and cheeks were red and puffy. She said it looked to her like an allergic reaction, and asked whether it would be all right to give him a dose of his antihistamine, which the school had on hand because of his history of allergic reactions. I told her to go ahead.

In the hours that followed, the same circular rash appeared on his thigh, on his groin, and behind his neck. The rash on his arm was about the size of a silver dollar; he remembered being bitten on the arm by a flying insect of some kind when he and his classmates had been playing near the town swimming hole. His face was flushed, although he was markedly pale around the mouth. By evening, he had developed a cold sore on his mouth. When he went to bed that night, Gil and I hoped that when he awakened the next morning, all would be back to normal. But it was not.

I woke up in the middle of the night to a sound, like someone walking on the stairs. I went down the hall and found Todd pacing the floor. He told me his head was killing him and he couldn't sleep. I had never seen him distraught like this. Nor had I had ever seen a child pacing a floor all night unable to sleep; it wasn't ordinary. Todd had never had insomnia, nor was he prone to headaches. He wasn't a complainer; if he was telling me he was in pain, it had to be bad. I felt so helpless, seeing him like that. I gave him an aspirin, tucked in his sheets, and put a fresh, cool pillowcase on his pillow and he got back in bed. I talked to him awhile, and when he seemed to be getting sleepier, I tiptoed out of his room.

We tried to reach our doctor because Todd was increasingly upset. He was irritable from lack of sleep and the headache. Our doctor was unavailable. The doctor who was covering for him couldn't see him until Monday. I don't remember ever seeing Todd so miserable.

Todd's insomnia and headache lasted all weekend. He had his appointment with the doctor and he was still very uncomfortable. He didn't want anyone to touch his skin anywhere, saying that it felt really weird. He had pain in his lower rib cage. The top of his head, the sides of his head, and the area around his ears hurt. His fever was just over 100. The doctor did a culture for strep and a urinalysis, and told me to keep Todd quiet and give him one and a half Tylenol every four hours for pain. Just the few minutes of sun exposure that Todd received walking to and from the car seemed to have made the ringlike rash more pronounced. Despite the Tylenol, his head pain continued that night, as did the rashes on his face, neck, legs, and arm. The rashes were flat and more ringlike now, less red in the center.

At graduation, Wendy looked lovely in her new long white eyelet dress, and she read her poem with perfect enunciation. No one would have guessed that just a short while before, she had sounded like one of the Munchkins in *The Wizard of Oz*. Todd, who had begged to go to graduation, sat in the hot auditorium holding his head in his hands. As soon as the ceremony was over, we took him home and got him into bed.

I called the doctor as requested and found out that Todd's urinalysis was normal, as was his strep culture. The doctor said the symptoms might well be due to the bug bites, or possibly fifth disease. (Also known as erythema infectiosum, fifth disease is a viral illness, caused by Parovirus B19, that in children usually manifests itself as a facial rash, but that may also have more serious symptoms, including acute, serious anemia.) He went on to say that fifth disease was not contagious, so that Todd could return to regular activities as soon as he felt up to it.

Gil awoke feeling achy and sore and stiff. He said he felt the way he had after an auto accident. He stayed in bed because of the fever. His right upper torso was stiff and sore, and it hurt to move his eyes. His neck, shoulder, and rib cage were affected. When his fever abated, he was up and around, but I knew he wasn't feeling well. I suggested that he consult a doctor, but he decided to wait and see. He denied his malaise, which was his way of coping. (Gil was probably as annoyed as I was that each new health problem only added to the family tension. We were all concerned about an unexpected change in his job, which had made us uneasy about our future.) Gil's soreness and stiffness lasted a week. At the time I knew that he was feeling miserable, but he hid from me the fact that he had an unusual rash in his shoulder area. When I finally saw it for myself I was alarmed. By then it was on his back, and I had never seen anything like it. I was angry and hurt that he hadn't told me about it sooner, and frustrated because it was obviously linked to the rashes that Todd and I had had. To hide it from me and from our doctors might make it harder to get to the root of what was ailing us.

Todd remarked that he had noticed the rash when he and Gil had gone swimming together and he, too, had been shocked by its severity. It seemed like a giant version of the ones he'd had. I asked Gil to see a doctor and have some tests done; he again decided to wait. (Later in the summer, when I asked him to write a description of his illness, he wrote that he had noticed "hivelike, horsefly bite–like red welts of rough pebble or Rice Krispies shape behind right armpit—ring formed around central welts and expanded like a rock-in-pond ripple to a size like a shoulder strap, ringing down two to three inches below armpit. Remained in evidence for about three weeks.")

Todd developed new circular rashes on his legs and feet. Canker sores appeared in his mouth and he was pale and not looking well. His earlier rashes were wider-ringed now and less red. He saw our regular doctor, who called the rash erythema circinatum (a red circular rash) or marginatum (a rash associated with rheumatic fever). (At the time of this appointment I did not know of Gil's rash.)

Wendy went out of town to visit a friend for several days. On July 8, she was limping because the ball of her foot was swollen. Several days later her tongue problem returned for a few days and then resolved.

Todd won a scholarship to a local summer outdoor science-education program for his project on lobster farming. That summer he also participated in a swimming program at the beach. His rashes appeared periodically, when he was in the sun or after a warm shower, but the excruciating headaches he'd had earlier in the month were gone. In late July, he and Wendy were scheduled to go to Block Island with a teacher and a small group of school friends on a bicycling and camping trip for several days. I continued my drawing and painting and gardening whenever I could fit them in. I exhibited in a gallery in Watch Hill, Rhode Island.

I had done several oil paintings of Watch Hill, as well as many drawings of children playing in the ocean and on the beach. Our family often went there on day trips over the years, and we would arrange to meet my brother's family when they came into the harbor on their sailboat.

Sandy was working again as a camp counselor.

Gil had recurrences of aches and flulike symptoms, and his rash was still visible. He described it as "faint pink subcutaneous blobs." A fever seemed to go along with his symptoms at the first recurrence; however, after that, his symptoms would come back almost like clockwork every ten to fourteen days, and without fever. All I could think of was that we had something, like malaria, that would present recurrent waves of illness. Perhaps something in our system was incubating over a certain amount of time, only to express symptoms when it reached a peak of toxicity. Gil's eyes ached; he had fluid in his left knee, a sore throat, and a hoarse voice. His symptoms were in so many respects like the ones I had

had over the years that I realized the illness couldn't be genetic. I was carefully documenting the symptoms on my calendar, and was distressed that Gil would not see a doctor and at least have a professional see the strange rash and hear of his recurrent illness. The issue became volatile between us.

MONDAY, JULY 28

Todd had a fever of 100 again for two days, and a severe jaw ache; he said it hurt to open his mouth. He had stiffness across his chest, neck, and back. The doctor noticed that his parotid glands were swollen. The attack lasted for five days. We decided to postpone his bicycle trip until the second scheduled trip, in August. Wendy went off on her bike with the group from school toward the ferry in New London the following Monday, with a disappointed brother watching her go.

MONDAY, AUGUST 11

We had planned a celebration for David's sixteenth birthday, but he had been home with fatigue and stiff neck and fever for four days. We had a party when he felt better.

WEDNESDAY, AUGUST 13

Todd's orthodontist told me that he didn't think our son looked well. Todd was to wear a plastic appliance in his mouth at night to straighten his teeth, and since he had been sick, he was having trouble with canker sores. After consulting with the orthodontist, we decided that Todd would stop wearing the appliance.

Gil finally went to the doctor and had some blood tests done. All results were negative. The doctor couldn't provide a definite diagnosis, but he thought that the rash might have been a reaction to an unrecollected bite by a spider.

My frustration was increasing with every day. It was becoming more and more obvious that our illnesses were related, not isolated occurrences stemming from different causes. We were all being exposed and re-exposed to some entity that was making us ill, but when I tried to explain my hunches, I got resistance from most everyone with whom I talked.

THURSDAY, AUGUST 14
Sandy woke up with his left knee stiff and sore. He had been jogging and practicing his soccer technique in preparation for the soccer team tryouts at Tufts University, where he would be a freshman, but he had no recollection of having wrenched his knee.

SATURDAY, AUGUST 16
Sandy had his required physical exam for college. With the exception of his knee, he was said to be in excellent health.

MONDAY, AUGUST 18
Sandy had felt achy and fatigued for two days.

THURSDAY, AUGUST 21
The camp director called to tell us that Sandy's knee was extremely swollen, the puffiness extending way up his thigh. He thought Sandy ought to see a doctor immediately. When I picked up Sandy at camp, I was astounded to see how badly swollen his knee was. It was grotesque.
At the clinic that evening, the doctor on duty took X rays which showed no traumatic injury. He suggested we make an appointment to see a specialist the next day. For now all he could suggest was that Sandy stay off the knee by resting or using crutches.

FRIDAY, AUGUST 22
It was the final day of camp, but Sandy had to miss the festivities and farewells because he had an appointment at two-thirty with Dr. Esbensen, the same specialist who had taken care of Gil's knee problems. The fluid was drained from the knee and sent for testing, and blood tests were done. He was given an antibiotic called cephradine, five hundred milligrams every six hours, and an anti-inflammatory drug, Indocin (indomethacin), twenty-five milligrams three times a day. His blood tests showed an elevated sedimentation rate and white blood cells in the joint fluid. He had no fever; however, his eyelid was swollen. If the knee swelling continued the following week, his knee would be re-cultured or biop-

sied. He was to have an eye examination the following Wednesday.

Todd, who had been on his trip to Block Island with the group from school, arrived home in the evening. He was very sunburned and had a blistered lip from the sun, but was full of enthusiasm for the time he'd had. I noticed that he had a strange mottled rash on the backs of his thighs.

SATURDAY, AUGUST 23

Sandy and Todd both slept late. When they arose, Gil and I were stunned to find that *both* were now afflicted with swollen knees. Todd couldn't walk on his right leg. The knee was puffy and stiff, bent in the position it had been in as he slept. His right shoulder and neck areas were affected, and he experienced pain when he took a deep breath. We decided that he should see our doctor. We had to carry him to the car because he couldn't bend his knee. The doctor suggested we schedule an appointment with Gil and Sandy's specialist, Dr. Esbensen, on Monday. We rented a pair of crutches for Todd.

MONDAY, AUGUST 25

Todd had blood tests at the lab. He saw Dr. Esbensen and was told that until the results came back, he should rest in bed, apply heat to the joints, and take aspirin to control the swelling and Maalox to help his stomach tolerate the aspirin.

Meanwhile, the dog developed a sore area on her body and was treated at the veterinarian. During the past summers Nanny had occasionally developed what the veterinarians in our area called "hot spots," and had been treated with medicine.

TUESDAY, AUGUST 26

Todd's right ankle was now swollen. I was becoming even more frantic over the situation. Our symptoms had certainly become pronounced over the summer. Even Nanny seemed to be ailing. She had had kidney problems off and on that summer and had been given medication. I was convinced that these episodes were related. Could it be something transmitted by deer flies, or those tiny little no-see-ums that could get through the screens at night, attracted by light? What about the biting knats and mosquitoes? The idea that ticks might be involved crossed my mind again, even though the tick-borne illnesses described in the medical books I'd read sounded different in many ways from what was happening to us. Still, ticks had been on the increase in recent years, and there seemed to be a great many baby ticks on the scene—either baby ticks or a smaller kind of tick, in shades of reddish-brown or black. Some people now called them seed ticks. Sometimes you could see them around the eyes and ears of dogs and cats. I had been used to seeing the larger ticks, but there seemed fewer of them now, and more of these tinier types.

I kept a chronological record of all the weird things that were happening to each of us, as well as what blood tests were done and what the results had been. Later I would use the library copy machine to make enough copies to send or give the doctors involved in our family's plight. To cut down on the chances of a doctor's thinking that I mistrusted his opinion and was therefore seeking another professional, I always told each doctor that I was communicating with the others.

Dr. Tellsey had called me a doctor-chaser; well, that summer I *was* one. And I would seek out the expertise of as many doctors as it took to make my family well. I knew that we were in some kind of medical limbo, outside the realm of easy diagnosis, and that I was going to have to push to get more professionals to roll up their sleeves and look into the enigma. What mother wouldn't, when her husband and children were waking up with crippling joint swelling?

I put a call in to Dr. Schur, and gave him a rundown of our symptoms. He said that he would be glad to go over the results of X rays and tests on all of us, and would see Sandy if he had further trouble while at college. I arranged to have these records sent, and wrote a long letter describing the bizarre rashes and other symptoms the family was experiencing. I awaited his reply.

WEDNESDAY, AUGUST 27

Sandy saw an ophthalmologist. He again had periorbital edema and general eye irritation. No significant eye changes were found. It had been explained to me that in certain arthritic conditions eye changes also occurred.

Sandy went to Dr. Esbensen for a follow-up visit. His swelling was down; he was taken off the antibiotic, as well as the Indocin, and told to take Bufferin. The doctor wanted to see him again before he went off to college.

During one of our visits Dr. Esbensen commented that sometimes when several members of one family have physical manifestations such as ours, a psychogenic factor may be involved. He didn't elaborate. At times he would even say, "Oh, no, not again," shaking his head and sighing with exasperation when we arrived at his office with a new round of symptoms.

During one visit I'd been telling him that another one of my sons was having the same symptoms as the son he was treating that day, and he became annoyed, telling me that he treated only one patient at a time and did not want to hear anything about anyone else. My anger and frustration welled up during these visits and I had to fight hard to keep them in check. It seemed obvious to me that these spontaneous rashes and intermittent fevers and joint swellings were most probably not random or isolated incidents but rather a pattern of recurrent symptoms of the same illness. Also obvious to me was that the illness seemed to be afflicting each member of my family over a period of years, and everyone was being diagnosed differently, if at all. Even Gil, the skeptic, was becoming frustrated with this nightmare that wouldn't end, and he was becoming more of an ally in my quest for answers. Gil and I were dumbfounded by Dr. Esbensen's lack of compassion and curiosity, but our situation was so frantic that we were incapable of looking for an alternative.

One morning before bringing Todd for a scheduled appointment, I called the doctor's office to ask whether he would be interested in seeing a rash that had just appeared and encircled Gil's swollen knee, because it seemed to me that Todd's and Gil's rashes were related. Dr. Esbensen said emphatically that he was not a dermatologist and had absolutely no interest in the various rashes that we were experiencing.

Gil had laryngitis, the same symptom as I had had in the past. His right elbow became swollen and sore, and his right jaw was painful. All his symptoms were on the right side of his body, as were his initial lesions in late June. We wondered if the illness was radiating out from those first lesions on the back of his right underarm.

Sandy and Todd both saw Dr. Esbensen. While there I asked why a study of our health problem couldn't be undertaken. He pointed out that research is extremely costly, and that conducting a study can often run into millions of dollars; he wanted to know who I thought was going to fund this proposed research of mine. I persisted because I felt strongly that research was warranted, and that perhaps rheumatologists at Robert B. Brigham Hospital in Boston could investigate. Whatever was affecting us was more than a mere annoyance, it was debilitating, and so far it was beyond anyone's explanation. Dr. Esbensen emphasized that although our (as he saw them) isolated, unrelated symptoms were annoying, they were not life-threatening. I thought about the other people I knew with these mysterious symptoms and wondered how the doctor could be so certain that these cases were unrelated.

I was hopeful that Dr. Schur would shed some light on all this, but in addition, I had thought that one of the doctors we had seen in Connecticut would be concerned enough—or just plain curious enough—to work with Dr. Schur or with colleagues in the area on gathering patient histories that fit the pattern of this emerging illness. It seemed as though there was so little communication between doctors, that it was usually the patient who had to tie things together.

This doctor evidently wasn't the man for the job, for he came right out and said that no such disease existed as I was suggesting.

"I suppose you think this is some new disease," he commented during one of the office visits. "Why, they might even call it Murray's disease." With each visit to him I became more determined to find our symptoms' cause.

My anxiety increased, too. For all my determination, it was tough to go against these doctors, who were a part of a profession I had always respected. Like anyone else, I wanted to feel supported in my endeavors. Now I had to realize that being intensely committed to something so nebulous would mean shutting myself off from others. Many would question my tenacity and would consider my involvement rather compulsive. Others would disagree with me, and I had to learn to deal with their skepticism. They didn't have what I had at stake. Still, it was devastating to have no one believe in you.

Gil and I discussed our predicament at length. Although earlier he had denied it, now he was involved in this mysterious ailment personally, and he also had become threatened. He wrote up his thoughts one Saturday as we sat at the kitchen table. He described my dilemma this way:

"You remind me of the lonely hero of a typical Hitchcock movie . . . who, having private knowledge of the villain and the villain's plot, is himself suspected of being the threat. The more he warns society of what he knows, the more deeply he becomes mired in accusation. The police, who should be his refuge, are now his enemies. His only salvation is to be pursuer and fugitive at the same time. He is truly alone and able to enlist society's protective arm only by becoming a more effective detective than the official detectives by proving his scenario unequivocally in incontrovertible terms the authorities can't help but accept."

As I had for many years now, I talked to any doctor who would listen. I also talked to other mothers. Once I started asking questions, I found that there were quite a few with almost the same story, although not with as many victims within the same family. I heard of eight cases occurring over a period of years, and diagnosed in different ways. I could see that the rash and later arthritis and neurological manifestations were all part of some cyclical pattern in this mysterious affliction. It definitely came in waves. I wondered what more could I do? I would wait to hear Dr. Schur's opinion.

Todd had a checkup with the ophthalmologist and his eyes were all right. He had increased swelling of the knee and was hobbling. And he had developed a rash on his chest. That night Sandy called from Boston to tell us that his symptoms had returned. He had severe swelling of his knee, and could hardly walk. His flare-up had hit at exactly the same time as Todd's. This news was unsettling. Again I wondered about the episodic nature of the illness. It almost seemed to me that the boys had been exposed to some infectious agent earlier in the year at the same time, and that the resultant incubation periods were similar, so that the two were reacting on similar timetables. It was very strange.

Sandy went to Robert Brigham Hospital. Dr. Schur could not fit him into his schedule, so he saw another doctor, who did X rays and blood tests and drained his knee. He was given an anti-inflammatory drug. The doctor told him that his condition was traumatic arthritis; he would have to give up sports and be very careful of his knee in the future in order not to cause permanent knee damage.

Todd's knee was worse and he saw Dr. Esbensen. More X rays were done, and he was to have more blood tests the following day. His knee was drained of fluid again. He was told to increase his aspirin dosage, use an elastic support bandage during the day, and walk with crutches. Again I went to the drugstore to rent crutches. I couldn't bring myself to buy him a pair. I think this was a way of avoiding the reality that we might well have a chronic problem on our hands. I didn't want to think about the idea that Todd might need them again.

We escaped to Watch Hill for a day away. The hot sun brought out the rashes.

MONDAY, SEPTEMBER 22

The doctor taking care of Sandy called to say that the joint fluid culture had shown *Escherichia coli* bacteria, which normally inhabit the intestine but can cause illness, and that he wanted to see Sandy again as soon as possible.

WEDNESDAY, SEPTEMBER 24

Sandy saw the doctor and knee fluid was withdrawn for more tests.

THURSDAY, SEPTEMBER 25

Sandy's test results were negative, and it was decided that the original test had been contaminated. He was told to continue his anti-inflammatory medicine, be very careful of his knee, and return to see the doctor in a month.

FRIDAY, SEPTEMBER 26

In desperation I had a sample of the well water tested. The results indicated nothing wrong.

TUESDAY, SEPTEMBER 30

Todd saw Dr. Esbensen, who concluded that Todd had juvenile rheumatoid arthritis and should be seen by a rheumatologist. His blood and joint tests were negative; he was permitted to resume sports and was to continue to take aspirin and Maalox. He complained of a sore elbow.

When I got home, I looked up juvenile rheumatoid arthritis in a medical text, and learned that it is a fairly rare disease. By definition, Sandy, being over sixteen years old, would not fit the diagnosis. Anyway, he was said to have possible infection, or trauma, even though his symptoms were almost identical to Todd's. And how did the joint swellings and rashes that Gil and I experienced fit into the total picture? The JRA diagnosis didn't make sense.

WEDNESDAY, OCTOBER 1

Todd awoke with severe pain in his elbow, which cracked when moved. He also had pain in his jaw and shoulder. His aspirin dosage was increased.

SATURDAY, OCTOBER 4

Gil had swelling and soreness in his elbow, and a rash that appeared in the morning, especially after a hot shower, just as Todd's rash did. Simultaneously, he had a sore neck, shoulder, and jaw. The rash seemed to follow the area of the pain. The incidents occurred in one joint and then another, and seemed to play out in a given joint before moving to another joint. The flare-ups were still coming cyclically, occurring every few weeks.

At this point, everyone in the family was simply reacting crisis by crisis; things were happening so fast there was hardly time to sort them out. The children didn't pause to reflect on what was happening; they just wanted the illness to go away. Yet there were always the nagging questions: What was causing all this to happen? Why here? What am I doing wrong? The guilt and self-doubt were enormous.

MONDAY, OCTOBER 6

I wrote a letter to Dr. Schur outlining recent events. Then I drove to New Haven to enter my large oil painting *In the Greenhouse* in the Members Show of the New Haven Paint and Clay Club.

FRIDAY, OCTOBER 10

I had a telephone call informing me that my painting had won an award at the show.

SUNDAY, OCTOBER 12

The family accompanied me to the opening at the New Haven Paint and Clay Club. It was an exciting exhibition, and receiving the award meant a lot to me. Watching others enjoy my painting at the exhibition made me want to paint again. I had worked in my

studio less in recent months, because the paint and solvents ex-
acerbated my hand problems, and I wanted to avoid exposure to
them for a while.

In fact, I had taken up a new hobby: I was learning how to restore antique dolls. My interest in the field was sparked when I in-
herited a bisque doll that had been in the family and needed
restoration. I read up on restoration techniques and studied the
history of doll making, which inspired me to make my own dolls. If
I couldn't fix our health problems, at least I might learn a new
craft and see some progress somewhere.

CHAPTER NINE

THE TURNING POINT

Do not fear to repeat what has already been said. Men need [the truth] dinned into their ears many times and from all sides. The first rumor makes them prick up their ears, the second registers, and the third enters.

RENÉ THÉOPHILE HYACINTHE LAËNNEC
(1781–1826)[1]

TUESDAY, OCTOBER 14

I called Dr. Schur to see if he had received my last letter outlining what was going on with us. I told him about Gil and Todd's continuing problems. He was at a loss. All possible tests had been done on everybody. I told him of the other similar cases I had heard of: four children in the East Haddam area and four in Lyme in addition to the Murrays. I asked if public health nurses or school nurses might be of help in finding out the incidence of arthritis in the various school systems. Dr. Schur explained that Todd's diagnosis of juvenile rheumatoid arthritis was the result of a process of elimination of other diagnoses; there was no specific test for JRA.

He also suggested that since local doctors were evidently unwilling to examine the possibility of a unique problem in our geographic area, perhaps I should take the initiative and call the Connecticut State Health Department with my concerns. He said that logistically it would be difficult for him to pursue the matter himself from Massachusetts. He didn't know what was causing the problems, but thought it could be viral, and that blood tests during both acute illness and convalescence should be conducted. Then the results are studied to see if there is an increase in antibodies to a particular infectious agent. He wished me luck in my pursuit for answers.

Again it was back to me to pursue the matter further. Dr. Schur was right; it wasn't practical for an out-of-state medical center to try to research the problem long distance, at least not until all other in-state avenues had been tried. I appreciated his suggestion that I call the State Health Department. Perhaps it had received other reports, and maybe it would do a viral survey. Dr. Schur, like me, thought the illness might be caused by some unknown infectious agent.

Todd was unable to play sports. His knee was blowing up again, and at times the aspirin therapy affected his stomach. For a boy his age to be shut off from athletics—not to mention all the other physical activities he and his friends engaged in, from bicycle riding to hiking—was psychologically and socially debilitating. In school some of his friends had coined for him the nicknames Hard Luck Murray and the Crip. When I thought of Dr. Esbensen's calling our symptoms merely "annoying," I felt like marching into his office and asking him if he would describe them that way if it were his child who was hobbling around, nauseated from too much aspirin.

WEDNESDAY, OCTOBER 15

Now Todd's other knee was swollen. I had to call the State Health Department. I couldn't wait any longer. I wrote up an outline of what I wanted to say. I was apprehensive. I called information and obtained the telephone number.

THURSDAY, OCTOBER 16

I knew that I was dealing with something that was on the one hand very real in terms of symptoms, but on the other hand didn't exist in the medical literature, and that I would therefore have to be collected and convincing to whoever was on the other end of the phone at the health department.

I told Gil that I had a feeling the call I was about to make might turn out to be an important one in the long run, and then I went into the study, spread my notes out before me on the desk, and dialed the number.

I reached an epidemiologist; in my nervousness I did not get his name. I introduced myself, and told him that I was a concerned mother who was witnessing a growing health problem in our area, and that I was calling in the hope that someone in the health department could investigate it. I informed him of the many tests that I had had over the years for collagen-type disorders, the hospitalizations at numerous medical centers, and the persistent episodic symptoms including fever, joint problems, rashes, headaches, neurological problems, sore throats, and gastrointestinal and inflammatory disorders.

I went on to tell him how, over the past few years, my oldest son, my youngest son, and my husband seemed to be falling victim to the same affliction. My daughter and other son may have had "whatever it was," too, though not as badly. I told him that in trying to figure out our own problems, I had talked with other mothers and had found that there was an unusually high incidence of joint problems in our area, and that doctors often diagnosed the affliction as rheumatic fever or juvenile rheumatoid arthritis. I conveyed that I knew that juvenile rheumatoid arthritis was considered to be a rare disease, and that it therefore seemed remarkable that in the East Haddam Elementary School in 1974–1975, there were four children aged seven to twelve who exhibited severe joint problems that lasted for months. Several had been hospitalized, and two of the children lived next door to each other. In addition, there were four others in Lyme who were afflicted.

I informed him that severe headaches had accompanied the joint involvement in some cases, and that the joint problems would migrate from joint to joint over time. I asked, "Does the State Health Department know of any unusual incidence of joint problems in the state? Have any viruses been reported to involve joints in this way? Has there been a higher than normal incidence of viral meningitis? Do they have any overview of health problems in our area of the state?"

I told him I wondered about some infectious agent, and asked if school nurses couldn't be enlisted to help in evaluating the extent of the problem.

The epidemiologist was polite but noncommittal. He told me that he was not aware of any other reports but would be on the lookout for any information that reinforced my findings. While he didn't sound entirely convinced, I figured that if further evidence came in to corroborate my findings, my phone call might help them to decide that a full-scale investigation was warranted.

On the same day that I made the phone call, Todd and I saw Dr. Esbensen at noon for our previously scheduled appointment. As he examined Todd's knee, which had pronounced swelling that day, I told him that I had consulted the State Health Department.

He was incensed. "By what authority did you do that?" he asked. "What are you doing, stirring up trouble?" He looked at us and said that he wanted us to find a rheumatologist by the time of our next appointment the following Tuesday.

I felt flushed with anger, and struggled to keep my composure and get through the unpleasant procedure of his draining the fluid from Todd's swollen knee. He gave me the syringe full of fluid to take over to a nearby lab for testing, and ordered further blood tests to be done at the lab.

When I get angry, I don't throw things across the room or kick walls; I cry. By the time we reached the car, I couldn't hold my anger back any longer. I handed Todd the syringe of his knee fluid to hold as I drove over to the lab, tears streaming down my cheeks. Todd, who had been quiet throughout the doctor's appointment, tried to soothe me by saying, "It will be okay, Mom. You're right. Don't let him upset you." Todd and I look back on that afternoon as one of the bleakest we'd experienced; although the intensity of our frustration could have moved mountains, the feeling of being utterly alone in this nightmare proved the stronger emotion.

FRIDAY, OCTOBER 17

Now the swelling was in Todd's left ankle and right knee; his jaw ached as well as his elbow. I gave in and went to the drugstore and bought a pair of crutches.

SUNDAY, OCTOBER 19

Todd stayed quiet over the weekend. I called a couple of friends who are doctors, one a neurosurgeon and the other the pathologist who had helped me get a second opinion back in 1971, and asked whether they could recommend a rheumatologist. Our regular doctor was away on vacation until the twenty-seventh of October, so we were at a standstill. Several rheumatologists in New London and New Haven were recommended. They also suggested that acute and convalescent blood tests be done on all of us.

TUESDAY, OCTOBER 21

I dreaded this final encounter with Dr. Esbensen. I had to tell him that we were in the process of deciding which rheumatologist to go to, and that we still felt that one doctor should be aware of the problems of the entire family. I reiterated my belief that the symptoms we were experiencing were all part of one disease process, not separate illnesses. He said that it would be impossible to get everything under one roof, so to speak, because juvenile rheumatoid arthritis was treated by its own specialist, and we all had so many different complaints. He said he would be glad to talk to whomever we decided to consult, and would pass the records on to him. He advised that Todd stay off the knee as long as swelling and stiffness persisted, and only when Todd was able to walk normally, without a bent knee, should he stop using the crutches. Todd was to continue his medication, and use an elastic support bandage when the swelling was pronounced.

SATURDAY, OCTOBER 25

Gil had pain and swelling in his neck, elbow, and shoulder, in the same areas where he had had rashes. His knuckles were also swollen.

MONDAY, OCTOBER 27

Our regular doctor was back in his office. I had given him some written information on what had taken place the past few weeks; I discussed this with him by phone and asked for his suggestions as to what our course of action should be. He concurred with the others that a unified assault should be made on the problem. He encouraged me to keep up my records of what was happening, and suggested I take photos of the rashes.

Our pathologist friend arranged an appointment for me with a

Dr. Robert H. Gifford, a rheumatologist at Yale University School of Medicine, to go over the entire situation. He told me that I should be at the rheumatology clinic at one-fifteen on November 20, with all pertinent information on hand. I tried not to get my hopes up.

I had not heard anything further from the State Health Department.

THURSDAY, OCTOBER 30

Todd had a stomach upset from the medication, and Gil awoke with a rash around his waist and on the front of his thighs.

EARLY NOVEMBER

I had entered a painting entitled *The Porch at Bobbie's,* which depicted Wendy on a friend's porch in Truro, in the Connecticut Women Artists Show at the Slater Museum. I was pleased to receive an honorable mention in the show, and attended the opening on November 2. My doll-restoration work kept me busy, as did getting ready for the annual crafts fair. Throughout it all, I anxiously awaited the appointment at Yale.

When the weather turned suddenly colder we had an influx of fleas into the house, despite the fact that Nanny wore a flea and tick collar. On the advice of our veterinarian, we used a special soap and spray to get rid of them. At the same time, the field mice decided it was time to come in from the cold—and into our house. Our neighbors complained of this, too, saying they also had to set traps nightly for a while. None of us had seen anything like it in the years we had been living in Lyme.

WEDNESDAY, NOVEMBER 5

At a crafts group meeting, and later at a large luncheon gathering of another group that I belonged to, I was able to compile a list of fourteen more people with joint problems. And I had a call from Dr. David Snydman in the State Epidemiology Department. He explained that he had been on vacation when I had called in October, and upon his return had received a message about my call. He asked me about the story I had reported earlier, and told me that he had recently heard of additional cases in Old Lyme. I said that I had been gathering information on others with similar symptoms, and said I'd continue to be on the lookout for further cases.

In the weeks since I'd first called the State Health Department, I had embarked on a telephone campaign. Each person I called seemed to know of someone else who had had similar ailments that had not been satisfactorily diagnosed. The accounts were hauntingly familiar: severe headaches, rashes, joint problems, and inflammations involving many systems of the body. One individual had had surgery. I wrote their stories down as they spoke, having gotten their permission to relay the information to the State Health Department and whatever other health organization might join the investigation.

I was more sure every day that something quite unusual was going on, something that involved many people and was being diagnosed in many different ways. And I had a hunch that there were many more people out there who were suffering and hadn't yet consulted their doctor about their symptoms.

SATURDAY, NOVEMBER 8

Todd had more stomach problems; on the advice of his doctor, we reduced his medication. Gil complained of feeling cold, and wore heavy sweaters in the house. He even kept a wool hat on all the time. I remembered how cold my hands and feet had been when I had been ill several years before. I had shivered a lot then. Gil had a stiff neck, scratchy throat, and a rash again.

MONDAY, NOVEMBER 10-FRIDAY, NOVEMBER 14

Gil's right wrist was painful, his sore throat continued, and by the end of the week he developed a rash on his torso. Todd complained of slight pain in his wrist and right elbow on Monday, and on Tuesday he had pain and stiffness in his elbow and was not able to hold his arm extended straight out. The doctor increased his dosage. By Thursday, he had pain in his right shoulder too and was wheezing on exertion. We put David on a train to Boston to visit Sandy at college.

Todd's swelling was diminishing, and he could move his right arm all the way out. But Gil's stiff neck was worse, and he now had difficulty opening his mouth because of pain in his teeth and his jaw.

I met David's train from Boston. The others had a quiet day at home.

David had been throwing up violently all the night before, and complained of severe abdominal pain. I got Todd off to school, and Gil went to his office, taking Wendy to her school bus in Old Lyme on his way. David was in a lot of pain. It reminded me of Gil's acute appendicitis in the spring of 1960. David was doubled over, and couldn't straighten up on his many trips to the bathroom. He had always been a stoic about physical problems, but now he assured me that the pain was bad. His father thought it was a reaction to partying at Sandy's college over the weekend.

As the morning progressed, and the pain moved from the center of his abdomen over toward the lower right side, I decided to call the doctor. He ordered medication and suggested we see what happened over the next few hours. Around lunchtime I decided that David really should be checked at the doctor's office. In 1960, Gil's appendix had ruptured before he arrived at the hospital, and I didn't want to go through a repeat of that. The doctor checked David over carefully, and felt that he should go into the hospital right away; he suspected appendicitis. He called the surgeon who had operated on Gil, and we planned to meet him at the hospital.

At the hospital the surgeon did blood work and evaluated the situation, saying that he wanted to watch David's blood count over a period of time before performing surgery. I called Gil and he came to be with us at the hospital. I arranged for a friend to care for Todd and Wendy after school. We ran into our friends the pathologist and the neurosurgeon, whom we had recently consulted about the family's problem with strange rashes and joint swellings. They told us of a girl from Old Lyme who had had a severe joint problem, and a boy, a soccer player, who was having knee troubles. I was reassured to know that the doctors were now aware and on the lookout for similar stories.

The vigil over David's appendix ended that night when the surgeon decided that he should have it removed. When a couple of nurses wheeled six-foot-six-inch David off to surgery on a stretcher, they actually had trouble fitting him into the elevator; they were chuckling as they maneuvered the stretcher, trying to find the right angle. It was a nice bit of comic relief. The operation went well.

TUESDAY, NOVEMBER 18

On my way into New London to visit David at the hospital, I had time to think about the appointment at Yale that was to take place on Thursday. I had a list of the cases I had reported to the State Health Department: the original four from East Haddam and the four from Lyme, in addition to our family. I now had a list of thirty-five additional people who were having problems or had had them in the past. I had brief case histories, as well as my own long case history and the detailed case histories of my family. I also had data on tests done, results of consultations, and diagnoses. This was to be the nucleus of what seems to have been a constant companion of mine ever since: my endless lists of data and piles of notes. David was doing well, and we had a good visit.

WEDNESDAY, NOVEMBER 19

We decreased the amount of Todd's medication because his stomach was upset. Gil felt feverish, with night sweats; he had a scratchy throat and his left knee was stiff and swollen. We visited David; he was progressing well.

THURSDAY, NOVEMBER 20

The appointment at Yale. It was the first thought that entered my mind when I woke up that morning. I hadn't driven to the hospital clinic before, so I allowed extra time in case I lost my way. It was a clear and crisp autumn day. I found a parking lot on Howard Avenue, and from there found the Dana Clinic, which was in a contemporary part of the hospital. I registered with the receptionist, and then sat down to wait, nervously flipping the pages of a magazine.

A nurse soon called my name; she walked me down a window-lined corridor and into a small examining room, where she introduced me to a kind-looking man in a white coat who looked to be in his early thirties. His name was Dr. Allen C. Steere. I was surprised that I was not seeing Dr. Gifford, the rheumatologist I was scheduled to see. My heart sank a bit; I thought that I was being put off once again.

Dr. Steere sat at a desk at one side of the small room and pulled a chair up for me to sit next to him. He opened the conversation by saying that he was going to take down the history of "what was going on in Lyme," and that I would meet with Dr. Gifford after he had taken some information. He asked me to start at the beginning. Right away I was struck by his openness. He was understanding and unhurried in his approach. I didn't feel that I had to rush through sentences; here was a doctor who was ready to listen, who was genuinely interested in the story.

He took notes as I talked; I gave him a copy of my medical history, and we carefully went over the outlines I had written up for Dr. Schur, detailing all the symptoms each one of us had had. I emphasized the severe joint swellings and the unusual rashes, especially Gil's enormous circular rash that curved from his underarm onto his back.

Dr. Steere said that he had never heard of so many bewildering, recurrent symptoms. We went over the notes I had compiled on the eight other cases I had first reported to the State Health Department in mid-October. We also went over page after page of my notes on the thirty-five other possible cases in our area that I had come across in the weeks since my call. I told him that I had found that it was not just children who were involved, but people of all ages. He asked questions about patients' ages and wrote notes on my notes as we went along. Dr. Steere said that he knew of no known disease that fit the description of what seemed to be happening in our geographic area, but he was anxious to study the problem.

(As I later learned, he had spent some time at the Centers for Disease Control in Atlanta, and had known Dr. Snydman there. Dr. Snydman had called him to tell him about our problems, and he had decided to investigate further. He had originally been planning to do research through a postdoctoral fellowship sponsored by the Connecticut Arthritis Foundation. He was studying how white blood cells influence inflammation.)

Other doctors came into the room. Among them were Dr. Stephen Malawista, chief of the section of rheumatology at Yale, and Dr. Robert Gifford. The small room became crowded. Dr. Steere summarized our conversation for them, and there was great interest in what was transpiring; the air seemed charged with it. "Isn't this exciting?" one doctor said. "There is certainly something unusual happening here. We must get into the field to investigate further. Bring in the patients to examine here at the clinic. We will map out the cases road by road." They were spirited, like archaeologists who'd unearthed an intriguing artifact, some bit of pottery that promises even greater riches will surface with just a few more turns of the spade.

I certainly shared their enthusiasm. On the other hand, I'd been "in the field" for a while, and I knew it wasn't going to be easy to figure everything out so fast. Whatever this illness was, it was complicated, in that it involved so many systems of the body, and my instincts told me it was going to elude definition for some time to come.

Dr. Steere went off to make copies of my notes; when he returned he said that he would call me the next day to set up an appointment to see Gil and Todd as soon as possible. I thanked him, and told him that I would cooperate in any way I could to help him investigate the enigma of what was occurring in Lyme, Old Lyme, and East Haddam. I said good-bye to the other doctors, and Dr. Steere walked me to the elevators.

When I looked out the window in the hospital lobby, I was surprised to find that the sky was dark; over three hours had passed. I phoned Gil to let him know that I was running late and that I was starting for home. He had been to see David in the hospital, and reported that he was doing well.

On my way out of New Haven, I turned on the car radio to hear the five o'clock news. As I spun the dial, I happened upon an old show tune. I let the music fill the car and hummed along. I was bursting with emotion, overwhelmed with a sense of having been liberated from the solitary confinement I'd been in all these years with respect to our family's health. I knew I had reached a turning point that afternoon. Something existed where it didn't before. Something had begun. To use Gil's analogy of my being like the lonely hero of a Hitchcock film, I had finally reached the part in the plot when the hero convinces the authorities that something is amiss. They finally listen to what she has to say, round up their men, and pursue the matter. They are finally on her side.

As I drove the last miles toward home, I cried—with relief, anger, anticipation, and most of all, joy.

CHAPTER TEN

THE YALE INVESTIGATION

We are still beset by plain diseases, and we do not control them; they are loose on their own, afflicting us unpredictably and haphazardly. We are only able to deal with them when they have made their appearance, and we must use the methods of medical care for this, as best we can, for better or worse.

LEWIS THOMAS, *THE LIVES OF A CELL: NOTES OF A BIOLOGY WATCHER*[1]

As I was drifting off to sleep that night after my meeting at Yale, it occurred to me that perhaps something inherent in the way medicine is practiced restricts physicians' thinking about new medical problems. Perhaps, being outside of the medical world, I had more freedom to see new possibilities; I had nothing invested in being an expert or in maintaining the image of the all-knowing doctor. For many doctors it may be easier to make up a diagnosis or blame the patient when she does not fit into an established entity. Some physicians may become complacent in the status quo, not wanting to challenge current disease classifications for fear of being wrong or opening a Pandora's box. Another problem is that many doctors are very specialized, so they may see only part of a given problem, therefore missing connections between different aspects of a complicated disease.

It is an unusual physician who says that he will listen to all in search of an answer and who acknowledges that perhaps the person living with the disease may be able to provide invaluable clues. The doctor who *listens* and *hears* is a good doctor.

After today's events, I knew that the skepticism I had faced would be replaced by original, creative thinking. No one knew what the future research had in store, but everyone was poised to watch and learn. The investigation into "Lyme arthritis" had begun, and with that; the feeling of isolation and despair I had lived with for so long was replaced with a feeling of support and respect.

FRIDAY, NOVEMBER 21

Gil had a pain in his right wrist, his right shoulder, the right side of his back, and the base of his neck. His jaw was better, although his throat was still scratchy. His left knee remained swollen, and he continued to have insomnia and night sweats. Dr. Steere asked that Gil come to the Dana Clinic on Monday.

SATURDAY, NOVEMBER 22

Todd's right elbow was slightly swollen again. Gil's right wrist was now swollen, but his throat was better; however, his left knee was still puffy.

SUNDAY, NOVEMBER 23

David came home from the hospital.

MONDAY, NOVEMBER 24

Gil had an interview with Dr. Steere at the Dana Clinic, during which he described his symptoms—his recurrent flulike illness, the joint stiffness and swelling, and the various rashes, including the circular rash that widened over time. A knee biopsy was done.

TUESDAY, NOVEMBER 25

Dr. Steere set up an appointment to see the entire family on Friday the twenty-eighth, the day after Thanksgiving, at which blood tests would be done on everyone.

THURSDAY, DECEMBER 4

Todd had an appointment with Dr. Gifford at the Dana Clinic. Aspirin dosage was reduced due to stomach upset.

SATURDAY, DECEMBER 13

Gil again awakened with a faint butterfly rash on his face (this faded as the morning wore on), a rash on his trunk, and slightly sore joints.

MONDAY, DECEMBER 15

Todd awoke with knee pain and couldn't bend one finger of his left hand.

WEDNESDAY, DECEMBER 17

I had swelling and skin eruption on a finger of my left hand.

FRIDAY, DECEMBER 19

Todd complained of a painful left wrist, left knee, and fingers, in addition to a scratchy throat and a hoarse voice.

TUESDAY, DECEMBER 30

Gil's lower back was tender, as was the left side of his heel. He had knee swelling off and on, and he limped occasionally. He had difficulty turning over in bed at night. He had had these symptoms for almost a week.

FRIDAY, JANUARY 2, 1976

The stiff neck that I had had for several days became severe overnight, and I could hear it crack whenever I turned my head. I used a heating pad and rested most of the day. My finger joints were full of fluid, a sore erupted in my mouth, and I felt achy.

SATURDAY, JANUARY 3

On awakening in the morning Todd had a stiff, sore, and slightly swollen left knee. He couldn't bend or straighten it.

SUNDAY, JANUARY 4

Gil's right wrist was swollen and painful and he was limping again. He noted that his swollen and tender joints cracked, the way my joints had when I was ill.

MONDAY, JANUARY 5

Todd complained of throbbing knees, shoulder, and one finger. He had a sore, irritated throat and hoarse voice.

WEDNESDAY, JANUARY 7

I wrote to Dr. Steere, informing him of our current symptoms.

FRIDAY, JANUARY 23

I received a letter from Dr. Steere. He now knew of thirty-nine people in the Lyme area who had our symptoms and had seen twenty-three of them. He said that all twenty-three seemed to have a similar type of arthritis. He felt that the cause was most likely a viral disease; they were continuing to test for such illnesses. He said, "There is an answer to this, and I still believe we will eventually find it." He ended the letter by saying that he would keep me informed of developments.

SUNDAY, JANUARY 25

Todd had an episode of soreness and slight swelling in both knees, and he complained of a sore jaw.

TUESDAY, JANUARY 27

Todd's symptoms were continuing, but he now had black-and-blue marks near his left knee joint, and he was back on crutches.

MONDAY, FEBRUARY 2

Todd could not straighten or bend his legs normally, and he was still on crutches. He felt cold a lot. Gil and I had had this feeling many times; it was as if the body's thermostat was impaired. The middle joints of Todd's fingers were now involved. He was irritable and depressed. His dosage of aspirin was increased.

TUESDAY, FEBRUARY 3

Todd's jaw and shoulder bothered him, and his knees were still swollen.

WEDNESDAY, FEBRUARY 4

I picked Todd up at school to take him to Yale–New Haven Hospital for an appointment with Dr. Steere. After the examination, Dr. Steere tapped his knee, did a tissue culture, and drained the knee fluid. On the way home from the hospital, Todd felt very achy.

FRIDAY, FEBRUARY 6

Todd's left knee suddenly became much more swollen. He felt terrible fatigue, and ached all over. He had a bad headache, and his jaw, lower back, shoulder, neck, left ankle, and thigh were sore. I tried to reach Dr. Steere and Todd's local doctor, but they were both off. I called Dr. Gifford, who had seen him earlier at the hospital, and he recommended that we increase Todd's dosage of aspirin. He also advised me to measure the amount of swelling that Todd was experiencing with a tape measure around the knee and around the thigh, and to be sure to measure the same area each time.

Todd never complained without good cause, and so when he did I respected his judgment. If Todd mentioned that he was having pain in a certain joint, that joint would invariably swell shortly thereafter. Irritability would also precede a joint flare-up.

TUESDAY, FEBRUARY 10

Dr. Steere came to the Old Lyme town hall to do skin and blood tests on his patients in the area. The number of these patients had been steadily increasing since November. I had been informing any victims who called me of the study being done at Yale. Dr. Steere increased Todd's dosage of aspirin to thirteen a day. He said to change to another form of aspirin called Ascriptin, which was easier on the stomach.

THURSDAY, FEBRUARY 12

Gil, Todd, and I had watched for reactions to the skin tests. We had varying degrees of positive reactions. Todd was still on crutches, and his knee swelling increased as the day progressed.

This was the same phenomenon I had experienced with my symptoms; whether joint pain or rashes, they were often more severe from about four o'clock in the afternoon on. Todd said he had ringing in the ears, a sign of aspirin overdose. So far, his stomach was all right. He developed dime-sized red spots—two on his right knee, one in a matching position on his left knee, and another fading one on the back of his thigh. When he took off his shirt we found another one on his torso. These looked like the same lesions I had had in earlier bouts of this mysterious ailment. Gil started an episode of symptoms: He had a swollen elbow, the backs of his hands were puffy, the knuckle of his left index finger was enlarged, and his whole right arm was swollen. These symptoms, which were painful, lasted a week.

FRIDAY, FEBRUARY 13

I talked to Dr. Steere and told him that Todd had had ringing in his ears. Dr. Steere said to cut his dosage back to ten Ascriptin a day. He also wanted our local doctor to order a salicylate (aspirin) level test to see if the aspirin was reaching toxic levels in Todd's system. He informed me of the normal range we should maintain, and said that if Todd's level was high, his dosage would have to be reduced further.

TUESDAY, FEBRUARY 17

I woke up to find the fingers of my left hand were swollen and sore. I drove Todd to the lab for his salicylate level test.

THURSDAY, FEBRUARY 19

I phoned Dr. Steere to let him know that Todd was generally much better and was able to walk without crutches. The circumference of his knee was down from 14 inches to 12¼, which matched his other knee. He was still taking aspirin. Dr. Steere said that Todd could resume taking gym classes at school. Todd was thrilled to hear the news.

THURSDAY, FEBRUARY 26

Todd was back on crutches. He had resumed sports and his right knee swelled again, making him very discouraged.

SUNDAY, FEBRUARY 29

Todd's swollen knee had a circumference of 13¾ inches. I spoke to our local doctor; he increased the Ascriptin dose to twelve a day. I noticed a bulge above the kneecap on the right side.

MONDAY, MARCH 1

I called Dr. Steere. He said Todd should continue to take twelve Ascriptin a day until the swelling is gone. A month after swelling is absent, Todd may be able to slowly resume sports again.

THURSDAY, MARCH 4

Todd had general aching, canker sores, insomnia, and little appetite. He was still taking twelve Ascriptin a day. He stayed home from school. The knee swelling was at 13¼ inches.

FRIDAY, MARCH 5

Todd was feverish, and his thigh was swollen above his especially painful knee. He had a throbbing headache around his ear. Canker sores still troubled him. Unable to reach Dr. Steere or our local doctor, I decided to cut back his aspirin level.

MONDAY, MARCH 8

I called Dr. Steere. Todd's fever and insomnia persisted and he looked very pale. Dr. Steere said Todd should take ten Ascriptin a day, stay off the knee, and remain home from school as long as he was running a fever. By Monday night his temperature was normal and he was anxious to return to school.

TUESDAY, MARCH 9

Todd went to school but felt achy in the afternoon. His knee remained swollen and he had a fever of 101 degrees that evening, so we planned to keep him out of school again.

THURSDAY, MARCH 11

I called the local doctor because Todd was still running a fever of 101 degrees and he had a nosebleed. I made an appointment for a checkup for Todd for the following day.

At the doctor's his blood count and urinalysis were fine. No evident symptoms except the fever and the arthritis.

Todd had a nosebleed and more knee swelling, but his fever was down.

Todd went back to school. A friend told me that there had been a seminar at Yale Medical School on "epidemic arthritis" in Lyme, Connecticut. Local doctors were alerted to the problem. Work on the mystery was moving along swiftly; more and more information was being gathered from near and far.

Later in the day, I called Dr. Steere, who said Todd should keep on taking ten Ascriptin a day, plus Maalox to coat his stomach, and should keep off his knee. He told me to keep track of Todd's nosebleeds and bruising and to call him next week. Todd should go to school only if he felt well enough. Dr. Steere suggested that I document the rash with color slides or prints.

He mentioned that the Yale Lyme Arthritis research group were now studying whether the disease was transmissible from one patient to another. They also were taking into consideration proximity to bodies of water, or a possible transmission through underground water. He said that an important factor in who was getting ill seemed to be a proximity to heavy brush and woodland. Dr. Steere now referred to the condition as "Lyme arthritis," saying that the episodic nature of the arthritis that accompanied the other symptoms is what made it different from other forms of arthritis.

He told me of a case in a nearby town starting in late May back in 1974. The patient had the mysterious expanding circular red rash and severe flulike symptoms; she had been hospitalized and given intravenous penicillin. Later, another member of the family came down with a similar ailment. Dr. Steere said the patient would like to talk to me, so I called her.

About this time a mother whose family had been afflicted with Lyme arthritis had told me that two dogs and a horse that she owned had gradually become lame, sickened, and died, and she had also noticed a squirrel and a mole that were acting ill and behaving strangely. This reminded me of a time when Gil and I were returning home late one night after a summer rainstorm, and we saw a group of mice erratically going around in circles in the middle of the road. When we first moved to Lyme, Iago, our bassett hound, a puppy at the time, had become severely lame one spring. He couldn't move his hind legs and dragged himself around. We worried that he might have been hit by a car; however, we could find no area of tenderness or evidence of abrasion. Within a day he was walking normally again. A number of years later Nanny also had these attacks. We would find her lying under a bush. Her legs would twitch at times. Sporadically, she also would not be able to climb the stairs. At other times she would be spry as a puppy, even when she was getting on in years.

I knew that the possibility of animal involvement might seem farfetched to many people, but I couldn't dismiss it. I decided to document any reference to pets being afflicted from then on.

I mentioned all this to Dr. Steere. He was open to the possibility that animals might be involved but said that at this point, his efforts were focused on the affliction in humans.

WEDNESDAY, MARCH 24

Gil's left knee was swollen, his left elbow hurt, and the left side of his neck was tender. He had to resort to using crutches. He was sleeping well again, and didn't feel as achy as he had been. He didn't have a fever. Todd was still on crutches and having headaches as well. His shoulder hurt, and the knee swelling was the same. Because his temperature was normal, he had been attending school. It was unseasonably hot; Todd took off his shirt while he was outside playing and got a strange pinpricklike rash from the sun.

MONDAY, MARCH 29

Todd's shoulder hurt and his knee was the same. Gil was still on crutches, and he was keeping his knee elevated as much as he could. The swelling had advanced into his thigh, and his left calf also hurt. His left ankle was so swollen that you couldn't see the ankle bone.

THURSDAY, APRIL 1

Gil had an inflammation over the top of his left foot, and was on crutches. He had bouts of insomnia again. Todd's condition was unchanged. The children were all back at school after spring vacations.

MONDAY, APRIL 5

I was doing errands in Saybrook and noticed Gil's car in the parking lot at the shopping center. I drove up next to it and found Gil fast asleep in the front seat. He confided that he had episodes of extreme drowsiness during the day, and told me that he felt exhausted all the time. He said that last Saturday he had been planning to drop David off in Saybrook—David was taking his college boards at the high school there—and then pick him up later, but instead he slept in the car in the parking lot for the three hours. The overwhelming lethargy and fatigue that are part of this illness is difficult to understand unless you have suffered them yourself.

WEDNESDAY, APRIL 7

Gil had tried walking again yesterday, and his leg was weak at first. His ankle swelling lessened, and although his knee swelling was worse, it was less painful. A rash appeared over his kneecap, and he experienced a burning, prickling sensation when it was touched. I had had that same sensation with the rash across my nose and cheeks.

Todd had an appointment with Dr. Steere at the hospital. He was given weight exercises to tighten his thigh muscles. They were to be done only if there was no pain, and increased very gradually. He was to stay off his crutches and do limited walking; running was forbidden.

Because an antihistamine prescribed for me when I had seen Dr. Schur had cut down the severity of my symptoms so considerably, I asked Dr. Steere if Todd might try a low dose of the same medication. (In addition to Todd's other ailments, he had hay fever and other allergies.) Dr. Steere agreed to give it a try, and we started Todd on one dose of Periactin (cyproheptadine hydrochloride) at bedtime.

THURSDAY, APRIL 8

Todd's swelling was a little worse. He started walking and doing his exercises, which made the knee feel very sore.

SATURDAY, APRIL 10

The soreness in Todd's knee had subsided; Todd said his knee felt stronger every day. Gil's knee was worse than ever, so he was back on crutches. He had a rash on his face in the morning. His hand and shoulder bothered him. Todd developed a rash on his torso. We put David on the train for Philadelphia, where he would work on a semester-long independent school project in an architect's office.

MONDAY, APRIL 12

Gil's ankle was better and his knee rash had receded. But Todd's wrist and shoulder were painful, and he awoke with an irritated throat and laryngitis. (This reminded me of all the throat problems and laryngitis I'd had in the early 1970s.) He didn't have a fever and wanted to go to school, so we sent him. At two o'clock I got a call from the school nurse saying Todd had a fever of 101, had lost his voice, and had a headache, so I picked him up and brought him home. He still had a pinprick-type rash on his torso. I called Dr. Steere, who said that Todd's blood test, taken the previous week, had shown a high white-cell count, an indication of an inflammatory response to some infectious agent.

TUESDAY, APRIL 13

Todd saw our local doctor for a blood count and a strep culture; both turned out negative. The doctor noted the fading pinprick rash and the canker sores in Todd's mouth, and he recommended we keep up the aspirin and the antihistamine and make sure Todd got plenty of rest at home.

Todd was still taking four aspirin with Maalox a day and had nausea and little appetite for several days. A pinprick rash appeared on his face.

Easter. A warm day. Todd lay in the sun on the deck. His back, neck, and arms broke out in the pinprick rash a little later. Our local doctor said to discontinue aspirin. I had a bad stiff neck, a face rash, a rash near both ankles, and eruptions on my hands.

When I called Dr. Steere to tell him that Todd's knee was swollen again, I asked him if perhaps the combination of medications might be making Todd's symptoms, especially his rash, worse. Dr. Steere said that was very unlikely.

Dr. Steere assured me that the rashes and symptoms were all part of the disease process of this mysterious affliction; other patients were describing these same symptoms. The rash seemed to be sun sensitive, rather like the rash of lupus.

The household was so different with David in Philadelphia and Sandy back at boarding school. Todd was taking two antihistamines a day, and no aspirin. We both started taking a daily vitamin. The rashes over his arms and torso were fading, but the rash over his legs and the tops of his feet continued. He had intermittent headaches, and shoulder and wrist pain.

Todd's appetite was better and his color was returning. He was doing his exercises and his symptoms seemed improved. Gil had been walking without crutches, and the knee felt stronger although it was still swollen. His shoulders still bothered him.

SATURDAY, APRIL 24

Gil awoke and couldn't move. He had pain and stiffness in both shoulders—especially on his left side—and down to his elbows. He couldn't lift his arms, had difficulty dressing, and walked very stiffly. He couldn't turn over in bed last night (a symptom that I had experienced several times in the past). He stayed quiet most of the day.

SUNDAY, APRIL 25

Gil was still very sick. He had a "malar," or butterfly, rash between his eyebrows, over the bridge of his nose and upper cheeks, reminiscent of my face rash. He was having chills, and wore two or three sweaters at a time to stay warm. His hands felt cold to the touch, just as mine had at various times. His left knee was swollen.

Todd, too, continued to have problems. I talked to Dr. Steere, who said to keep up Todd's antihistamine, keep him off his feet, and forbid exercise. He was to do only limited walking. Dr. Steere told me that he was going to speak at an epidemiology meeting at Johns Hopkins the next day. They were working hard on plans to try and isolate the cause of our ailments. Many specialists were now working on the problem.

MONDAY, APRIL 26

Gil's right side was better, but the pain and stiffness on his left side now extended down to his wrist. Todd had problems with his right knee, ankle, and shoulder.

SUNDAY, MAY 2

Todd had been taking two antihistamines a day plus vitamins for a week. He was walking almost normally, although there was residual swelling in his knee and right wrist. Gil had a severe episode over the weekend and stayed flat in bed most of the time. His right elbow was grotesquely swollen, and what looked like a Ping-Pong ball of fluid protruded off the end of the elbow. It was sore to the touch and painful to move. The pain in his lower back was extreme; it hurt him to get out of bed, go up or down the stairs, sit down, or turn his body in any direction. He had no rash or fever at this time. His left elbow also became affected, and he couldn't straighten his arm.

MONDAY, MAY 3

Wendy's fifteenth birthday. Such an effervescent time of life, and what a shame that we were so preoccupied with all these physical problems. Wendy and David had separated themselves from the rest of us, considering themselves to be "the wellies" (versus "the sickies") in the family. They tried to live as normal a life as they could under the circumstances. Wendy had cultivated quite a baby-sitting career, which allowed her to get off on her own. David was still in Philadelphia and learning a great deal from the experience of being in a busy architectural office.

I called Dr. Steere to inform him of Gil's worsening symptoms. He told me about the medical meeting; most of the authorities felt that Lyme arthritis was most likely an insect- or arthropod-transmitted infectious disease. He and his colleagues were busy setting up research plans and obtaining funding, as well as setting up protocols for the studies. He wanted to see Gil at the Dana Clinic the following Friday for more tests and examinations of his joints.

FRIDAY, MAY 7

Gil and I met Dr. Steere at the clinic. He did blood and kidney-function tests, all of which were normal, gave Gil a thorough checkup, and saw the remaining lump of fluid on the end of Gil's elbow. He didn't do further X rays. We discussed the Yale research. I told him that I felt there was a tremendous need to make the local doctors fully aware of the presenting symptoms of the disease, and that all clinics and emergency rooms should be knowledgeable about it, too, and willing to refer patients to the research team at Yale for evaluation.

I told him how earlier that spring I had been at the local clinic with David after he had caught a basketball the wrong way and ended up with a badly swollen finger. As we sat in our cubicle waiting for the results of the X ray (which ended up showing no fracture) I overheard an interview in the next cubicle concerning a child from Lyme who had had a fever, rashes, and joint swellings. The doctor planned to admit the child to a local hospital for further tests, with a possible diagnosis of juvenile rheumatoid arthritis or rheumatic fever. I wondered if the child might have our mysterious ailment. The history was so similar to ours, it was all I could do to keep from speaking out about the research at Yale.

Why couldn't the Yale team come set up a clinic in the heart of the problem area? Why couldn't the state make Lyme arthritis a reportable disease? (As such, doctors in the state would be given information on the disease and would be required to report cases to the State Health Department.) Why couldn't doctors who saw symptoms that might be related to the disease feed the data into a central computer?

I gave Dr. Steere my notes on new cases that had come my way by telephone. In recent weeks I had received a lot of phone calls from people telling of their similar ailments, some of them going back to the 1960s, some possibly before that. It was unbelievable to listen to the tales of suffering so similar to ours. Many people had been given serious diagnoses; one had even had orthopedic surgery. They wanted me to relay their information to Dr. Steere.

THURSDAY, MAY 13

Todd seemed a little better. Gil told me by phone that his symptoms were still severe, especially his back and knees. He not only had to suffer his physical problems but also had recently changed his business endeavors to a company near Boston. He planned to live in the Boston area during the week and be home Wednesday nights and weekends. This had followed a very stressful time for him, and of course was a major adjustment for the entire family, emotionally and financially.

As time went on the tension between us had become more and more intolerable. The separation was helpful to me, because I felt that I could get back some control in my life. However, the more independent I became, the wider was the gulf between us.

SATURDAY, MAY 15

Gil was flat in bed. His back was very painful; he was stiff, and had difficulty moving at all, and this time he felt an incapacitating fatigue, chills, and general malaise. Both knees were very swollen.

WEDNESDAY, MAY 19

We received a letter from the doctors at Yale to all participants in the study. It read:

> *After 6 months, we have finished the first phase of our study of patients with "Lyme arthritis." To date, we have identified 51 residents (39 children and 12 adults) in Old Lyme, Lyme, and East Haddam, Connecticut, who have an apparently similar type of arthritis. It is characterized by usually short and mild but often recurrent attacks of pain and swelling in a relatively few large joints, especially the knees, with longer intervening periods of no symptoms at all. No patients have had permanent injury to joints. Although almost half the patients described only joint symptoms, others described fever, headaches, weakness, and a skin rash as well. Some felt weak for long periods of time even though joint symptoms were absent. One-quarter of the patients described an unusual skin lesion before the onset of joint symptoms. The lesion started as a red papule but then developed into an expanding, raised red circle. Some patients had nausea and vomiting, headache, fever, and a stiff neck along with the skin lesion.*
>
> *Overall, at least 4 per 1,000 residents seemed to have this illness. However, marked geographic clustering was observed. Many of the affected residents lived near heavily wooded, more sparsely settled areas. On some roads, as many as 1 in 10 children were affected. In contrast, almost no one had the illness who lived along the shore or in the town centers of Old Lyme or East Haddam. Six families had more than one affected member. In addition, many of the affected residents had the onset of their symptoms in the summer or early fall.*
>
> *All of the results of your laboratory tests are listed on the last*

page. In general, patients had few abnormal tests. No one had an elevated white blood cell count (these counts are often elevated with bacterial infections), and no one was anemic. During symptomatic periods, many patients had an elevated erythrocyte sedimentation rate and some had a low serum complement (these results are suggestive of inflammation, but the tests are not specific). Specimens of synovium (the affected tissue in the joint) examined microscopically showed a heavy infiltration of inflammatory cells. All of our cultures of joint, throat, and rectal swab specimens showed no abnormal microorganism, and the results of serological testing of blood samples did not suggest infection with any bacteria or virus known to cause arthritis.

How do we interpret these findings? Many of the children have been thought to have juvenile rheumatoid arthritis and in an individual patient the distinction may be very difficult to make. However, against that diagnosis are (1) the usual short duration of joint effusions, (2) the higher prevalence in males, (3) the occurrence in 12 adults, (4) the lack of iridocyclitis (inflammation of the eye) or positive blood tests for antinuclear antibody, (5) the seasonal occurrence, and (6) the high prevalence of the disease in 3 communities and within 6 families. The geographic and seasonal clustering of patients definitely suggests an infectious cause of the illness. However, all tests for agents known to cause arthritis have been negative. Still, we believe that "Lyme arthritis" is most likely caused by an infectious agent that has not yet been identified. Furthermore, the geographic clustering of patients in heavily wooded areas rather than in town centers, the peak occurrence in summer months, and the usual lack of close temporal onset in those living close together are best explained by transmission of an agent by an insect vector. In this regard, the occurrence of an unusual expanding lesion before the onset of arthritis in one-quarter of the patients is particularly intriguing. This lesion fits the description of an entity that is usually thought to be caused by a tick bite.

The best treatment for the usually mild symptoms of arthritis is not yet clear. At present, we suggest taking only aspirin during symptomatic periods. In a few patients, knee swelling has persisted for months. Should this occur, we believe that continuing care by a physician is important.

In summary, we believe that this type of arthritis is a previously unrecognized clinical entity and have called it "Lyme arthritis" after the community where we first studied it. We have seen patients from other parts of Connecticut and Rhode Island who seem to have the same illness, and so we believe that the illness is not just confined to your communities. Because we think that "Lyme arthritis" is probably transmitted by an insect vector, we are beginning to study insects in the Lyme area.

We would appreciate your continuing support for this study in 3 ways. First, we feel fortunate to have been able to arrange for a special laboratory to do a test called HLA typing.* This test gives information on predisposition to certain infections. Because the test needs to be done very soon after a blood sample is drawn, we will be contacting you to see if you would be willing to have another blood sample drawn. There is no charge to you for the test.

Second, we do not know how long "Lyme arthritis" lasts. Therefore, we would appreciate your keeping track of your joint symptoms as shown on the following page. We would like to collect this information from you about every 6 months. Third, if we are unable to collect adequate insect specimens, we may ask for some of you to help us by saving insects (particularly ticks) that bite you and your family. Should you prefer not to continue in the study, your decision will, of course, be honored and will not affect subsequent treatment at this institution.

We would like to re-emphasize that we believe "Lyme arthritis" to be a relatively mild type of arthritis which may be self-limited. We can hope that patients will have no permanent difficulty from it. We greatly appreciate your participation in this study, and if you have any questions, please feel free to call or write us.

---

*This is an immune-cell typing test. Some diseases, such as diabetes mellitus, multiple sclerosis, rheumatoid arthritis, Reiter's syndrome, ankylosing spondylitis, and, as it turned out, "Lyme arthritis," are associated with specific HLA types.

THURSDAY, MAY 20

After reading the letter from Dr. Steere and Dr. Malawista, I couldn't help but think that they were playing down the severity of the illness. The letter didn't take into account how debilitating the symptoms became when one lived with them day in and day out for months, even years, on end. The concluding paragraph of the letter, which stated that they "believe[d] 'Lyme arthritis' to be a relatively mild type of arthritis which may be self-limited," did not match my experience or my family's experience at all. Granted, they didn't want a case of mass hysteria on their hands, but it seemed that there was room to acknowledge that the ailment could be rather serious.

I didn't speak to Dr. Steere directly about the matter, but in my meetings or phone discussions with him from then on, I made a point of continuing to describe all the symptoms very accurately, and didn't shy away from letting him know just how painful, swollen, debilitating, and so on, they had been. And I continued to tell Dr. Steere of all the symptoms that I surmised were a part of the disease process.

To me, the fact that some cases seemed to be chronic, lasting for many years, meant that somehow the infection smoldered in some patients and was set off by an immune reaction, or perhaps patients were being repeatedly re-infected by the organism. I wondered about Gil's donating blood during the Red Cross drive as he had done in the past, before he became ill. Years earlier, when I started having my strange recurrent symptoms I had decided not to give blood. Now I convinced Gil that it was better not to risk transmitting our malady, feeling that not enough was known yet and it would be wise to stop.

FRIDAY, MAY 21

Gil arrived home from Boston to say that both knees had been so swollen all week that he had had a hard time getting around. I talked to Dr. Steere on the phone. He planned to come to the Old Lyme town hall to do some more blood tests, and wanted Todd and me to come in at eight in the morning on Wednesday. He told me how to collect live ticks in the little bottles that Yale had distributed. I could bring any samples in on Wednesday. An acquaintance in Lyme had told me that she had seen a kind of very small tick on her cats and other animals. She also had heard that deer were found to be loaded with ticks. I informed Dr. Steere that she would help in any way she could. We then discussed some of the people who had called me for information and referral.

SATURDAY, MAY 22

I had purchased a power lawn mower the previous Thursday because I realized that I would probably be doing most of the grass cutting, now that Gil was away so much of the time and was often incapacitated. Gil was against the use of power mowers and I had to override him on the decision to purchase one. Todd wanted to learn to use it, and when his knees were able, he worked hard cutting grass for people in the neighborhood. Sandy did some neighborhood gardening, worked as a busboy for a while, and was planning to work as a camp counselor again. David persuaded him to come to Philadelphia, and so both boys planned to get jobs there during the summer. David had lined up a construction job for himself, and was due home for the last few weeks of school before returning to Philadelphia. He had been elected student trustee at his school for his senior year.

CHAPTER ELEVEN

MEDIA BLITZ

Disease is very old and nothing about it has changed. It is we who change as we learn to recognize what was formerly imperceptible.
JOHN MARTIN CHARCOT (1825–1893), *DE L'EXPECTATION EN MÉDECINE*

MONDAY, MAY 24

I was driving along Route 156 in Old Lyme on my way to the Lyme school to pick up Todd, when I heard a report on CBS out of New York concerning a mysterious new disease that had been identified in the small, affluent towns of Lyme, Old Lyme, and East Haddam, Connecticut. The news report stated that the illness was being studied by a team of doctors at Yale University. Hearing the story coming from such an official source as CBS radio hit me hard. It gave the disease a validation, an indisputable reality that even the research at Yale hadn't given it. Tears welled up in my eyes. I hadn't felt such a wave of emotion since last November, when I had driven home after my first meeting with Dr. Steere. "The problem in Lyme" had come of age.

It seemed incredible that the study had been going on all these months, and yet the town officials didn't know about it. Well, they'd know about it now, now that the story was coming over the radio waves from New York City and into their living rooms.

The phone was ringing as I came into the house after retrieving Todd at school; a reporter was on the line, wanting to hear our family's story. I answered a few questions, but asked him not to use our name. I wanted to talk to Dr. Steere about how he wanted me to handle this kind of thing.

TUESDAY, MAY 25

The story hit all of the local area papers, in New London, New Haven, Middletown, Norwich, and Hartford. Todd and I saw Dr. Steere for tests for HLA typing. Todd was still taking one antihistamine daily, and he was walking with less of a limp.

TUESDAY, JUNE 1

Todd and Gil's symptoms were improved, although both still had transient pinprick rashes and swellings, and Gil now had an eruption on his hands almost identical to mine over the years. He had had several tiny tick bites with a localized reaction.

WEDNESDAY, JUNE 2

Todd was under a lot of pressure in school and seemed depressed. Having the older boys around again had been an adjustment. They were planning to leave for Philadelphia the following Wednesday. I was elected an artist member of Connecticut Women Artists, and wondered if I would ever get the time to get back to painting again.

Dr. Steere called to say that NBC television had contacted him and his colleagues about doing a story on "Lyme arthritis" for Frank Field's scientific portion of the morning news. NBC thought the story was big enough to warrant a film interview, and the doctors had decided to do it. He said that NBC wished to interview our family, too, and that I should call the producers to set up a time for them to come to Lyme. NBC would do some filming and interviewing at Yale first, and then come to our house with Dr. Steere to film the rest of the story.

THURSDAY, JUNE 3

I reached the producer, Larry Schultz, in New York, and arranged for the film crew to come to the house with Dr. Steere at two the next afternoon. I promised to have Sandy and Todd here for the interview. Gil would not have returned to Lyme from Boston. Then I went into a frenzy trying to get the place shaped up. My car had to go to the garage across the river in the morning, the lawn needed cutting, the house needed cleaning, and I had no idea what I was getting into. I tore around like mad and somehow managed to get ready. I planned to get the car repaired and pick Todd up at school before the reporters arrived. The garden was at its prettiest, with masses of iris and coral bells blooming, and I hoped for a sunny day.

FRIDAY, JUNE 4

The day of the interview was beautiful and breezy and clear. I tore over to the garage, thinking that it wouldn't take too long to fix the car. I sat patiently in the waiting room, and after three-quarters of an hour they hadn't yet so much as glanced at my car. I started to wonder if I was going to make it back to the house in time. I didn't dare tell them to please hurry up, so I sat some more. I read *Popular Mechanics* cover to cover. Time passed, and nothing was done. Finally it looked as if my car would be next in line. It wasn't. I was getting more anxious. At last they started working on my car, but it seemed to take an unbelievably long time. It was now twelve-thirty. Panicking, I told them that NBC television was due to arrive at my house in a little over an hour. They hurried the job and sent me on my way, probably thinking that I was a little balmy. I had a quick lunch with Sandy, picked Todd up at school, and rushed home just in time. Shortly thereafter two sleek black cars with New York license plates drove in the driveway along with Dr. Steere in his car.

After introductions we came into the house to discuss how the interview would be conducted. Numerous cameramen were setting up equipment outside. Dr. Steere looked at me and said, "Well, Mrs. Murray, this is it. After this there is no turning back."

The NBC interviewers had each of us stand out in the garden while we spoke about the newly recognized illness. Naturally they wanted the segment to be as "candid" and as lively as possible, so they assigned each of us different activities. Sandy and Todd, for example, were to walk through the front gate and across the lawn—and they did so, for several takes. When my turn came, they had me watering the garden and picking flowers as I spoke. Sounds picturesque, perhaps, but "burlesque" was more like it. After nearly drowning the flowers in one area of the garden where they had focused the cameras, I went to pick some iris that were plentifully in bloom, and I ended up getting into this on-camera tug-of-war with an iris stem or two before realizing that they were too tough to pick without scissors. I moved on to fairer game, the camera still rolling, and had to pick just about every pickable flower in my garden before they called it quits!

When I finished with my screen debut, it was Dr. Steere's turn in front of the camera's eye. The cameraman had him stand in front of a bed of newly planted marigolds.

When Dr. Steere said that the illness seemed to be self-limiting, and that aspirin was helpful in its treatment, I felt that he wasn't telling the full story. Later, other Lyme arthritis patients expressed this same concern, saying that their symptoms were far more severe than the researchers were telling the public. Still, we were all grateful that the research had begun, and we understood that the doctors didn't want to release information prematurely without sufficient documentation.

Recently, I had discussed with Dr. Steere my belief that the sooner people could be warned about this mysterious affliction, the better. He had informed me that proper medical protocol dictated that information on a research project not be released to the public until it had passed peer review and been published in a medical journal. I understood this intellectually, but not emotionally. Although I recognized that this rigorous system helped to safeguard the public against improper medical research, it seemed unfair to the victims and future victims who were left in the dark while the report made its way into print.

After the NBC interview, I attended the opening of the Essex Art Association's members' show, where I was exhibiting two paintings, one of Todd and Wendy on the sea wall at Watch Hill, and another painting of Wendy on the phone, which is where, being a young teenager, she could be found about twenty-three hours of the day.

SATURDAY, JUNE 5

I finally had a chance to read a report in the June 3 *Gazette* (a newspaper serving the lower Connecticut River Valley). Reporters Kyn Tolson and David Holahan told the following story:

"A Lyme man whose knee began to swell in April 1974 from a bite received the previous fall was on crutches and out of work for four months.

"In August 1973 a local doctor diagnosed as an 'allergic reaction' the swelling which stretched eight inches along the man's arm after he was bitten by a spider. The Lyme resident said headaches accompanied the inflammation.

"Three times during the same winter the man experienced week-long periods in which his jaw muscles were so painful he could not close his mouth.

"In a subsequent examination a New London orthopedic doctor diagnosed the pain and swelling as rheumatoid arthritis. When the symptoms disappeared a year after the bite the doctor discounted his previous diagnosis but was unable to find a cause for the affliction."

Other cases mentioned in the article were those of "a student who missed the majority of the school year" and "a man who was forced to quit his job as a salesman and take up a more sedentary type of employment."

SUNDAY, JUNE 6

Todd was in the sun today and developed a rash. Gil had right and left knee swelling, as well as a rash on his fingers and the back of his hand. Todd had had several tiny tick bites, over the weekend, and one had a red pinprick kind of rash around it. He was doing his exercises and walking with less of a limp. His mouth erupted with another canker sore.

WEDNESDAY, JUNE 9

The two older boys left for Philadelphia; David had a job, and Sandy hoped to find one. Todd, Wendy, and I drove to my sister and brother-in-law's house in Westchester because we wanted to see the NBC segment and couldn't get it on our TV. We saw the report the following morning. One of the first to tell the public of the mysterious ailment, it reached a very large audience.

SUNDAY, JUNE 13

Todd now had a rash on his knees and one encircling his right arm, like a bracelet. I took some pictures, as Dr. Steere had suggested. Although it was a warm, sunny day, Todd felt chilled, and his hands and feet were cold. Gil had a tiny tick bite under his arm.

I continued to get many calls from people who believed they had the disease, and I relayed their case histories to Dr. Steere. It was noticed that a good number of children riding the school bus had reported "water on the knee" and some were on crutches. One mother in another town said that the epidemic was especially poignant when one saw the number of children on crutches at large gatherings like sports events.

I found out that the child that I had heard discussed at the clinic after David's finger accident had indeed been hospitalized and diagnosed with juvenile rheumatoid arthritis (JRA). Later this diagnosis was changed to Lyme arthritis.

People in town complained to me of unusual foot swellings (like mine) and episodes of rashes that, before the discovery of Lyme arthritis, they had attributed to some kind of sun poisoning.

I heard of another child in town who had been diagnosed with JRA several years before. Still another child, whom I used to drive in a car pool, had supposedly had JRA for three years. One woman had rashes and numbness down one side of her body, as well as joint involvement and vasculitis. She also had been hospitalized for evaluation and been given a questionable diagnosis. A friend's husband had had hand problems identical to mine, as well as Bell's palsy, a sudden-onset paralysis of one side of the face. More reports of cases of lupus and butterfly rashes were made. One person with knee problems and rashes had also had pericarditis, for which a temporary pacemaker was used. Women with the disease complained that their symptoms were made worse by their periods. Some people had muscle twitching that they had never had before. All of us had had annoying eyelid twitching.

Those in the area who had Lyme arthritis were, naturally, appreciative of the Yale research. But on the other end of the spectrum, I came across people who resented the fact that their town had been put on the map by a disease, and they didn't mind telling me so. One man walked right up to me in the A & P parking lot and told me that thanks to the recent publicity his children and grandchildren wouldn't come east to visit him for fear of Lyme arthritis. He wanted a letter of reassurance to them from the State Health Department or from the researchers. I told him that I sympathized with him, but that to write such a letter would be like guaranteeing that there would not be any future tornadoes in Kansas!

MONDAY, JUNE 21

Gil's knee was still swollen. My hands were both inflamed, had been bad for a week, and I had a rash on my chest.

TUESDAY, JUNE 22

Now that the media had found out about Lyme arthritis, the calls from magazine, newspaper, and television reporters and people who thought they might have the disease were constant. At times I felt as if I were running a telethon.

MONDAY, JUNE 28

Todd was stung on his toe by a honeybee. The area around the bite swelled and redness began to move up his foot. He was given antihistamine, and later the antibiotic erythromycin. At around this time Dr. Steere came by one night with Boyce Rensberger, a science reporter for *The New York Times*. Rensberger listened to our story.

WEDNESDAY, JUNE 30

Sandy arrived home from Philadelphia, having had no luck in finding a job, and was pleased to find employment here in Lyme as a carpenter's helper. He told me that his knee hurt if he did any exercise.

For the last week or so, Gil and I had had a bad flare-up of symptoms, and Wendy developed a sore throat for which she was given penicillin. We all had episodes of joint pain, stiffness, and bizarre rashes.

During this time I received a telephone call from a woman in a northeastern city who had heard the story of my involvement with Lyme arthritis. She said that she had mysterious symptoms, which had begun ten or eleven days after a mosquito or flea bite: She had joint pain and swelling, swollen fingers, muscle weakness, insomnia, black-and-blue marks, blisters, skin sensitivities, nausea, vomiting, flulike aches, abdominal cramps and leg cramps, and muscle twitching; it hurt to breathe. She went on to tell me that when the doctors couldn't diagnose her problems, they suggested that she see a psychiatrist, saying that she was under stress and depressed.

The irony of it was that she herself was a distinguished psychiatrist, and a teacher in a medical school. As I listened to her story, I couldn't believe that even a woman with her credentials was vulnerable to the medical profession's trigger-happy approach to diagnosing unusual illness as psychosomatic.

She told me she was now crippled in her joints, and felt "toxic." She admitted that she was very depressed as a result of being ill and misunderstood. I could certainly sympathize with her plight. She couldn't function the way she always had, and she was convinced that her problems were not psychosomatic. She was extremely discouraged by the attitude of her medical colleagues. She asked me how I had had the courage to buck the medical establishment and insist on getting answers to what was occurring in Lyme. She told me that I was very fortunate to have found such an open, supportive psychiatrist in my search for the cause of our sickness.

The conversation was rather emotional for me—after all the times I had been called neurotic, it was quite a turnaround to have a psychiatrist asking me for advice on how to handle a similar predicament. I encouraged her to keep seeking answers, and we later corresponded with each other a few times.

SATURDAY, JULY 3

I had written to Mrs. Aladjem earlier with the story of Lyme arthritis; she called and said that she was fascinated by the story and wanted to be kept up-to-date with new developments.

SUNDAY, JULY 4

I had a purple pinprick rash over my lower legs and ankles.

MONDAY, JULY 5

Early in the summer investigators from Yale and from the Connecticut Agricultural Experiment Station started a study of insects and other wildlife at various spots in the area of the Yale study.

Dr. Kirby Kloter, a research assistant from Yale, was in charge of trapping mammals in order to study them for parasites and ill health. He would come just about every morning at eight to check the traps and take whatever animals were caught back to the lab. (He would later return them to their natural habitat.)

The scientists were studying patterns of pet ownership, water sources, food and drug history, and past illnesses among the disease victims. At Yale they were testing for all known bacteria and viruses.

Special steel light traps were installed to attract mosquitoes and other insects. The researchers dragged the lawn and brush at different sites by pulling behind them a wide white flannellike cloth to which the ticks would attach. They then inspected the cloth for insects and arthropods, especially for ticks. Dr. John Anderson and Dr. Louis Magnarelli of the experiment station were studying the ticks and other possible vectors. Scientists such as Dr. Thomas H. G. Aitken, a senior research associate in epidemiology, examined and identified these specimens under a microscope. Afterward, a "soup" was made from the specimens for further experimentation at growing organisms. If they yielded any organism, the plan was to test it with blood sera from Lyme patients to see if they had antibodies to the new organism. Dr. Warren A. Andiman, a postdoctoral fellow in pediatrics and epidemiology, was working on this phase of the research.

At that point, they were especially on the lookout for a virus. The theory that it was a virus didn't add up to me, because from what I had heard, viruses do not respond to antibiotic treatment, yet I always felt much better with antibiotics. Sandy had had antibiotics, and he was doing better than either Gil or Todd.

I asked Dr. Steere if they had tried using antibiotics on any of their cases with the peculiar circular rash. The Yale researchers at that time felt that antibiotics did not work. They saw no difference between those treated or not treated with antibiotics.

TUESDAY, JULY 6

Sandy had been installing a roof on a new house in the hot sun; he became dizzy and nauseated and developed a terrible headache. He rested, drank lots of fluids, and wore a hat for the remainder of the workday.

FRIDAY, JULY 16

It had been a bad week. Gil and Todd's symptoms continued and Wendy was sick with a sore throat. Mono? Strep? She was given penicillin.

SUNDAY, JULY 18

The New York Times ran a front-page story on Lyme arthritis and our phone rang off the hook. I was interested to learn from the article that Judith Mensch of Old Lyme had called medical authorities in November 1975. Anne Mensch, Judith Mensch's then-eight-year-old daughter, was hospitalized with a very swollen knee thought to be osteomyelitis and was put on a course of intravenous antibiotics for a number of days; however, the treatment was stopped and her diagnosis changed to juvenile rheumatoid arthritis.[1]

(Over the years I have read other accounts of what took place, and I interviewed Judith Mensch in December 1994. The story, based on this research, is as follows: Anne Mensch was given large doses of intravenous antibiotics by her orthopedic surgeon at Lawrence and Memorial Hospital in New London, and tests were run to find the bacterial cause of her infection. Knee fluid was tested. In addition, Dr. Arthur Mensch, Anne's father, who was a staff pathologist at the hospital, had ordered a series of tests for viral infections. [Dr. Mensch worked in the same department as the staff pathologist who had advised us about our mysterious ailment over the years and who in October 1975 had helped to set up my first appointment at the Yale Rheumatology Clinic.] The tests came back negative, but Anne's other knee swelled. The diagnosis was then changed to JRA; Anne was sent home in a wheelchair and was prescribed aspirin therapy, standard treatment for JRA.

Judith Mensch questioned the JRA diagnosis because, like me, she had observed a number of children and adults with arthritis in her rural neighborhood in Old Lyme. She also knew that JRA was a rare disease, and as I had been, she was skeptical that so many cases of it could be occurring within such a small area. In early November, she talked to local doctors and, finding their response frustrating, followed up by calling the Connecticut Department of Health Services.[2] "They said juvenile rheumatoid arthritis was not a reportable disease, and that I was a hysterical mother and there was nothing that they could do. . . . They [the State Health Department] did nothing at all for me, and they deserve no credit."[3] "I called the Communicable Disease Center [now known as the Centers for Disease Control] in Atlanta and was told much the same thing. I was very emotional and used language that I would rather forget. I was put on hold and eventually spoke to a physician who tried to calm me down. I do not know whether he was an epidemiologist or a psychiatrist, but he did calm me down. He suggested I call Dr. Allen Steere at Yale."[4] Dr. Steere had had training at the Epidemic Intelligence Service of the CDC.

Meanwhile Dr. David Snydman, Connecticut's acting director of preventable diseases, who had been on vacation when Judy Mensch and I phoned the Connecticut Department of Health, returned to the office and, on finding out about our calls from the man who had been covering for him, did take an interest and agreed that we were right to be concerned: He knew that clustering of arthritis was very unusual and should be investigated. As an

epidemiologist trained at the CDC, he also knew of Dr. Allen
Steere, and after preliminary investigations in the three-town area,
called him and proposed that a further investigation be undertaken. Steere recalled that "David called and said, 'I've had these
two calls from mothers who say there's been an outbreak of juvenile rheumatoid arthritis. What do you think of that?' and I said,
'Well, if it's true, it's never happened before.' " Dr. Stephen E.
Malawista, Yale's chief of rheumatology, agreed that an investigation was warranted.[5] According to a 1994 report in *The Day,* Dr.
Steere said that without Judith Mensch and me, it probably would
have been years before anyone identified Lyme, a disease now
known around the world.[6]

MONDAY, JULY 19
    A very hot day and Sandy had another reaction while in the sun.
His face became an alarming purple-red and he spiked a fever. His
knee was painful again, and he decided to find a another job that
would be out of the sun. Dr. Steere told me that other patients had
complained of sun sensitivity. He prescribed the use of sunscreens.

TUESDAY, JULY 20
    Sandy was still sick. David arrived home from Philadelphia be-
cause of a layoff due to a strike. He decided to take over Sandy's
job. Todd left for another bike trip to Block Island with a school
group organized by his science teacher and the teacher's wife, who
had led the group the previous summer. Sandy left for Boston to
find another job.

FRIDAY, JULY 23
    We met Todd's Block Island ferry in New London because he
had called and told us that his knee had swelled and we didn't
think he should bike the twenty miles home to Lyme. He had a
pinprick rash on his legs and feet, but had had a great time.

TUESDAY, JULY 27
    A writer from *Good Housekeeping* came to interview me, and I
persuaded her to attend the public meeting on Lyme arthritis at

the high school in Old Lyme that evening. My reason for agreeing to tell the story to the women's magazine was that as soon as possible I wanted to reach others who might be suffering. The readership of *Good Housekeeping* is enormous, and I knew that if I communicated the story of a family living with the disease, plenty of people out there were bound to benefit, whether they had Lyme arthritis or some other mysterious medical condition.

I arrived at the meeting in Old Lyme to find a crowd of nearly four hundred people, some from as far away as Rhode Island and Norwalk, Connecticut. The state health commissioner, Douglas Lloyd, and the Yale researchers were there, along with State Senator Richard Schneller of Essex, who had called me earlier and offered his support. Dr. John Lewis, director of the Connecticut Department of Health's preventable-diseases division, and Brian Cartier, of the Connecticut chapter of the Arthritis Foundation, were also present.

Lieutenant Commander William E. Mast, Medical Corps, United States Naval Reserve, attended from the Submarine Medical Center in Groton, Connecticut. He mentioned that since the summer of 1975 he had been studying ten patients who had exhibited the expanding circular lesion described by Dr. Steere as erythema chronicum migrans, or ECM. He and Dr. William Burrows, a dermatologist, had learned that the rash had been described many times in the European medical literature. He had treated his patients with antibiotics and the results were good. He said that only two of the ten people went on to develop arthritislike symptoms.[7]

I knew that when Dr. Steere had consulted fellow physicians about the unusual rash, Dr. Martin Carter, a dermatologist at Yale, recognized it as ECM. With a Danish dermatology resident, Dr. Thomas Hansen, Dr. Carter had attended a meeting at Yale at which Mast and Burroughs presented their case. It was at that meeting that Dr. Hansen had pointed out ECM as very similar to a European ECM. The ECM rash, described first in 1910 by Dr. Arvid Afzelius in Sweden, was associated with a preceding *Ixodes ricinus* (sheep tick) bite.[8] (In 1986, it was suggested by Dr. Klaus Weber of West Germany that the name be changed to erythema migrans [EM] because the rash was now not considered to be chronic in most cases. For those cases that do become chronic, lasting over four weeks, then the term ECM should be used.) The first recorded description of this rash in the U.S. medical literature was by R. J. Scrimenti, M.D., in 1970 in Wisconsin. The victim was a fifty-seven-year-old physician who was hunting grouse in Medford, in north-central Wisconsin, and had been bitten by a tick.[9] In November 1976, three doctors from Hyannis, Massachusetts, wrote to *The Journal of the American Medical Association* describing how in the summer of 1975 they had diagnosed two vacationing children as possibly having erysipeloid (fish handler's disease). The children had frequently swum around fishing piers; they developed expanding ringlike rashes and difficulty walking. The doctors found that months later, back at their winter homes in Connecticut and Massachusetts, the children had developed episodes of arthritis. These doctors now thought that the children probably had "Lyme arthritis" instead of erysipeloid.[10]

I was interested to hear Dr. Mast's statement that he felt antibiotics might well be an effective treatment. It was right in line with what I had observed in my own case and in other family members, even though Dr. Steere did not think antibiotic treatment helped.

Some people at the meeting expressed concern that Lyme arthritis was not being taken seriously enough, and that area physicians must be made aware of it in order to properly diagnose it. Others worried about the adverse publicity the disease was bringing to the towns involved.

Dr. Steere urged people to come in to the clinic at Yale to be evaluated if they were suffering from symptoms that fit the description of Lyme arthritis.

TUESDAY, AUGUST 3
I found a tiny tick embedded in the skin behind my knee, and removed it. Todd had a flare-up, his right knee badly swollen, and Gil had a swollen left knee after suffering several tiny tick bites. Being bitten, even if one removed the tick promptly, seemed to trigger symptoms immediately.

I awoke feeling terrible. It hurt to get out of bed. I had an ache in my lower back so severe I could hardly move. My hands were throbbing and swollen, my eyes were gooky, and my lips were sore also. Gil saw Dr. Steere for HLA testing and a checkup.

Todd's elbow was swollen, and I was still sick. My hands were so bad that I went back to using ointment and cotton gloves or bandages. Gil also had similar problems with his hands.

My symptoms continued. I saw a dermatologist at Yale about my hands. He prescribed more cortisone ointment.

I ran into Dr. Malawista and in the course of our conversation I explained to him that I thought there were other rashes associated with Lyme arthritis, not just the ECM. I told him how Todd had recently had what our doctor called cellulitis—a large, red, slightly raised area on his forearm, with no obvious center, as if due to a bite. When we had flare-ups we had also noticed tiny pinpricklike dots of blood under the skin; measleslike blotches; butterfly rashes; hot, burning sensations; numbness; and even black-and-blue marks and blisters. I told him I was convinced that a flulike illness, including recurrent sore throat, gastrointestinal problems, and fever, was also a part of the syndrome. I suggested that he and the other doctors at Yale be on the lookout for the symptoms we had had and for those being described to me daily by people on the phone.

I also explained to him that Gil's knees continued to be swollen, and that he had had a pinprick rash over his kneecaps.

Todd had a checkup with his doctor and his elbow was found to be swollen.

I spoke with Dr. Steere, telling him that Gil and Todd had severe swellings. Dr. Steere said that the researchers were working on a blood test. He explained that circulating immune complexes in the serum of blood are present when the body is mounting an immune (antibody) response to an infectious agent. Serum cryoglobulins are formed and the detection of their presence indicates active infection. The doctors at Yale had found cryoglobulins in the serum of patients with active Lyme rash, joint swellings, and other symptoms. As the symptoms improved, the presence of cryoglobulins lessened or disappeared. He said that I had shown cryoglobulins in my blood serum.

Todd fell and hurt his knee, causing even more swelling.

The barrage of publicity that summer left its mark on Lyme, Connecticut. Several people approached me to tell me they were upset that the town had been identified with a disease. I never knew quite how to respond. I told them of the long-established medical custom of naming a newly identified medical problem for the community or area in which it is initially found, and cited examples such as coxsackievirus, identified in Coxsackie, New York; Rocky Mountain spotted fever; tularemia, for Tulare County in California; and Legionnaires' disease, first found in a group of members of the American Legion attending a meeting in Philadelphia. My little pep talks didn't mollify them entirely.

I myself questioned whether this custom of naming diseases for the place of outbreak is a good one. It seems eventually to lead to confusion, for the disease is often later found in other groups or areas, even in other countries. In addition, naming diseases after places gives the general public the misleading impression that the disease actually originated in whatever town the first cluster of cases was found. This may stigmatize the town and those who live there.

People in the area worried that a kind of *Jaws* scenario would ensue, causing real estate values and tourism to plummet. I even heard from some skeptics that Lyme arthritis was nothing more than a case of mass hysteria. Meanwhile, calls were coming in to me from all over the country from people who suspected they had the disease.

CHAPTER TWELVE

THE FALL OF 1976

Man is inevitably a boarding-house: he sickens when he entertains the wrong guests.

GEDDES SMITH, *PLAGUE ON US*[1]

MONDAY, SEPTEMBER 27

Gil found a tick embedded in his back; there was redness around the bite. We sent the tick to Yale for the study.

THURSDAY, OCTOBER 14

Wendy still had swollen glands, but tests for mono and strep were negative. She said that her glands would swell the minute she was in the least run down from too little sleep. She wasn't herself. Gil had a bad flare-up, with swelling of his right knee, and pain and stiffness in his left neck and shoulder, along with devastating fatigue. His voice was off, and it bothered him to take a deep breath. Todd had had slight knee swelling. Dr. Steere scheduled an appointment with Todd, Gil, and me on Saturday, the sixteenth, at three P.M.

SATURDAY, OCTOBER 16

Dr. Steere took blood samples from all of us. We had a general discussion about the state of the research, and Dr. Steere said that cases were now being identified in shoreline communities of Massachusetts, Rhode Island, Connecticut, and New York, as well as on the islands off these states. "The tick is highly suspect," he said, "for the rashes are often in those areas preferred by ticks: the shoulder, underarm, back, thigh, and back of knee." He mentioned that the tiny type of tick we had noticed in recent years did indeed seem to be more prevalent than the larger dog tick. The researchers planned to step up their efforts to find out more about this tick and its habits. When we discussed Gil's and Todd's knee swelling, he told us that the Yale team had had success with an operation called a synovectomy (surgical removal of the synovial membrane of the knee), which had been performed on one Lyme patient whose knee had been severely swollen for a year. They had discovered that the synovial tissue was inflamed. He hoped Gil and Todd could avoid the operation, but it was a viable last resort if their swelling continued.

Dr. Steere told us that heart inflammation as well as Bell's palsy and meningitis had been found to be a part of the disease. He said that this would explain the excruciating headaches we had experienced. Spinal taps were positive in several patients, which indicated that the infection was in the nervous system. The doctors had seen also the sore throats, gastrointestinal problems, and swollen lymph glands that I had described.

As we were leaving, Dr. Steere mentioned that Dr. Malawista had told him, in essence, "You know, last year when Mrs. Murray was in here describing the illness and symptoms as she knew them, we couldn't relate a lot of what she said to Lyme arthritis. She always said that Lyme arthritis is a more serious illness than we described. Now, as we are further along in our research and have seen clinically here at Yale many of the things she mentioned, we realize that everything she said has proved out, and we are looking at Lyme arthritis as a more serious disease than we had originally. Now that we are aware of these other ramifications of the disease, we will be looking for them in new patients."

FRIDAY, OCTOBER 22

Gil and I attended a large cocktail party. At the party, a doctor friend brought me to meet an eminent medical colleague of his, introducing me as the mother who had first recognized the problem in the Lyme area and notified authorities the year before. The doctor nodded, and what I first thought was a smile of approval became a sneer. He then said something to the effect that the whole hoopla over Lyme arthritis was a lot of nonsense. Those guys in New Haven didn't know a simple case of gonorrhea when they were looking at it. And then he abruptly walked away. Everyone who had been clustered around him—indeed, everyone within earshot—just stood there with mouths hanging open in disbelief.

Like Dr. Tellsey, this doctor had used a venereal disease, I think, for its shock value. And of course, it expressed his disdain beautifully.

This kind of resistance was a common reaction to the early reports of the disease. One individual had dismissed it by saying that every so many years some unusual illness surfaces, gets a lot of attention for a while, and then quickly disappears. Others insisted that Lyme arthritis was misdiagnosed lupus. Some thought it might be another type of strep infection.

SATURDAY, OCTOBER 23

Todd had a tick bite on his back.

WEDNESDAY, NOVEMBER 3

Todd had a bad relapse. He had had pains in his joints for the past few weeks, but with no swelling. On November 2, he experienced throbbing pain in his ankles, knees, and hips, and I gave him aspirin. He went to school on the third, but the nurse called me around noon to report that he was in great distress.

I picked him up at school. He held his head very stiffly as he walked to the car, as though he were trying to balance a book on top of it. Whenever the car hit even the slightest bump in the road on the drive home, he winced. He said he couldn't move his head at all without agonizing pain. He would have terrible spasms and not be able to move his head forward or back. He was depressed and teary, and he felt cold. I got him under blankets and put a heating pad beneath his head. His temperature was subnormal. I called Dr. Steere and reported Todd's symptoms.

Dr. Steere wanted me to bring Todd to the hospital right away. Getting him back into the car was difficult, for he was in so much pain. It reminded me of times when I had had the same unbelievable neck pain and, like Todd, needed help getting up.

At the hospital the doctors noticed a slightly swollen neck

gland; they took blood and diagnosed acute meningitis. Dr. Steere said that these episodes of acute meningitis can last from four to five hours to several days. He added that the Lyme researchers had found disease evidence when they had done lumbar punctures on some patients. Todd mentioned that he had a headache and dizziness at times, too.

Dr. Steere told me that the results of the blood tests done on us on October 16 were negative, which surprised him because we had active symptoms. He checked Todd's eyes and joints, and they were okay. I mentioned a friend who had had Lyme arthritis–like symptoms for years and had developed a serious eye condition, compromising her vision. She had swelling of the forehead and eye, and atrophy of the iris from an unknown cause. Dr. Steere was interested to hear the story, and told of a case of eye atrophy that had been reported in Germany.

I asked him whether it was possible that my bleeding trouble had been caused by a cervix inflamed by the disease. It seemed to make sense, in light of the fact that they had now found inflammation in so many areas of the body. He didn't think so, but he said it was possible.

WEDNESDAY, NOVEMBER 10

Toward evening, as Todd ran through the woods with a friend toward home, he was poked in the eye by a tree branch that snapped back at him. The eye looked a little red, and Todd complained of a great deal of pain. He was seen immediately at a local clinic. Drops were administered, the eye was examined with some kind of special light, and the injury was thought to be superficial. A patch was put on for him to wear over the next twenty-four hours.

THURSDAY, NOVEMBER 11

I called the clinic to say that Todd was having vision problems, which we'd noticed as soon as the patch was taken off. The staff thought it was due to drops they had used when they examined him. If it had not improved by Monday, we were to see an ophthalmologist.

I called Dr. Steere. He said that no cryoglobulins were found in the November 3 sample of Todd's blood, which surprised him. He thought that it might be a lab error. Perhaps the cryoglobulins were only there for a very short time, or perhaps Todd was at a more advanced stage of the illness. He wanted to see any of us right away if we had symptoms. I mentioned Todd's eye accident.

Todd's vision was no better, so I brought him to our ophthalmologist. At first she agreed that the problem was a slight abrasion to the outside of his eye, causing redness; however, after she tested his vision, she realized there was a far more serious problem. She said that he showed signs of early optic atrophy or optic neuritis. She knew of his joint and neurological symptoms due to Lyme arthritis. Todd was put on prednisone until he could be seen at Yale. I called Dr. Steere. Todd's accident was devastating to us all. He had been through so much already.

Todd was evaluated by Yale ophthalmologists, and the opinion was that the accidental trauma to the eye had caused the damage, and that his Lyme arthritis infection was not related to this problem. Due to the severity of the injury to the back of his eye, his central vision was found to be greatly diminished. There was also a danger of retinal detachment, and he was told to keep very quiet. Todd's eye was to be closely followed at Yale—weekly at first, and then periodically over the next several years, until the situation stabilized.

David visited a school friend who lived in Branford, a town on the outskirts of New Haven. As he was passing through her father's study, a wall display of insect specimens and vials caught his eye. He looked more closely and saw one exhibit labeled "Murray Property, Lyme, Ct." His friend hummed a few bars of the theme song from *Twilight Zone* and told him her father was a researcher working on our problem in Lyme. When he arrived home later that afternoon, she introduced him to David and they had a lengthy discussion about the mysterious affliction.

MONDAY, NOVEMBER 22

I saw Dr. Steere following Todd's appointment with the ophthalmologist. I gave him a batch of clippings on Lyme arthritis. Todd had had symptoms for the past week, and so Dr. Steere examined him. I had a swollen lip and was not feeling well myself.

I spoke to Dr. Steere about the insomnia that Gil, Todd, and I had all suffered when we were sickest with the disease. I was convinced that it was due to the disease's effect on the nervous system, not just to the underlying anxiety of being ill.

He said that I had intuition and insight into the disease that no one else had, and that just because no one had thus far mentioned it to him, nor had he asked anyone directly about it, that didn't mean that insomnia was not associated with the illness.

As Todd and I were leaving, Dr. Steere said, "You know, you really should write a book yourself." He encouraged me to tell of the struggle to be diagnosed, and to describe the illness from the patient's perspective. "I'd like to," I replied, thanking him for the idea and his kind words, and then Todd and I headed home.

CHAPTER THIRTEEN

EXPLAINING THE RIDDLE:
1977–1983

1977

Ill-favored ticks, the foulest and nastiest creatures that be.
PLINY THE ELDER (23–79 A.D.), *NATURAL HISTORY*

This small vile creature [the tick] may, in the future, cause the inhabitants of this land [the present-day United States] great damage unless a method is discovered which will prevent it from increasing at such a shocking rate.
PEHR KALM, 1754, *MEMOIRS OF THE SWEDISH ACADEMY OF SCIENCE*

According to a UPI account of December 11, 1976, the Yale researchers reported on Lyme arthritis to the Arthritis Foundation, describing a little girl, aged three, who developed an ECM lesion which was followed in the next four days by twenty additional expanding lesions on many parts of her body. At the same time, she also had a flulike illness, including fatigue, fever, stiff neck, nausea, and headache. Her symptoms disappeared after a week; however, three months after her first illness, her right knee became inflamed with arthritis.

The UPI reporter told of another case. An East Lyme independent investment and insurance agent by the name of Garry Granai said he almost went broke when he, his wife, Pauline, and their sons, Jason, nine, and Jeffrey, four, came down with the illness in September 1975.

"I developed a problem in my leg and back which another

doctor diagnosed as a slipped disc. In January I had swelling in the joints. I was bedridden for about a month and I was on crutches for a long time," Granai said.

He was not well enough to work more than a few days a week from September until February 6, 1976, and his wife had to take over all the driving and family care.

On the Murray home front, the right side of Gil's leg above and in back of the knee became extremely swollen during the first week of January 1977. Gil was limping and in pain. I heard of others in town having similar flare-ups.

On Friday the fourteenth, I was at Yale–New Haven Hospital for Todd's eye appointment and afterward dropped by to see Dr. Steere; he said Gil's swelling was a Baker's cyst and that there was a danger that with increased swelling that the knee joint's synovial sac could actually burst, allowing fluid to disseminate downward in the leg to the ankle. He had seen this occur in other Lyme arthritis patients. The result can mimic phlebitis.

Dr. Steere told me that the first report on Lyme arthritis would soon be published in the journal *Arthritis and Rheumatism.* Entitled "Lyme Arthritis: An Epidemic of Oligoarticular Arthritis in Children and Adults in Three Connecticut Communities," it focused primarily on the arthritis.[1]

SATURDAY, JANUARY 29

Gil and I had an appointment with Dr. Steere. Gil had an electrocardiogram, blood tests, and knee X rays. Both knees had been swollen over the past month, and Dr. Steere urged him to restrict exercise.

Gil had become an exercise and yoga devotee. He spent hours every day swimming in the summer, jogging, and lifting leg weights to strengthen his knee muscles. He seemed to be trying to combat the disease with exercise. I worried that he was overdoing it and might do damage to his joints. At the time, he did not want to take any medications to alleviate the symptoms. He had also become very preoccupied with his diet. He was eating large amounts of certain foods, so his diet was not well balanced. This, combined with the exercise, had made him lose considerable weight.

Gil's X ray showed no bone damage, and there was no cryo-precipitate in his blood. His heart was normal. During February he improved for a while, only to relapse suddenly at the end of the month with fevers, general achiness, and swellings, which several times forced him to give in and take bed rest. He had insomnia, as I had had.

Wendy had a sore throat again, and a face rash. She saw our local doctor. I tried to keep up with my work, doing doll, antique and painting shows and doll-restoration work, in order to earn money. I had started to design and make cloth dolls as well. The children's schedules were filled to the brim, as usual. David got his driver's license, and was busy having interviews and applying to colleges. He started work as a busboy at a nearby inn on weekends. The children's earnings would help toward their education costs.

THURSDAY, MARCH 10

We had an appointment with Dr. Steere. The *Good Housekeeping* article had come out, and I had been inundated with phone calls and letters.[2] New cases in the community were also increasing. I received calls constantly; with permission I reported all cases to Dr. Steere, and I gradually answered all the letters. More and more calls came from reporters.

Dr. Steere said that he had now seen a great many cases, and that he was sure that they were just the tip of the iceberg. He was certain that if other areas were studied carefully, clusters would be found as they had been in our three-town area. The researchers now realized that neurological problems such as Bell's palsy, pares-thesias (distortions of sensation, such as burning and prickling), headache, and meningitis are part of the disease. Palpitations and irregular heart rhythms had also been detected in Lyme arthritis patients.

Dr. Steere told us that several medical articles would be published soon with good clinical descriptions of the disease, including photos of the rash, microscopic findings, photos of swellings, and test results. The Yale researchers had found in the German medical literature mention of a rash and neurological syndrome as a result of the bite of a certain kind of tick.

We discussed the skepticism that we had both encountered when explaining the illness to others. I guess it's human nature for people to deny the problem and think, "It can't happen to me." People in our part of Connecticut love their beaches, woods, marshes, riverfront, lakes and gardens—all reasons for their choosing to live here—and anything that threatens the healthfulness and security of the area is difficult to accept.

I mentioned to Dr. Steere that I felt that physician and public awareness of Lyme arthritis were extremely important. He said that perhaps another public meeting would be a good idea. The Yale researchers were still looking to identify a virus in patients' serum, and that was their main focus.

TUESDAY, MARCH 15

Gil now had severe swelling in both knees, and the swelling extended all the way up his thigh. He was told to rest rather than risk rupturing the Baker's cyst. Looking very thin and drawn, he had a rash on his nose and cheeks, terrible fatigue, and stayed in bed.

THURSDAY, MARCH 24

I had an appointment to see Dr. Steere. I explained to him that I had had shortness of breath and soreness in my rib area for several weeks—it hurt to take a deep breath—as well as the recurrent rash on my ankles and feet, which looked like bleeding under the skin.

I also told him that in my work on Lyme arthritis, I had become more and more aware that many people in our society suffer from undiagnosable problems. Most doctors are overloaded in just trying to alleviate known problems, thereby making it difficult for anyone with a new set of symptoms to compete for the clinician's time.

I shared with Dr. Steere my idea that there might one day be a clearinghouse of sorts for people with undiagnosed symptoms. Patients would be given support and their cases would be reviewed by several experts. Undiagnosed patients would be given hope and concern rather than being put off into a medical no-man's-land.

He said that perhaps, in the future, computerization of information on undiagnosable illness might lead to answers on other unidentified diseases.

I also asked if dermatologists, especially in our area, were being alerted to the rash, because the rash was such a clear-cut symptom of this malady.

SATURDAY, APRIL 30

Gil had a sore throat, fatigue, and fever, and was limping. He had that terrible stiffness again, so it hurt to get in and out of chairs.

Todd had seen the eye doctor at Yale monthly, and the injured area was scarring normally.

MONDAY, MAY 16

Dr. Steere and I decided that I would come with Gil to the hospital on Saturday to see him. Two hundred patients, ranging in age from two to seventy-three, had now been seen. The doctors at Yale were planning a news release soon on Lyme arthritis awareness and early recognition.

Dr. Steere had consulted recently with local doctors and the nearby clinic. He and the other researchers wanted to see patients and any ticks that had bitten them.

WEDNESDAY, MAY 18

I was contacted by the friend who, back in July 1972, feared her husband had suffered a stroke when she saw his face droop as he ate lunch. She told me that the publicity about the Lyme arthritis rash helped her to recall that a few days before the facial paralysis, her husband had had a peculiar rash on his midriff. She reminded me that he had been out spraying poison ivy vines along the edge of their property, and afterward had shown her a large ringlike rash. He saw a dermatologist, who had no idea what the rash was; it was no skin disease he knew of. My friend's husband felt tired and unwell when he had the rash. Then he had the strokelike episode and went to the hospital. She wanted me to pass the information on to Dr. Steere. (Years later, in 1989, I met with this friend again and she said that several years following her husband's hospitalizations for neurological symptoms, he had developed severe swelling in one knee and ankle, which was thought to be phlebitis. I wondered if it could have been a Baker's cyst that had ruptured. In 1987, he had heart block, a conduction system disturbance that has been associated with Lyme disease—the heart rhythm is slowed because of faulty conduction of electrical signals to the heart—and a pacemaker was installed. He also had suffered a stroke. She had been infected by ticks three times, but her illnesses were treated with antibiotic immediately and she has not suffered later problems.)

SATURDAY, MAY 21

We spent several hours with Dr. Steere at the hospital that Saturday afternoon. He talked more about the knee operation called a synovectomy. It had been successfully performed on a patient with long-term knee swelling due to Lyme arthritis. Joint damage not seen on X ray was noted at the time of surgery.

Dr. Steere checked Gil over carefully, noting his butterfly rash and the cyst. He told us that he felt that it was very important for him to follow all his patients on a continuous basis in order to know the stages of the disease. Just seeing a patient once, it was impossible to learn the pattern of the illness. He said the researchers were documenting in others many of the symptoms described by us, and they are still learning about all the manifestations of the disease.

I gave him my breakdown of responses to the *Good Housekeeping* article; there were fifty-nine letters and phone calls, coming from a total of twenty-three states.

THURSDAY, JUNE 2

I had a very sore elbow that was to last several weeks. Todd had been having nosebleeds and a rash on his nose and cheeks.

SATURDAY, JUNE 4

The Day, a daily newspaper published in New London, Connecticut, reported that Dr. John Lewis, director of the state's preventable disease department, had initiated a telephone survey of doctors to discover how much arthritis is occurring in children and what proportion may be due to Lyme arthritis. Lewis said that "doctors in 20 towns in Southeastern Connecticut and 29 towns in Northwestern Connecticut will receive additional information from the state [health] department and will be asked to report all cases of nontraumatic arthritis in children under age 18."

Todd had more nosebleeds and, though there was no history of trauma, the bridge of his nose was black and blue. The following week he had four more bad nosebleeds. I heard of others who had experienced difficulty swallowing, black-and-blue eruptions, and blurred vision.

I tried to keep up my business of doll and antique shows, and entered paintings in several exhibits. David and Wendy were now working at the inn, and Todd was cutting grass to earn money. Sandy was working in Boston. The symptoms continued all summer. Gil lost his voice. His knees were so bad that he was limping a great deal of the time.

I was doing all the house and yard work, plus some necessary house-interior painting, and was exhausted. I resigned from several volunteer posts. David was getting ready to go off to Rhode Island School of Design, and Sandy would be a junior at Tufts University. Wendy now had her license, so she could drive Todd to school.

Coping with Lyme arthritis, I'd had times when my mind didn't act as quickly as it had earlier in my life. Some days the symptoms seemed worse than others. It was difficult to concentrate. I couldn't remember things; I wrote lists for every purpose and sometimes when I was writing I got letters mixed up. My handwriting had changed. Sometimes my sense of balance seemed off. Sometimes I'd mix up words. Names were impossible to recall. Now I could see Gil doing the same thing. There were notes and reminders everywhere. Todd also said that he reversed the beginnings of words and often couldn't find the next word he wanted to say, sometimes stammering.

I saw Dr. Steere at his new office and met Elise Taylor for the first time on October 25. She worked closely with him on his research and communicated with his patients. I wrote Dr. Steere shortly after our visit to ask him about the State Health Department's function in tracking down cases. Given how important it is to know how many cases there are and where they are occurring, I asked whether mandatory reporting might be initiated. I asked if we could talk about this at our next meeting.

On November 15, Wendy, Todd, and I had tests down at the hospital and met with Dr. Steere. In answer to my question about reporting Lyme arthritis, he said that reporting of some serious, highly contagious, or life-threatening illnesses such as venereal disease and tuberculosis is mandatory; however, Lyme arthritis was not in that category.

I mentioned to him that my neck had been bothering me and my fingers were sometimes numb. It hurt to lift anything, my hands and arms were weak, and my hands were shaking. It seemed strange, but at times my limbs seemed to "go to sleep" on me. After our conversation Dr. Steere said that he wanted to see Gil and me at the hospital on November 25.

During that visit, I wasn't feeling well. I had a low-grade fever, headache, and neck pain, and my eyes burned. My left knee ached and I felt nauseated. Dr. Steere drew blood from both of us. I asked whether he thought there was a correlation between households with pets and the incidence of Lyme arthritis. (In 1978, Steere et al. found that more Lyme patients owned cats than neighbors who didn't have Lyme disease.)

It was now the hunting season, and I read in the papers that scientists at state deer check stations were examining the deer brought there by hunters for evidence of ticks and illness.

On December 4, there was a Lupus Foundation meeting at the University of Connecticut Health Center in Farmington, and Henrietta Aladjem was there from Boston. I, too, attended and talked with Dr. Naomi Rothfield about my idea of having a support group for undiagnosed patients, especially those with collagen-vascular disease. These people might be in the early stages of serious disease, before tests would register positive, or they might have some disease previously unrecognized, as in the case of Lyme arthritis.

Such a group might ease the anxiety and loneliness of these patients. I told Dr. Rothfield about my vision of a clearinghouse for undiagnosed patients. Often patterns show up when there are more cases to examine for clues. Doctors, I should think, would feel that sending a patient to such a clinic or center would be a logical next step if they couldn't diagnose an ailment. Also, patients might find support in knowing that there are others in the same limbo, and might gain from sharing frustrations and problems. I felt that this support should not have the stigma of a psychiatric association.

Dr. Rothfield suggested that perhaps a nurse practitioner might set up a program in a hospital or clinic to which the undiagnosable could turn for emotional support.

It was good to speak with Henrietta Aladjem again. She told of her upcoming speech to psychiatrists and psychologists and her plan to question the treatment of undiagnosed lupus patients who all too often were labeled neurotic or worse, some even ending up in mental hospitals. She encouraged me in my work with Lyme arthritis.

MONDAY, DECEMBER 5

I had a temperature of 100, and had extreme fleeting headaches when I moved my head at all. It was an effort to hold my head up, and it hurt to brush my hair or put a bobby pin in because of the sensitivity all over my scalp. My eyes felt "off," I had little appetite, and I felt dizzy and weak at times.

TUESDAY, DECEMBER 13

I called Dr. Steere for the test results of November 25, and he said that they weren't in yet but that he would call soon with the results. Several days later he called to say that both Gil and I were positive for cryoglobulins, which suggested that we had active disease.

I struggled through the holiday preparations and continued to have very painful neck spasms and headaches. My neck now hurt if I turned my head to the right, and the problem seemed to get worse as the day went on. Lifting my head up from a horizontal position was agony. I rested with a heating pad as much as possible, and drove only when absolutely necessary. I had pain in the back of my head if I touched my forehead or face or if I moved my jaw or sneezed, and I continued to have a low fever. Gil had large swollen knees and achiness. I tried to call Dr. Steere, but found that he was off until the beginning of January. I hoped that the new year would be better.

1978

I called Dr. Steere on January 3 to let him know about my stiff neck and low fever, which I couldn't seem to shake. He suggested that I come for a checkup, and he would run an EEG (a brain-wave test), and take some X rays.

At the January 12 appointment, I told him it was extremely painful to turn my head to the left; I had tried resting and using a heating pad, but the pain just seemed to be getting progressively worse. I wasn't sleeping well, because I couldn't get my neck into a comfortable position. I described how I'd been dogged by a low fever since late November, and how if I touched my forehead or chin, I felt pain down the back of my neck. One of my fingers had also been numb.

Dr. Steere hoped an EEG would turn up some answers. He recommended that I take six aspirin a day, and arranged for me to see a physical therapist at the hospital the following week.

On February 6, Dr. Steere called to let me know that my EEG showed a diffuse, abnormally slow rhythm. He said he had seen this slow rhythm in other Lyme arthritis patients who were having neurological complications. He said he wasn't worried about it at all, and thought that I should have an EEG done again when all my symptoms were gone to evaluate any change.

February was a rugged month. There was a record-breaking blizzard in the Northeast. Boston was hit particularly hard; Gil couldn't get home for quite a while. When he did arrive home for the weekend, he was exhausted. He had strained his knee while shoveling snow, and was limping. He looked alarmingly thin. At six feet four inches, he was down to 163 pounds. One evening he was helping me carry some things down steps and his bad knee completely gave out on him. He went sprawling. It was awful.

Gil went back on crutches. He was fatigued and depressed. His insomnia returned. He felt achy and experienced the same strange sore scalp that I'd had at various times. He had put off going for a checkup with Dr. Steere since November, but decided he ought to have an evaluation.

At the February 20 appointment, Gil's knee fluid was tapped. Dr. Steere gave him a shot of cortisone into the knee joint. Blood tests were done on both of us, and Dr. Steere planned a program of physical therapy for Gil.

A few weeks later, Gil had an acute tooth abscess; following surgery, he was put on a long course of penicillin by his dentist in Boston. He stayed in Boston while he was recuperating.

Meanwhile, Wendy was home from school with mononucleosis. Todd continued to have sporadic knee swelling. I saw Dr. Steere on April 6; on the eighteenth I had another EEG at the hospital, which showed no change.

On May 12, Gil and I had an appointment with Dr. Steere. Gil had started aspirin therapy in the middle of April. Dr. Steere again mentioned that Gil might have to have a synovectomy. Five such operations had now been done on Lyme arthritis patients. Gil wanted to wait until fall to see if his knees would improve on their own. Because Todd and I had felt better after taking the antihistamine Periactin, which I had originally been given by Dr. Schur to help with allergic reactions, I again asked Dr. Steere if Gil might not try the medication. With the exception of our family, patients with Lyme arthritis had not been given this drug. However, I felt that it might be worth a try with Gil, and despite being hesitant about taking medication, he decided to try it. The Periactin helped combat his insomnia; for the first time in two years he slept for eight hours straight. He continued taking the medication and with increased rest he felt better. He confessed to me that he wished he hadn't resisted Dr. Steere's suggestion that he take medication as long as he had.

During the summer of 1977, the doctors at Yale had seen a

man named Joe Dowhan who had come in to the hospital with a tiny tick he had removed from his knee. He also had a bite on his neck. A scientist for the U.S. Fish and Wildlife Service, Joe Dowhan had been working with a group of biologists along the Connecticut shore on a coastal ecological study when he was bitten. Several days later he developed malaise, swollen glands, stiff jaw muscles, and swelling and redness in his knees, hips, shoulders, and elbows. He had heard about Lyme arthritis in the media, and found his way to Dr. Steere.

Joe Dowhan's tick, a member of the species *Ixodes scapularis* (the black-legged tick), was the smoking gun that Dr. Steere and his colleagues had been looking for. This was the first time they had actual proof of what kind of tick transmitted Lyme arthritis. Dr. Steere and his team had paid special attention to the *Ixodes* genus over the past few years of research, because Connecticut scientists had found that the *Ixodes scapularis* ticks were twelve to sixteen times more plentiful in towns on the eastern side of the Connecticut River, where Lyme arthritis was more prevalent, than in towns on the western side. Smaller than a dog tick or a wood tick, *Ixodes scapularis* is commonly called a deer tick.

Scientists had noted for many years that *Ixodes* ticks cause illness in humans. In Europe *Ixodes ricinus,* commonly called the sheep tick, was linked to the ECM rash and to neurological symptoms. In California a patient with ECM had also kept the tick after being bitten, and it was identified as *Ixodes pacificus,* a tick common on the West Coast.

In light of the evidence that Joe Dowhan brought to Yale, Connecticut researchers began requesting that patients collect ticks that had bitten them, putting the ticks in bottles along with a blade of grass to provide moisture to keep the tick alive. These samples would be retrieved and taken to New Haven for study. Entomologists continued to monitor our property and others in the lower valley.

During May and early June the news of the discovery of the culprit in Lyme arthritis transmission was published in all the papers. A reporter who had written one of the first news accounts of the disease called me for an interview. He wanted to know my reaction to the research thus far. I said that I was very encouraged at the progress the researchers had made into describing the disease. I said that my hunch was that the scope of the disease was even more complicated than the myriad symptoms documented so far. I told him that I was convinced that in the future there would be many other symptoms linked to the disease that were now noted only by the patients themselves.

Due to publicity and through the patient grapevine, I was getting many phone calls from people in the area who were plagued with symptoms similar to the ones that I and others had experienced. One woman reported a sensitivity to the sun she'd never had before. Many people reported swellings of the fingers, toes, wrist, ankle, or elbows. Some had rashes appear on their face, either with puffiness or in the butterfly pattern of lupus. Rashes appeared on most areas of the body, and several people had the hands-to-elbow distribution that I had. A few told of neurological problems. Others had reported chronic recurrent sore throats; one reported difficulty swallowing. Some reported illnesses in their animals. Depressing as these reports were, at least this communication indicated that the disease would one day be more completely described. In a strange way, it was comforting to me to hear these stories because, being consistent with the peculiar symptomatology that I and my family had struggled with for so long, they reinforced my perceptions. Definite patterns in the illness were emerging. And patients were relieved to talk to someone who understood the self-doubts one had to deal with in explaining the changes that they felt were affecting their body. I sensed that often patients felt more comfortable asking me about their strange symptoms than asking their doctors. They felt less apprehensive; to me they could reveal their fleeting symptoms, which spanned so many areas of their body, without the worry of feeling foolish or coming up against a physician's skepticism.

Articles on Lyme arthritis were now published frequently in medical journals. As a result, media attention increased, as did phone calls to the house and requests for interviews. A major textbook in pediatrics planned to include an entry on Lyme arthritis.

Sandy had been in England for a semester his junior year and had gone off to Nantucket to work for the summer, planning to go to Paris in the fall for his senior year as part of a Tufts University program. David would be home, working at the inn. After school let out, Todd was planning to be in Cambridge, Massachusetts, as a camp counselor.

On June 2, when I pulled in to the driveway after going shopping for groceries, David came to meet me. With a weird, excited expression on his face, he informed me that I had had a call from Walter Cronkite's *CBS Evening News* office. "Stop pulling my leg," I said, handing him a bag of groceries to carry. David said, "No, it's for real," and I should call them back. I called CBS. They were doing a segment on Lyme arthritis and wanted to send a reporter to the house to interview me the following Monday. I said that I would be happy to be a part of it. Luckily, I was madly getting ready to participate in a doll show that weekend, so I didn't have time to get nervous about the upcoming interview.

The filming went well, this time with a backdrop of our stone wall and the woods. CBS also interviewed the researchers at Yale, and the piece aired on *CBS Morning News* shortly thereafter.

In late May and early June the nymphal stage of the ticks became plentiful. I found a few on me after walking at a friend's house. We were all now finding them crawling on us after just walking across the lawn to the driveway. The children and I never sat on the grass anymore.

We did careful tick checks, but even so we occasionally missed ticks because they were in a place that was hard to see, like the back of the armpit. Sometimes the ticks were stopped by the elastic of a bra, pants, or a belt, and began feeding there. I found that a full-length mirror was very helpful.

Hoping to reduce the number of ticks, I decided to clear the brush between the lawn and the woods on our property. I also began wearing protective gear when working outside. Because one can see ticks more readily on light-colored clothing, I bought a pair of white painter's pants, which I wore with a white long-sleeved shirt. I donned a kerchief over my hair and wore high boots.

When bitten, we carefully removed the ticks with tweezers and saved them in little bottles marked with the name of the person bitten, the date of the bite, and the area of the body where the bite was. The researchers would later study these specimens. Because the nymphal *Ixodes* tick is so small and difficult to see—it's the size of a typed period—and the bite is usually not felt, often one notices the tick only because of the redness that sometimes comes after it has latched on. Some people, perhaps those who have become sensitive to the bite, have itching, which alerts them to the presence of the tick. Each time Gil, Todd, and I were bitten, aches and fatigue were triggered; in fact, these symptoms might alert us to a bite. The situation could be very discouraging.

Gil felt cold all the time, and he wore a heavy sweater throughout the summer. He was fatigued and slept a lot now. He told me that when I'd had these symptoms he had not understood my suffering. It was only when he had the disease that he could truly understand what we were all going through.

That summer I continued my work with dolls, and at a local library I exhibited my drawings of children at the beach. A painting of mine won an award in a shoreline exhibit, and a story on my dolls appeared in a New Haven paper.

Wendy flew to Seattle to baby-sit for a couple who had moved there from Lyme, and it was an enjoyable experience for her. Todd and I went on a day trip to Block Island. I asked our taxi tour guide about the prevalence of deer there; she told us the island did not have any deer until eight were brought to the island around 1967. Since then the population had increased dramatically. The Lyme arthritis tick spends the winter feeding and mating on the deer, so often where there are many deer there are also cases of Lyme disease. This was certainly true of Block Island.

The aspirin Gil was taking progressively affected his hearing and caused ringing in his ears, so he had to cut back on his dose. He saw an ear doctor. He had rashes on both hands in September and October. He was bitten again in October, and this was followed by another flulike illness. He had blood tests done. A dime-sized lesion appeared on his thigh for three weeks, and his knees were still swollen and giving him trouble. He did a lot of swimming and physical therapy. I noticed that in order to get up from a chair, he had to push hard with his arms.

Todd was having nosebleeds again and had a checkup. He had knee pain but no swelling, and had to give up playing soccer because it aggravated his problem.

On November 20, Gil and I drove to New Haven for Gil's appointment with Dr. Steere. We were to go to the X-ray department first, and then have a consultation with an orthopedic surgeon and Dr. Steere. After the X rays had been evaluated and Gil had been examined, he and the doctors decided not to go through with the operation, but instead to try the anti-inflammatory drug Indocin, which Sandy had taken for his knee problems in 1975. We discussed the Lyme arthritis research, the HLA testing that had been done on a number of patients, and how the ticks seemed to heavily infest certain areas and not others. Dr. Steere felt that the infestation patterns probably were a random phenomenon, depending on where the engorged, fertilized female tick dropped off a deer or other host animal and eventually laid her eggs. I had noticed that the deer on our property had paths that they took regularly, and they were seen mostly on one corner of our land. The ticks and deerflies were definitely more plentiful in that area. If you walked during the summer in that spot, deerflies would attack your head and eyes.

I mentioned to Dr. Steere that I had heard from a woman in Lyme whose severe Lyme arthritis symptoms had improved rapidly after she was given a tetracycline drug. Dr. Steere responded that there was no noticeable effect from tetracycline on the later symptoms of the Lyme syndrome.

In December, Wendy and I made trips to numerous colleges for her interviews, and she was busy writing essays for applications. I was getting ready for the upcoming holiday season. Sandy would not be home from Paris, and we would miss him.

1979

I continued to get calls from people who wanted me to relay information to Dr. Steere, which I did regularly. Dr. Steere and colleagues planned to study nymphal ticks, which were plentiful during mid-May, June, and into July in the Northeast, a time when many cases of ECM were reported each year. Ticks would be routinely collected and studied by entomologists, so the researchers would rely less on the patient's collection of the ticks. In an AP story printed in the February 10 *Day*, Frederick W. Schofield, a Mystic, Connecticut, man who had been treated for Lyme arthritis since 1976, was quoted as saying: "I'm having trouble talking and eating, and I can't open or close my mouth completely. When a year goes by they [the Yale researchers] add another year to the time it [the illness] takes to run its course." From my own experience talking to people, a certain number of them told me that they wondered when and if they would be free of the disease and its debilitating symptoms.

On the evening of March 9, Todd complained of pain in the lower spinal area of his back. The following day he was seen by a doctor and told he needed to be flat in bed. X rays were done and he was found to have a minimal scoliosis. He was given a muscle relaxant and painkiller and stayed flat. Gradually, over the next five days, he improved. We heard from Sandy, who was studying in Paris, that he had had a week of swelling in one knee.

In April, researchers as well as townspeople began noticing a dramatic increase in the number of ticks. In an April 3 article in *The Day*, a Dr. Anderson of the Connecticut Agricultural Experiment Station said that the tick population was new to the state. In early reports by the Insect Identification Center, which began its work fifty years ago, "you seldom find mention of ticks. If they had been around in any numbers you'd find them in the reports."

I mentioned to Dr. Steere that I thought that a support group affiliated with the hospital would be a good idea. I also suggested that perhaps a brochure on Lyme arthritis could be prepared in order to get the word out, especially to libraries, schools, doctors' offices, drugstores, and tourist bureaus. I asked Dr. Steere whether someone who had the Lyme infection and was bitten again by a disease-carrying tick would find their symptoms reappearing, triggered by the new bite. I had observed the phenomenon in our household.

On April 24, I talked to Dr. Steere and relayed information

from people who had called me. I told him of Todd's back episode. He felt that it might have been due to a flare-up of Lyme arthritis. On May 25, I had Todd's X rays sent to him.

The spring months were busy with trips to colleges as Wendy decided which one to attend. (She chose Vassar.) I had a twenty-fifth anniversary reunion at my college, at which I had to give a talk about my creative endeavors, so that took a lot of preparation. My dolls were selling, which made me happy. I exhibited paintings and participated in doll and antique shows. Wendy was in a dance recital at school and would be graduating in June. The children were all growing up so fast. Sandy would be arriving home from France in June. David planned to work in New York City for the summer; Sandy would be helping me paint the house; Todd would be a counselor in Cambridge again; and Wendy would be working at the inn.

As a result of a news release from Yale, on June 7 many of the papers ran stories telling of some important findings in the evolving story of Lyme arthritis. The disease was far more complicated than the researchers had originally thought; it involved many systems of the body, and therefore they were going to rename it Lyme disease. They had also found that they had been wrong in thinking that *Ixodes scapularis* was the culprit. The "smoking gun" tick had been misidentified. Instead, a closely related tick was identified by Dr. Andrew Spielman of Harvard as the real culprit. This tick was named *Ixodes dammini,* after the distinguished Dr. Gustave J. Dammin, professor emeritus of the Harvard School of Public Health, who had been working on research on babesiosis, another disease transmitted by the same tick and studied on the islands off Massachusetts. Though so far there had been no cases of babesiosis in Connecticut, now, with the increased *Ixodes dammini* population here, infection in our state was possible. Dr. Spielman said that *Ixodes dammini* is dependent on the deer population, and that Nantucket had had no deer for many years prior to the 1920s. (The deer had all been killed for food.) In 1927, deer were reintroduced to Nantucket from Michigan. Since then the deer population has increased a great deal, and tick-borne diseases have appeared as a consequence.

The Yale group described the heart symptoms (irregular heart-beat and heart block) and neurological symptoms (Bell's palsy, brain inflammation, uncontrolled muscle movements, loss of balance, and bowel and bladder dysfunction) that they had found were also part of the disease. The arthritis was now believed to become chronic in some patients, and to damage the cartilage of the knee.

In August, our family had more blood tests for research on Lyme disease by Dr. Robert Winchester at the Rockefeller Institute in New York City, who was studying the genetic aspects of Lyme arthritis.

I had symptoms again during the summer, and in August Wendy was bitten by an *Ixodes dammini* tick. Fortunately, she had been taking tetracycline for acne for quite a while and continued to take it.

She was getting ready to go to college; Gil, Todd, and I drove her to Vassar late in August. I was busy with my work whenever I had a chance, and participated in several antique and doll shows.

During her first month at college Wendy developed four lesions; one, silver-dollar-sized, on her lower leg; one red ring on her neck and up over her jawbone; and one on each thigh. The heat of the shower would bring out her rashes. They didn't itch, but felt prickly. Gil and I had had such rashes. Wendy also had a recurrent sore throat, her jaw was slightly stiff and sore, she had a few dizzy spells, and her eyelid was again swollen and twitched a lot. A dermatologist at college could not diagnose her rashes and gave her cortisone cream. I told Dr. Steere of her problems.

Gil had started out the year taking Indocin and Periactin. Beginning in April he started jogging again. By August he had stopped taking Indocin and was down to one Periactin a day. The following month he stopped all medication and began lifting weights with his legs. He worked out very often and was extremely thin. In 1978, he had refused to walk in areas where there might be ticks, but this year he was jogging through the woods again and was careless about checking for ticks. This became a great concern of mine; I worried, too, about his preoccupation with yoga and diet, because he looked so fatigued and exhausted all the time. He had always wanted to rely on his own resources rather than take the advice of others. To him, nature was the great healer. He was making fewer trips back from Boston to Lyme.

Reports of Lyme disease were coming from Cape Cod, the islands off the New England coast, Long Island, and all along the shoreline. In the November 1979 *Annals of Internal Medicine,* Drs. Steere and Malawista reported that there were now 512 known cases in the United States; through August 1979, 365 of them had been seen at Yale.[3]

When I took Todd for an appointment with Dr. Steere in November, we discussed the current research and the neurological report that had been published in July; I told him that I identified with a lot of the neurological symptomatology described. I asked if any of the patients with neurological symptoms and general slowing on the EEG had improved after the acute episode. He said that several had continued residual slowing on their EEG, as he thought was the case with me, and that he had believed all along that the disease manifested itself in me with more neurological symptoms.

During December Todd was looking forward to taking his driver's test, having recently turned sixteen, and he was working hard in school. My dolls were for sale in a New York City shop specializing in dolls, which was exciting. Wendy was getting out on vacation from college, so I drove to Vassar to pick her up, and soon we all were busy getting ready for the holidays.

1980

In January, I went with Wendy to see the doctor who was treating her acne. Wendy mentioned that she'd had ring rashes and jaw stiffness during the fall, and that the symptoms had subsided. He seemed skeptical of Lyme disease, saying that he and the doctors in his practice had found that the illness wasn't serious in children and that many cases of Lyme disease would turn out to be JRA and lupus. He had seen Dr. Steere recently and had been told that studies at Yale now supported the use of antibiotics for early disease and found that it prevented later arthritis. I was interested to hear this because as far as I knew, Dr. Steere had been doubtful about it. Wendy was encouraged to hear of this finding, because she was on a prolonged course of tetracycline at the time she contracted Lyme disease. (Indeed, she never did develop the severe symptoms others in the family had experienced.) The following day she went to a scheduled appointment with Dr. Steere at Yale, and had blood drawn for testing for evidence of Lyme disease.

On February 20, *The Gazette* published an article by Judy Urband about Dr. Paul Urband, a veterinarian in East Haddam who was treating a dozen or so dogs afflicted with an illness very much like Lyme disease. I was encouraged to learn that he had been in touch with Dr. Steere. I decided to call Dr. Urband to tell him of other Lyme disease–like symptoms in animals that had been reported to me, and of how our own cat had become lame and our dog had stiffened with arthritis and had kidney problems during the year when we were all hit with symptoms. I told him of unusual ailments I had heard about in local horses. I also related to him the details of a letter I'd received in 1977 from Mary Jo Everson, a woman who had worked for a veterinarian on Cape Cod. She had said that "during and following the 'tick season,' several dogs were brought to us with a vast assortment of puzzling and unusual symptoms that didn't add up. Among these were: acute high fever, seizures, *low persistent fever, joint stiffness and pain, muscle spasms,* nervous tics, etc." As with the dogs Dr. Urband had treated, X rays of the Cape Cod dogs failed to show any known disease.

Dr. Urband told me he strongly suspected that pets in our area did in fact have Lyme disease. Determined to pursue the mystery further, he had consulted with veterinarians in other areas of the state and found the problem to be focused on the area around Lyme. I mentioned that I had read about cases of dogs with lupus, so I knew that sometimes people and animals do get the same diseases. I wondered if a veterinary college couldn't undertake research into the problem of this Lyme-like illness in animals.

In late March, Todd complained of intermittent pain in his ears and a slight loss of hearing. The condition persisted, so in early May his local doctor gave him a three-week course of antibiotics. In late May, Todd was still disturbed by loss of hearing and tinnitus—ringing—in his left ear; after three more weeks on antibiotics, the symptoms finally improved.

Aside from the ear trouble, Todd was feeling pretty healthy. He now had his driver's license and was driving to school each day in the White Flash (a nickname he and Wendy bestowed upon our secondhand white Toyota during the days when Wendy was driving them to school).

About this time, Gil received a letter from Dr. Steere, who said:

> *As you know, you and Mrs. Murray are the ones that started me out on the pursuit of Lyme disease. I well remember your initial description of your illness, the first that I ever heard of the disease.*
>
> *I am most grateful for your clues, the pursuit of which have [sic] continued to occupy most of my time for the past five years. However, I remain convinced that Lyme disease is a solvable problem and look forward someday to discussing with you how it all works.*

Todd was elected student trustee of the school for his senior year. I think he missed having his brothers and sister around, but for the most part, he was relishing his independence.

Late in May newspapers carried articles about the Yale finding that penicillin administered early in Lyme disease was beneficial, and helped to prevent the later development of arthritis. In the June 6 issue of *The Journal of the American Medical Association,* George E. Ehrlich, M.D., wrote that "the discovery and description of Lyme arthritis thus seems to be the major accomplishment of rheumatology in the second half of the 1970s, just as HLA-B27 was the story of the first half."[4]

In addition to my volunteer work with Lyme disease, I kept busy with my doll making. My relationship with Gil had become still more estranged; we were each consciously and unconsciously trying to lead more separate lives. We talked of divorce, but I guess neither one of us was quite ready, emotionally or financially. We wanted to stay together, to keep some semblance of family, until the children were all out on their own.

As much as we each tried to keep the peace during the weekends Gil was home, our differences in temperament and philosophy flared often. I felt I didn't know my husband anymore; he seemed like a changed person. His devil-may-care attitude about Lyme disease continued. He'd lie in the grass to read the newspaper, encourage Todd to camp out, and go barefoot all the time; he didn't check regularly for ticks. Again he resisted treatment for his symptoms, saying he was too busy and unwilling to see Dr. Steere. We were angry at each other, of course, and so we each got more entrenched and protective of our separate stands. The more I realized the potential seriousness of Lyme disease and the more I took steps to guard against it—clearing land, and so on—the more Gil threw caution to the winds. This frightened me. And I, in turn became more determined to keep the household on an even keel. I continued to get professional counseling to help me cope, which was helpful to me. Gil and I decided that starting in January it would be best to see each other only on family birthdays and during holidays. We were relieved; this arrangement would give us each the freedom to pursue endeavors important to us without apology, without hassles.

To try to cut down on the ticks on our property, I hired professionals to clear a large portion of the land surrounding our house. (I had given up my earlier plan to do this work myself.) In one day, with heavy equipment, they were able to open up the property. They left an enormous area of smoothed dirt cluttered with roots and rocks; over the next few weeks Todd, David, and I worked hard and planted an extended area of lawn. The larger lawn kept the animal and tick populations farther from the house and enabled more breezes to reach the house from the river. I bought a ride-on mower so that I would reduce my exposure to ticks.

That summer Todd was working at the inn in Old Lyme; Wendy was working as a waitress in Woods Hole, Massachusetts; and Sandy was working in Boston. David started volunteer work in the emergency room at Bellevue Hospital and at the Chinatown

Health Clinic in New York because during the past year he had decided to go into medicine. He took first-aid and CPR courses as well. He planned to finish his major in photography at Rhode Island School of Design while taking premed courses at Brown University. He had worked on a project with a doctor there the past semester.

On July 2, *The Gazette* reporter Doug Tift wrote that a woman in the Becket Hill area of Lyme estimated that "almost half of the residents there have been afflicted by Lyme disease. . . . All of the local doctors were aware of the recently-released study indicating that early treatment with penicillin seemed to reduce the symptoms. One doctor had used this treatment with some success in the past and was not surprised by the Yale study. Another doctor, however, treated some patients with penicillin and did not use penicillin on others, but found there was no difference in the extent or severity of symptoms several weeks later."

The ticks were very plentiful; I constantly had calls from area residents about the problem. I accompanied some friends in to see Dr. Steere on July 14. One friend, who had a history of knee swelling, was given an antibiotic. I told Dr. Steere that I had heard about others with gynecological symptoms and Lyme disease. He had recently seen a patient with an inflammation of the bowel.

I mentioned that I felt the public needed education about ticks. Dr. Steere told me that Dr. Spielman was studying the relationship among deer and ticks and people with the disease on an island off Cape Cod. Research into pets and Lyme disease was being planned. Because the disease responded to penicillin, at least at the beginning of infection, Dr. Steere now thought it was caused by a bacterium.

Doctors in our area reported an increase in cases. The ticks, deer population, humidity, and temperature in our region were the right combination of factors to foster the disease.

On July 17, I attended an informative lecture by Dr. Andrew Main, an assistant professor of medical entomology at Yale University School of Medicine, on the various ticks that cause human disease in this country. Dr. Main described the life cycle of a tick. During the question-and-answer period after the lecture, one woman said that the tick population on the shoreline had grown tremendously from 1950 on. At first she noticed them in the marshes, and then in the woods. Some parents said they took nine or ten ticks a day off their children. Someone wanted to know if certain people chemically attracted ticks more than others. One man wanted to know if the decision to ban burning of the fields because of air pollution had triggered the increase in ticks.

In August, Todd and I made a trip to Cape Cod to see Wendy for a few days. David and Wendy were both home for a while before returning to college, and Todd was arranging for his upcoming college interviews and working on applications. His health was much improved, and I wondered if the six-week course of antibiotics his local doctor had prescribed for his ear condition back in May and June had helped him to get better.

1981

To discover the agent of disease and death depends on a patient piecing together of many seemingly distinct and unrelated facts developed through a vast amount of research in widely separated fields.
RACHEL CARSON, *SILENT SPRING*[5]

In early April, Todd was accepted at Brown University; he graduated from high school in early June. Wendy had decided to spend a year at Wesleyan University in Middletown, Connecticut, on a junior-year exchange program. David still needed to take premed courses before applying to medical school; he went off to work as a waiter in New Haven for a few months, and then headed for Massachusetts, where he worked in a psychiatric facility to gain experience toward his medical career and to save money for tuition costs.

During the spring Dr. Steere was quoted by David H. Rhinelander of *The Hartford Courant* as follows: "I no longer believe Lyme disease is caused by a virus. . . . Because antibiotics like penicillin and tetracycline are effective, it's most likely caused by a bacterium. A fungus is still a possibility, although a remote one."

In the June 4, 1981, *The New England Journal of Medicine* there appeared an article entitled "The Physician and the Hypochondriacal Patient," by Gerald Adler, M.D. Dr. Adler described the hypochondriacal patient and the difficulties the medical profession had in understanding the needs of this category of patient.[6] I wrote the following letter to the editor:

> *It was interesting to read the fine article by Gerald Adler, M.D., in the June 4 issue of the* Journal *concerning the hypochondriacal patient.*
>
> *Before enough information had been gathered prior to my discovery of Lyme disease in 1975 and the initiation of the study at Yale University, I had consulted many doctors concerning first my symptoms and then those of my family. Some of the doctors that I saw were supportive and open to the possibility of the unknown, that something wrong did exist; however, they and medical science as yet could not figure out what our trouble was. On the other hand, many of the physicians that I encountered tended to fit me into the category of a hypochondriac. It was suggested that I was obsessed, bored, depressed, bothering busy doctors, and later some suggested that the entire family had a psychogenic problem. I will admit that my behavior became insistent and constantly questioning.*
>
> *The many periodic, multisystem symptoms of Lyme disease can be easily confused with somatization disorder, hypochondriasis, conversion disorders and psychogenic pain disorder.*
>
> *I would like to emphasize Dr. Adler's statement that "these somatoform disorders must be distinguished from true physical diseases that often initially present with vague, confusing symptoms." I would urge that doctors be extremely careful before labeling a patient hypochondriacal. There now being over 600 cases of Lyme disease under study over the past six years at Yale University, time has proven that my family was not hypochondriacal. The myriad of symptoms that we exhibited over*

a period of years have since been seen clinically and are well documented by the numbers of patients now studied. Having talked with many patients affected by Lyme disease, I have found that their numerous physicians, faced with a disease that is not widely understood, reacted initially with a suggestion that the patient might be having a psychogenic problem. I would urge the physician to listen to the patient. Perhaps the patient's multi-system involvement of symptoms does have a true physical basis. The anger, depression, hopelessness, and helplessness might all be explained by the frustrations of the undiagnosed illness coupled with the physical effects of the undefined disease. Instead of anger, rejection and withdrawal by the doctor, I certainly would urge, as Dr. Adler suggests, compassion, concern, and respect for the patient and that the patient be taken seriously.

Perhaps there is a possibility that the physician, when confronted with symptoms he can't readily explain, will reject the patient and wrongly label the patient hypochondriacal as his only way of dealing with that patient. It is to this possibility that I speak. In some instances, could it be that it is not a hypo-chondriacal patient, but a doctor who chooses not to confront the unknown?

A certain amount of the hypochondriacal patient's need for emotional support can be found in many sick people. Part of good healing comes from the formation of a supportive rela-tionship with the doctor, nurse, or anyone who is attending the needs of the patient. The growth of patient support groups now speaks for this basic need of the patient with an illness for understanding as well as medicine.

I showed Dr. Steere the letter before sending it. His response was as follows:

Thank you very much for the chance to read your letter. I think it is very good and hope that the Journal likes it. I think that your experience in being labelled a hypochondriacal patient when, in fact, you had Lyme disease is an important example to bring before physicians.

My letter was published in early October in the following form:

> *Before it was recognized that I had what became known as Lyme disease, I had consulted many doctors, first about my symptoms and then about those of my family. Some of the doctors whom I saw were supportive and open to the possibility of the unknown; however, they and medical science could not figure out what our trouble was. On the other hand, many of the physicians I encountered tended to fit me into the category of a hypochondriac. It was suggested that I was obsessed, bored, and depressed and that I was bothering busy doctors; some later suggested that the entire family had a psychogenic problem. I will admit that my behavior became insistent and constantly questioning.*
>
> *Perhaps there is a possibility that the physician, when confronted with symptoms that cannot be readily explained, will reject the patient and wrongly use the label "hypochondriacal" as the only way of dealing with that patient. In some instances, could it be that it is not a hypochondriacal patient but a doctor who chooses not to confront the unknown?*[7]

While I was pleased to have my letter published, I was disappointed by how much had been cut from my original letter.

I received a number of responses, one from a doctor on Cape Cod who had framed my letter to hang on the wall in his office.

Interesting work on Lyme disease had been done by doctors on Long Island. According to a Long Island newspaper account, in May 1975 a Dr. Edgar Grunwaldt had started a medical practice on Shelter Island, a small island off Long Island. He noted a strange rash on some of his patients, found that penicillin helped them, and after doing some research was able to link the rash with the European ECM and with ticks. He couldn't understand why doc-

tors before him hadn't questioned the unusual rash. Dr. Grunwaldt also found that some of the patients with ECM also had a
disease called babesiosis. In 1977, he had a paper on babesiosis in
New York State published in a medical journal. Early in 1977, when
Dr. Steere published his first paper on Lyme arthritis, describing
the ECM rash, Dr. Grunwaldt realized that they were both interested in the same disease.

Jorge Benach, a researcher from the New York State Health
Department and the department of pathology at Stony Brook,
Long Island, was doing work on tick-borne diseases, and he contacted Dr. Grunwaldt after reading his paper in the medical journal. They then worked together on the tick disease problem, and
started a tick collection program on Shelter Island. The Shelter
Island ticks were sent to the Rocky Mountain Laboratories,
in Hamilton, Montana, where a renowned tick specialist named
Dr. Willy Burgdorfer was doing research on Rocky Mountain
spotted fever for the National Institute of Allergy and Infectious
Diseases.[8]

In the early fall of 1981, adult *Ixodes dammini* were collected by
flagging, a process by which a flag of white soft flannel is dragged
over vegetation in order to collect ticks. According to Dr. Burgdorfer's account in a speech given on Plant Science Day, August
10, 1983, at the Connecticut Agricultural Experiment Station:

"For several years, I have been collaborating with Dr. Jorge Benach from the State of New York Department of Health in studies
related to spotted fever on Long Island. One of the questions
under investigation concerned the potential role of the deer tick,
I. dammini, as a vector of the spotted-fever agent, *R. rickettsii*. Although we had already tested several hundred ticks without finding evidence of rickettsial infection, one additional shipment was
received in September 1981. While examining the tick blood
(hemolymph) for rickettsiae, I twice encountered the advanced
stages of a microfilaria [the prelarval stage of the threadlike worms
called nematodes]. Eager to find the younger developmental
stages of this nematode, I dissected both ticks and prepared
smears."[9]

Burgdorfer described the historic moment in the following way: "Tick surgery is what we do, and what I've done for the last 30 years or so, ever since I started in this game. . . . You take the tick and fix its legs in paraffin on a plate and when the paraffin cools . . . you take an eye scalpel [the sort used by eye surgeons] and cut." Burgdorfer didn't find any developing nematodes, but with his trained eye he found slowly moving spirochetes. Dissecting more and more of the ticks from Shelter Island, he found spirochetes in the midgut of more than half of them. He was convinced that he had happened upon the cause of Lyme disease.[10] He remembered that in 1948, a researcher named Carl Lennhoff had linked spirochetes with the ECM, although other scientists subsequently could not duplicate Lennhoff's work.

The scientific investigation of the spirochete and its role in Lyme disease initiated by Dr. Burgdorfer and several colleagues would now be formally written up for submission to a scientific journal and peer review and publication, a process that would take months.

Over eight hundred cases of Lyme disease had now been reported in the United States, and the discovery of the etiological agent was an exciting time for all involved in the illness's unfolding story.

Once again the element of chance had played a part in medical discovery. The lucky chance of evidence suddenly being presented to a prepared and receptive mind had culminated in the discovery of the cause of the disease. The course of scientific investigation can be unpredictable, and sometimes it is hindered by the territorial boundaries and limitations of the investigators, who fail to see the total picture. For this reason, open dialogue is so very important for true understanding.

1982

The first few months of 1982, I was adjusting to being on my own, now that the children were all away from home and Gil and I were leading separate lives. I did volunteer work, continued my antiques shows and doll making, and kept busy working on the house.

During the spring Sandy and Gil had knee problems again, and I also had strange symptoms, including "lightning pains." I awoke one morning in early June and had trouble hearing out of my left ear. My left eye was blurry and my balance was off. I felt disoriented, and I was running a slight fever. My jaw was cracking again. I checked with my local doctor. He thought it might be a viral illness.

I called Gil and persuaded him to write down his Lyme symptoms and send them to me so that I could inform Dr. Steere of them. In February he had a butterfly rash on his face along with a feverish feeling, and he, too, was experiencing lightning or stitch-like pains, which affected his neck, shoulder, and lumbar regions. In his notes, Gil said that by April he had "extreme pain and swelling in right ankle and right mid foot. Pronounced limp, feverish feeling, general stiffness and slowness in all actions." He "ceased all weight-bearing exercises. In bed when possible." By May 2 he was normal again, only to relapse after being "out in the sun for prolonged exposure," which led to "feverish feeling, general stiffness and slowness of action. Right shoulder blade and shoulder socket extremely painful. Right neck rear had stabbing pain on turning head." By May 14 he was normal again. He told me that he didn't realize how much he had changed physically until one day he was shocked to see his reflection in a window as he walked along a street in Boston.

On June 18, the article "Lyme Disease—A Tick-Borne Spirochetosis?" by Dr. Burgdorfer and his colleagues was published in the journal *Science*. The findings were widely picked up by the media.[11]

On Monday, June 28, I had an appointment with Dr. Steere, during which I brought him up-to-date on the symptoms that Sandy, Gil, and I had been having. We discussed the spirochete, which he said acts in many ways more like spirochetes of the genus *Borrelia* than like those of the genus *Treponema*, one of which [*T. pallidum*] causes syphilis. Dr. Steere said, "This has been in existence for many, many years and never fully understood. It is probably worldwide.''

Later I would read in the medical literature that acrodermatitis chronica atrophicans (ACA), a late-stage rash of Lyme disease, was found to have been mentioned in 1883 by a German doctor, Alfred Buchwald.[12] In 1909 a Dr. Arvid Afzelius in Sweden described the ECM and related it to an *Ixodes* tick bite.[13] In 1923, Dr. B. Lipschütz of Germany suspected a bacterium as the cause of the rash,[14] while in 1950 a Dr. Hellerström described the ECM and neurological symptoms as the result of an *Ixodes* tick bite[15] and mentioned that a colleague named Hollström had treated the infection successfully with penicillin. Dr. Hollström had suspected a spirochetal cause of the infection, following Dr. Lennhoff's theory.[16] In 1955, a Dr. Binder and his colleagues had managed to transfer the infection by transplanting pieces of the rash into the skin of three volunteers, who in one to three weeks then developed the ECM infection. All were successfully treated immediately with penicillin.[17] I was also fascinated by a 1965 paper by C. E. Sonck, of Finland. Sonck described the pinprick-type rash that our family had observed as ''small petechia-like effusions of blood which remained when pressed with a glass spatula.'' He also stated that the rash ''could be brought out by sunshine or a hot bath even long after it had apparently vanished,'' just as we had experienced in our family. A two-and-a-half-year-old boy Sonck studied developed braceletlike ring rashes on his arm, similar to the one Todd had had circling his wrist. Penicillin was used to cure these patients.[18]

This earlier research had pointed to different parts of the total story of what was now called Lyme disease, and now the causative *Borrelia* spirochete had been identified. The researchers at Yale were trying to isolate it from Lyme disease patients.

I asked Dr. Steere about the development of a Lyme disease brochure, and he told me that the Pfizer pharmaceutical company had funded the printing of a brochure developed with the Arthritis Foundation's Connecticut chapter. I told him I would contact Nancy Considine, who developed programs for public education at the foundation, and offer to distribute the brochures locally.

I explained to Dr. Steere the strange symptoms described by

some people who talked to me, including appetite changes, food cravings, sudden anxieties and fears (such as fear of heights), mood changes, hyperactivity and irritability. I shared with Dr. Steere the incredible strain that the disease had put our family under, and I wondered how many other families were stressed and in a state of upheaval from living with its unknowns.

David returned to Lyme to work at the inn and planned to enter the Columbia School of General Studies in January to complete his premed courses. He would help me work on the house and save money toward tuition. I kept busy with shows and caring for my father and my recently hospitalized aunt. Wendy returned to Vassar for her senior year.

In the November 18 *New York Times* the health reporter Jane E. Brody wrote: "Researchers said yesterday they believed they had discovered the cause of Lyme disease.

"Finding the bacterium in patients with Lyme disease . . . in a sense brings the researcher's detective work full circle; from victim, to a tick that carried the bacterium and transmitted it and now, finally, to finding that same bacterium in the victim."

As Brody explained, "Dr. Bernard Ackerman, a dermatopathologist at New York University, said in an interview that he and his colleagues had found the bacterium, a type known as spirochete, in human skin specimens sent to them by Dr. Bernard Berger, a dermatologist from Southhampton, L. I., who is affiliated with the university. The specimens were taken from a red skin lesion that is characteristic of Lyme disease.

"Dr. Ackerman said identification of the spirochete in patients was made possible by a special technique using Warthin-Starry silver stain, which highlights the organisms, which are otherwise difficult or impossible to see under a microscope."

In late November, *The Pictorial,* a shoreline paper, reported on a local case of Lyme disease with eye symptoms. According to reporter Martha Davidson, a young boy who resided in Lyme said, "I can't see. Cut my hair." The story continued: "But it wasn't his hair at all. They discovered the boy was suffering from Lyme disease which had affected him behind his eyes impairing his vision."

The reporter added that the boy had been treated at Yale several times.

I had wondered about the effect of the spirochete on the function of the eye. In our family we had some puzzling eye symptoms. Both David and I found that our pupils were different sizes; he had a wandering eye for a while; we all had bouts of conjunctivitis; I'd had subconjunctival hemorrhages; and Sandy, Wendy, and I had swelling and drooping of the eyelid. We all also had uncontrolled twitching of the eyelid during Lyme disease flare-ups. With the knowledge that Lyme disease can cause damage in so many areas of the body, it seemed reasonable that the eye could be affected. I had heard anecdotally of others being afflicted with eye symptoms. I felt that doctors noticing eye symptoms that accompanied Lyme disease infection should report their findings to the Lyme Disease Clinic at Yale. I hoped that opthalmologists would research the effect of Lyme disease on the eyes.

1983

Following the holidays it was soon time to take Wendy and Todd back to their colleges and to drive David to Manhattan, where he would begin the general studies program at Columbia. I spent the rest of January working on dolls. The next few months were very busy, as I had scheduled quite a few weekend shows.

The New England Journal of Medicine published the research of Yale and New York investigators in its March 31 issue. When I picked Todd up for spring vacation, we went to the Brown University library so I could read the long-awaited article.

The report stated that out of a total of eighty-four patients enrolled in two studies, investigators were able to isolate the spirochete in only five. This finding made it clear that the *Borrelia* spirochete was going to be difficult to culture routinely. (Yale researchers had found it in the blood of one patient, the spinal fluid of another, and the skin biopsy from the periphery of the ECM rash of a third. The New York researchers found the spirochete in the blood of two patients.)[19]

That same issue of the *New England Journal* included an editorial by Edward D. Harris, Jr., M.D., that began, "Lyme disease belongs to the people," and ended with the following words:

"There is something very satisfying about the progress that has been made since the summer of 1975, when the Lyme mothers recognized a pattern of disease in their town's children. The triumph belongs to the inquisitiveness and determination of clinical and laboratory investigators in medicine. The efforts of unfettered investigators, who had time to plan careful epidemiologic and etiologic studies, and a spirit of collaboration among scientists of many disciplines have led to the probable cause and cure of Lyme disease."[20]

When the *New England Journal* report was released on March 30, I was interviewed by David Collins of *The Day*. When he asked me what I thought about the new research findings, I was reminded of Dr. Peter Schur's encouraging words, back in 1973, and told him that one of the doctors that I had consulted told me that someday we would be able to look back and see how the pieces of the puzzle of my mysterious disease fit together. I guessed he was right. It was a wonderful thing that the research had come this far in so short a time.

During the spring I distributed Lyme disease brochures to area drugstores and libraries. The importance of getting the information to doctors and the public was illustrated in an April 24 account in *The New York Times*. A doctor in Katonah, New York, was puzzled by a strange rash on one of his young patients. He consulted a colleague, who quickly recognized the rash because he had seen a photograph of it in information put out by the New York State Health Department.

The *Times* article reminded me of a woman in the Northwest who had contacted me in 1979 or 1980. She'd told me that she had been hospitalized for neurological symptoms and had a very unusual rash at the time. Her doctors could not diagnose her problem. Still not feeling well, she was recuperating in a rented vacation house, where she began leafing through a two- or three-year-old copy of *Good Housekeeping* that had been left by previous occupants. Enticed by the headline "Mrs. Murray's Mystery Disease," she started reading the article. By the time she finished she was almost certain she'd discovered what was ailing her. After telling me her story, she asked for advice. I put her in touch with the experts on the disease. Over the years I heard of many more serendipitous accounts of people finding out that their illness might, in fact, be Lyme disease.

Wendy was working very hard on her thesis, a collection of short stories. We all attended her graduation in May, where she received honors for her work. Soon after graduation she took off for New York City to pursue a career in publishing and to continue her own writing. Todd planned to work in Providence for the summer, and David was taking more premed courses at Columbia.

During the summer there were several forums on Lyme disease in our area in order to heighten awareness. Westchester County in New York was increasing public awareness efforts, too. In August Dr. Willy Burgdorfer lectured at Plant Science Day at the Connecticut Agricultural Experiment Station in Hamden. He gave an interesting talk entitled "Ticks—An Ever Increasing Public Health Problem." I introduced myself to him after the lecture and also talked to Dr. John Anderson and Dr. Louis Magnarelli. They were attempting to isolate the spirochete from animals and to measure antibodies to the spirochete. Human tests for antibodies were being done by researchers at the experiment station. Scientists there were studying species of birds that were carrying ticks and the infection to new areas.

I discussed with them an idea I had of putting together educational exhibits including vials of *Ixodes dammini* specimens in their larval, nymphal, adult, and engorged state to circulate in schools and libraries in endemic areas. I had found that people had trouble identifying the Lyme disease–carrying tick, and that seeing specimens of different stages of the tick's life cycle illuminated the reality of the disease. Photos of the tick were helpful but not as effective. Dr. Magnarelli said he would help me with this project and supply the tick specimens.

It was a busy summer for me; I spent a lot of time traveling to

New Jersey to help my father, who had been hospitalized. I also worked on my paintings and arranged with a gallery in Old Lyme to handle my work. I was coping with odd symptoms, too. In the spring I had a return of eye swelling, bursitis, stiffness, and fatigue, and now I had trouble with numbness and weakness in my hands, which often made me drop things. Jitteriness and insomnia returned.

I was disturbed to hear of several instances of the ECM rash being mistaken for an insect or spider bite by medical professionals. Some of the misdiagnosed patients went on to develop other Lyme disease symptoms before they were finally able to obtain a correct diagnosis and treatment. I wished that emergency rooms and clinics would post photos of the rashes and a list of the ways the disease might present itself—including heart block, meningitis, encephalitis, and extreme knee swelling—for both patients and staff members. Posting this information seemed especially important during peak Lyme disease season. I supposed it all would take time.

An article by Roberta Tuttle on August 17, 1983, in *The Day* reported that signs of Lyme disease were being found in area dogs. A veterinarian named Dr. Leo L. Lieberman had supplied blood samples to Dr. Magnarelli and animal researchers at the Connecticut Agricultural Experiment Station in New Haven, and they found that as many as 25 percent of the dogs in the region had antibodies to the spirochete. Dr. Magnarelli suggested that in endemic areas, pets having joint lameness, stiffness, and loss of appetite during the tick season should be tested for the disease.

In November, I attended the first international symposium on Lyme disease at Yale University. I was honored to have been invited. On the first day of the meeting I met several women doctors from Sweden. During the first coffee break I spoke with Dr. Klaus Weber of West Germany about auditory-nerve involvement, mentioned that morning in the Swedish neurological report. I told him that I knew of several cases of hearing loss. I also mentioned that when my son David was a young boy, he'd had a swollen, red earlobe that looked very much like the slide of the borrelia lymphocytoma of the earlobe that Weber had shown during his lecture. I was intrigued that he had ventured the possibility of tracheolaryngitis (inflammation of the trachea and larynx resulting in loss of voice) associated with the disease.

The research papers and discussions during the afternoon session focused on the biology of the ticks and the spirochete. The time went very fast all day and I met a great many people.

I was staying at Elise Taylor's apartment during the conference. Not only does she work with Dr. Steere but she is also an accomplished painter and quilt maker; we had become good friends over the years. Elise had recently suggested that we have a show of our work, her quilts and my dolls, at a gallery in New Haven, and we had decided to work toward the possibility. We drove to her place to get ready for a dinner at the Graduate Club. When we arrived at the dinner, the festivities were in full swing. I was greeted by Dr. Steere and was glad to see his nice wife, Margie, whom I hadn't seen since the summer of 1976, when she attended the first public meeting on "Lyme arthritis" in Old Lyme.

I spoke with a man who has spent many summers on Great Island, off Cape Cod. He and his family and fellow islanders had suffered from perplexing ailments over the years, and had had to deal with the frustrations of being misdiagnosed or undiagnosed at various medical centers. Great Island was another place where there was a clustering of Lyme disease cases, and it was now the location of a long-term Lyme disease study.

After speaking with him we all sat down to dinner. I met doctors from all over the world. There were speeches and entertainment. I felt elated at being so warmly included in the conference. When the evening came to a close, Elise and I walked the short distance back to her apartment. The crisp November air felt good.

The following day went quickly and I had conversations with a doctor from Moodus, Connecticut, who had sent many patients to Yale from his general practice. With Harvard's Dr. Andrew Spielman I discussed the overpopulation of deer in the region, and its role in spreading Lyme disease. I met Dr. Andrew Kornblatt, a veterinarian at Yale, who was doing a study of dogs and Lyme disease. (Later I would help him enroll a control group of healthy dogs for his study.)

I was particularly interested in the presentation by Dr. John Anderson from the Connecticut Agricultural Experiment Station. He said that the reservoir for the infection is in many mammals and birds right in our backyard.

In the East, white-footed mice are the chief source of the spirochetal infection (woodrats are the chief source in the West). Larval ticks, newly hatched from eggs, feed on the mice and pick up the spirochetes. Larval ticks also feed on birds and small mammals. The larval tick molts to the nymphal stage, and when feeding on their next host, the nymphal ticks carry the spirochetes to birds, man, and other mammals such as squirrels, chipmunks, and raccoons, as well as to domestic animals—dogs, cats, horses, and cows. After feeding, the nymphs molt to adults beginning in late August. From early fall and through the winter, the adult ticks mostly feed on deer, and incidentally on man and dogs. Mating occurs on the deer, and in early spring the female drops off the deer and lays her eggs, which completes the two-year life cycle of the tick.

Dr. Anderson reported that in 1983 in East Haddam, Connecticut, *Ixodes* ticks were found on twenty-seven different species of birds, and a number of them were infected with the spirochetes. It was obvious from this information that birds are a factor in the spread of infected ticks to new areas.

The conference broke for the day around five-thirty. A doctor from New Jersey gave Elise and me a ride to her apartment. As we drove through the streets of New Haven, I could see the lights still burning in the office of the psychiatrist who had helped me so much with his understanding and encouragement. I thought of how far I had come since my arrival in his office after my hospitalization in Boston the fall of 1971.

On the shuttle bus to the symposium the next morning, the final day of the conference, I hurriedly revised my notes of what I wanted to convey should the opportunity arise. Dr. Steere had encouraged me to speak up at the symposium, and said he hoped he'd hear from me. I wanted to be prepared.

Some of my questions had been answered during the conference. For example, I had wanted to ask why the disease couldn't be made reportable in each state, or to the CDC, so that a more accurate accounting of its incidence could be tallied and so that doctors would be more aware of it. At the conference I had learned that indeed, some state health departments were working toward making the disease reportable.

As the bus made its way through the rush-hour traffic, I tested some of my ideas out on Elise. She was encouraging; she could see that I was tense. Since I am a shy person, the thought of speaking before so many learned and renowned doctors made me reel with nervousness.

The conference went quickly that morning as epidemiological studies from New York, Great Island, Minnesota, and Wisconsin were presented. Dr. Steere delivered a fine summary of the conference, after which there was a discussion about the disease's name, which at this point varied from country to country. Doctors from different areas of the world gave their views. Dr. Malawista suggested that we wait awhile before naming the disease until further research is done and we know more of the variations and similarities of the disease as it manifests itself around the world.

Dr. Steere then announced that the spirochete would be named in honor of Dr. Willy Burgdorfer: *Borrelia burgdorferi*. Dr. Burgdorger stood up and gratefully acknowledged the honor. Then Dr. Kari Hovind-Hougen of Copenhagen took the microphone and paid tribute to the early epidemiological work done by the mothers in Lyme. Her words were very kind, and I felt the glances of some in the crowd as she spoke. I knew that my time to speak was now or never, so I raised my hand. Dr. Steere said, "Oh, Polly, I'm so glad that we are going to hear from you." I walked to the microphone, my notes in one hand and my knees shaking so that I felt they might give out entirely.

I thanked the organizers of the symposium for including me and said that I would like to talk from the perspective of the patient concerning areas of future endeavor. I suggested that more thorough public education about the disease be initiated, encompassing such methods as the distribution of pamphlets, like the Connecticut one put out by Pfizer, Yale, and the Connecticut Arthritis Foundation, to schools, libraries, and drugstore counters, as well as doctors' offices. I mentioned the idea of making up traveling educational displays that would include specimens of the ticks.

I stated that I felt that further study of the psychological ramifications of the disease—including behavior changes, irritability, and depression—was desperately needed, and that there should be more thorough description of the many symptoms of this multisystem disease. More dermatologic presentations should be documented, and the effect of the disease on the genito-urinary system should be studied.

I felt strongly that during tick season a medical hotline should be established, to operate seven days a week, if only for a limited time each day.

I went on to say that perhaps patient support groups could be established through hospitals in endemic areas. Many people had nowhere to go to find information and understanding. The research centers were being swamped with calls, which took time away from their investigations.

After I spoke, Dr. Malawista remarked that "knowing Mrs. Murray's track record, all of these things may very well get done over the next years."

The conference came to an end, and after some time talking with many people whom I had not had a chance to meet before, I said good-bye to the organizers. As it turned out, some of the foreign doctors wanted to see the Lyme area, so Dr. Steere, Elise, and I offered to take them on a tour, and we drove to Lyme, stopping for lunch on our way.

Dr. Weber and Elise rode in my car, and we had an interesting conversation. Dr. Weber said that he had never gone along with the theory that Lyme disease was a viral infection; from his observations he had always felt it was bacterial. As we drove up I-95, he was interested in the topography of the land, the marshes, meadow, brush, and trees. We talked of the probability that pets picked up ticks while with their owners on vacation, only to bring the ticks back home with them. I said that one reason the disease had not been noticed earlier was that in our coastal area patients would choose to go to so many different medical centers for treatment— Boston, New Haven, Middletown, Hartford, New London, and even New York. No one medical center saw enough cases to raise eyebrows, and the different symptoms were misdiagnosed as a great number of other diseases.

When we reached Lyme, I showed the visitors a view of the river valley from near Joshua Rock, and we discussed the deer and tick populations and the roads where the first cases were noted. Then we all went to my house for tea and coffee. Dr. Steere said that it was fitting that we end up here, where he and I had started out back in 1976 when *The New York Times* and NBC had done stories. He noticed that I had cleared a large area of our property since then. The doctors wanted to know how often I saw deer. After they took photographs and we said a lot of good-byes, they headed off to New Haven. As I turned around in the afterglow of a beautiful sunset, I spotted a deer slowly moving about twenty feet from me in the field. They are never far away; I wished the doctors could have seen the deer.

It was wonderful to see my children the following week at Thanksgiving when the family gathered at Larchmont. I had been busy with interviews, my dolls, and getting paintings ready to go to the Shippee Gallery on Fifty-seventh Street in New York.

I had arranged to see Dr. Steere on December 2 and told him then that my left hand was painful and weak. During the examination he said that he was glad to have put together the symposium because it brought together for the first time over a hundred people directly involved and interested in the disease. "This is the end of the first chapter in the story of Lyme disease, and I anticipate new research and findings in the years to come as we piece together the story." He said he was pleased to have brought some of the European doctors to Lyme, and in the future might suggest that others take a look at where the first clustering was identified. I told him I'd be more than happy to see anyone who wanted a tour of the area.

Dr. Steere told me that he would be leaving Yale next summer for a sabbatical year in California, where he would continue his writing. He suggested that I find a general internist thoroughly familiar with Lyme disease for my total medical care. He felt I seemed to have hypersensitive reactions, as a certain number of his patients did.

After my appointment I went to his office while he finished in the clinic. Hoping that a diagnostic questionnaire could be developed for the disease, I had compiled a composite list of the symptoms cited by the many people who had talked to me over the years, and I had organized it into the different areas of the body that were afflicted. Elise made copies of the lists and other information on deer control and ticks that I had brought.

I later met Dr. Steere for lunch in the cafeteria to go over a lot of other information I had brought with me. We talked of the possibility of establishing support groups and a hotline, the formation of a foundation for Lyme disease, and further areas of research, especially neurological and psychiatric. Dr. Steere now felt that the use of intravenous penicillin in Lyme disease would reach certain symptoms better than oral medications did. He was glad that there was such interest in the neurological problems in Germany and Sweden, and hoped that more research could be done on these subjects in the United States. I told him that I knew a number of people now who had skin problems on the hands and arms similar to the ones that I'd had. He said that numbers like these sometimes add up; at first things seem unrelated, but that as you see more and more problems related directly to the onset of Lyme disease, you begin to wonder.

As we walked back to his office after lunch, Dr. Steere commented on how we had come together on this matter—in a way, just as randomly and accidentally as the spirochete moves and invades. It seems to be that things happen only when the climate and timing are right. I had spent years moving around with information that had fallen on deaf ears, until he happened along at a time in his career when he hadn't yet committed himself to his new research. We recalled how he had recently arrived at Yale from the Centers for Disease Control; there he had known Dr. Snydman, who in 1975 was at the Connecticut Department of Health Services, and had contacted him about the unusual medical enigma around Lyme. Dr. Steere had been intrigued by the epidemiological problem, so our histories miraculously fell together.

Back at his office, I reminded him that at the symposium he had invited me to come and see the *Borrelia burgdorferi* spirochetes at the lab. He kindly said he would show them to me now, and prepared a slide from a vial of live spirochetes in solution. It was both fascinating and unsettling to see these live, spiraling organisms, which could cause such devastation. Dr. Steere explained that they kept reproducing, and under the right conditions could survive for years. He explained that high temperatures, such as fevers of 105 or 106, would kill them, and mentioned induced fever therapy, an earlier treatment for syphilis (which is also a spirochetal illness): a treatment now considered primitive because of antibiotics.

I thanked him for all the time he had spent with me, and apologized for always being so full of questions. He said he didn't mind at all. I said, "I'll keep working on the problem of Lyme disease," and he answered, "So will I."

As I left the hospital, I thought about Dr. Steere's statement that we were at the end of the first chapter on Lyme disease. Everyone had high expectations that in the future treatment would cure all patients, accurate diagnostic tests would be found, tick control measures would be implemented, and a vaccine would eventually be developed for animals and humans.

PART TWO

———— ⚬⚬⚬ ————

THE SCOPE BROADENS

In the decade since that first Lyme disease conference at Yale University in 1983, the work of U.S. clinicians, scientists, politicians, laypeople, and the media combined to spread the word about the disease throughout the world. Lyme disease was found not to be a "new disease." The Europeans had conducted research on Ixodes-related illness, especially the skin manifestations, for many years prior to the American "discovery." What we now know as neurological symptoms of Lyme disease were described over the past century in Europe in many different ways, and known by many different names.[1] The research focus on Lyme arthritis in the 1970s initiated a closer look at a tick-borne illness that had been recognized in a rather piecemeal fashion since the late 1800s.

The medical community's attention on the cluster of cases in Lyme, Old Lyme, and East Haddam, Connecticut, in 1975 had been a catalyst for the growth of worldwide medical interest in tick-related illness and borreliosis. More research was devoted to the disease; as a result, the number of published medical articles on Lyme disease has been greatly accelerating ever since.

The road toward the development of a vaccine, accurate diagnostic tests, tick control measures, and treatment leading to a cure of the disease has been found to be longer and more difficult than was at first expected.

CHAPTER FOURTEEN

GETTING THE WORD OUT

I continued to promote public awareness about Lyme disease, and to try to give emotional support to the people who called and wrote to me about their illnesses. I encouraged them to keep pursuing a diagnosis. If they had diagnosed Lyme disease and had persistent symptoms following treatment, or developed late-stage symptoms, or were re-infected, I suggested that they talk to their doctor about further treatment. So that patients could pass on a full picture of their health to their doctors, I always urged them to keep a diary of symptoms and the results of treatment, and to photograph their Lyme disease rashes if their doctor had not already done so. In the future the photographs might help to substantiate previous Lyme disease infection. In addition to aiding their doctors, the diary often helps the patient deal with illness. Patients can go crazy trying to remember when and for how long they took medication, their responses to medications, and the sequence of symptoms. If more than one member of a family is afflicted, recordkeeping becomes even more necessary. Writing the medical history down and having it to refer to helps alleviate anxiety. If they change physicians, they will always have their own personal records.

I promoted public awareness by circulating Lyme disease informational exhibits I had put together, doing volunteer work for the Arthritis Foundation, distributing pamphlets, and attending health fairs and public information meetings.

Through my work, I had the opportunity to get to know a number of researchers who came to Lyme because they wanted to see the area where the disease was first identified in the United States.

In late August 1984, Dr. Eva Asbrink and her husband, who were both visiting the United States from Sweden, came to the

Lyme area and I showed them both around. Dr. Asbrink studies the skin manifestations of Lyme disease. We discussed the fact that some Swedish Lyme disease patients develop acrodermatitis chronica atrophicans (ACA) in the late stage of the disease, and Dr. Asbrink showed me many interesting pictures of this complication, which so far has not been seen very often in the United States. (Years later, in December 1992, I heard that a woman in southeastern Connecticut had been diagnosed with ACA. Hers was the first case that I had heard of in our area. Many years before that, she had complained of neurological problems in her legs as well as knee swelling; these symptoms had been diagnosed as Lyme disease and treated with antibiotics. When ACA arose, the patient was given a longer-term course of antibiotic treatment, which helped to alleviate the pain and swelling.)

CONFERENCES

In order to keep up with research worldwide, I went to a number of local and international medical conferences on Lyme disease in Washington, D.C.; New York; Connecticut; Rhode Island; and New Jersey. Starting with the third international conference, in New York City in 1987, more laypeople attended conferences. Some had been active in raising public awareness in numerous states; others were Lyme disease patients seeking up-to-date information. Karen Forschner of Tolland, Connecticut, who later started the Lyme Borreliosis Foundation (now known as the Lyme Disease Foundation), attended the New York meeting in the hopes of finding help for her toddler-age son, Jamie, who she believed had been afflicted with Lyme disease in the womb. Karen and family pets had also been affected by the disease. One patient had come east from California. She had seen thirteen doctors over a three-year period until she was finally diagnosed. Many of us had corresponded before meeting in person at the conference. Each year more and more patient and support-group representatives attended these conferences.

In October 1988, I attended a conference at Pfizer Central Research in Groton, Connecticut, and immediately afterward went to another, sponsored by the newly formed Lyme Borreliosis Foundation. At that meeting, where I received an award, I was especially encouraged to find that in New York State doctors were asked by the State Health Department to review the records of cases of juvenile rheumatoid arthritis from 1975 on to make sure that the patients did not instead have Lyme disease. This reminded me that in 1986, the Connecticut chapter of the Arthritis Foundation had published a startling finding in its Lyme disease brochure: "At the Newington Children's Hospital, in 1984 and 1985, a group of 60 children who had the symptoms of arthritis were given the blood test, and all were found to have Lyme disease. Of those, 70% had not had, or had not detected, the red skin rash which is an early symptom characteristic of Lyme disease. In many of those cases, the arthritis symptoms were arrested through antibiotic therapy."[1]

In November 1988, I had a call from Dr. Robert Quackenbush of the National Institute of Allergy and Infectious Diseases at the National Institutes of Health. I had met him at the October conferences. He informed me that in Bethesda, Maryland, on December 13, 14, and 15 the National Institute of Allergy and Infectious Diseases and the National Institute of Arthritis and Musculoskeletal and Skin Diseases would hold a scientific workshop on Lyme disease, to be chaired by Dr. Lawrence E. Shulman and Dr. John R. La Montagne. Dr. Quackenbush told me that the institutes hoped I would be their guest at the conference, and that the allergy institute would present an award to me following the banquet at the conference. Would I be able to attend? I said that I would be honored.

I traveled to Washington by train, and visited on the trip with my friend Marge Anderson from Pfizer, who was also a member of the Lyme Disease Awareness Task Force. We found our way to Bethesda on the subway, and soon saw many friends who were also arriving the night before the conference. There were 119 participants from all over the world, plus 45 from the National Institutes of Health.

The first day of the conference I had a chance to talk to Judith Mensch, the other mother who called medical authorities back in the fall of 1975. I had not met her before, because she had moved from Old Lyme to Maryland back in 1976 or 1977. (Because her daughter had been treated with intravenous antibiotics for a knee infection by the orthopedic surgeon at Lawrence and Memorial Hospital in the fall of 1975, she had not had any recurrence of symptoms during the years since then.) After chatting with Judith during a coffee break at the conference, I thought that I would see her again, but couldn't find her. On the night of the banquet, awards were presented to Dr. Allen Steere, Dr. Willy Burgdorfer, and me. Judith Mensch was given her award in absentia. At the last minute something had come up and she was unable to receive her award in person, which was too bad.

In June 1990, I traveled to the fourth international Lyme disease conference, in Stockholm, where over five hundred participants had gathered from seventy-two countries. The number of registrants for the international conferences had grown dramatically, from 150 at the first Yale conference in 1983, to 854 at the fifth international conference, in Arlington in 1992 (115 of these were from twenty-three foreign countries). Nearly four hundred papers were presented at the fifth conference. By 1992, a total of over 2,500 scientific papers on Lyme disease had been published.[2]

I tried to keep up with the medical literature, especially those papers on the clinical aspects of the disease. Many articles were sent to me, and I also frequented the medical library at Yale to keep abreast of new developments.

SPEAKING ENGAGEMENTS

In 1984, I was given another opportunity to speak publicly about Lyme disease. In addition to his premed studies, my son David had been doing work at Columbia University on a research project in epidemiology, through which he met a number of doctors at the School of Public Health. One day in August he called me and told me that they were interested in my coming down to speak to a class of epidemiology students about my involvement in

Lyme disease. I quaked at the thought of public speaking, but David was very persuasive, joking and egging me on, and I agreed to give a short lecture.

I went down to New York City on September 20, armed with slides, a display, and reference materials. I'd practiced my speech for days, but I was still plenty nervous. Before meeting the doctors at the Health Science Center at Columbia University, David said, "Mom, do you want to see where you will be speaking?" and opened the door to this enormous modern lecture hall. I couldn't believe what I had gotten myself into. David smiled and said, "You can do it. You'll be fine."

Time passed quickly as I was introduced to doctors, set up my display, and arranged my slides. Students and doctors filled the huge hall. Somehow I made it through and answered questions for quite a while afterward. The students and doctors showed a lot of interest, and many of them came up to talk to me. Giving the talk was a big hurdle for me, and I was happy that I had done it. The following month I had a call from the doctor who had arranged for me to talk at Columbia, inviting me to come back in February of 1985 to give a presentation to medical students. I accepted. I later gave a third talk in the fall of 1985.

In May 1987, I visited Case Western Reserve Medical School in Cleveland to lecture on Lyme disease. (David was then a second-year student at Case Western.) At the time I wasn't feeling very well as I was being treated again for Lyme disease. I borrowed slides from researchers, including a Lyme area doctor's recent slides of the different presentations of the Lyme rash, and took the tick exhibit there as well. Before the lecture, I really enjoyed getting to know David's friends.

The day of the lecture was beautiful and warm, so I wore a short-sleeved dress. Afterward a medical student came up and said, "Mrs. Murray, pardon my asking, but is that an ECM on your arm?" I told him yes; I was still being treated, and the warmth of the sun had made the rash more visible. The faculty and students were all very interested to hear the story of Lyme disease. Paul Aronowitz, a Case Western Reserve medical student, later received

an honorable mention in a medical essay contest with an article on
Lyme disease; it was published by *The Pharos of Alpha Omega Alpha*
(Medical Honor Society) in the fall of 1989.[3]

MEDIA COVERAGE

From 1983 on, media attention to Lyme disease increased;
after 1987 there was a virtual explosion of interest. Even cartoon-
ists got into the act. To further awareness, bumper stickers, bal-
loons, T-shirts, and children's coloring books were introduced.
Lyme disease began to be included in a number of works of fiction
on TV and in magazines as well, including a John Updike story,
"Wildlife."[4]

I gave a great many interviews to national magazines, newspapers, book authors, Lyme historians, and radio. I wrote a brief
chapter for a book on Lyme disease that was published in Germany in 1991, and contributed information to Dr. Derrick Brewerton of London, England, for his book *All About Arthritis, Past,
Present, Future.*[5] I contributed a guest editorial to *Connecticut Medicine* in 1989.[6] In the 1980s, I gave TV interviews in the United
States and was interviewed for one Canadian and several British
documentaries.

One such interview was in March of 1985. Marge Noyes of the
Yale School of Medicine had asked me to participate in a *Horizon*
BBC television production. (In the United States, the documentary would air on *Nova.*) The story of Lyme disease would be part of
an hour-long documentary on arthritis entitled *Riddle of the Joints.*
Marge told me that if I was willing, I would be interviewed by Michael Coyle from the BBC at my home. Thinking the project
sounded interesting, I agreed.

Shortly thereafter I met with Michael; we discussed his plans
for the interview, and I familiarized him with the Lyme area. Several days later he returned with his crew to do the filming.

After they'd set up all the equipment, Michael had me sit in a
chair in the backyard and began the interview. Just as we got rolling, the sound man called out, "Stop!" and made us wait until an

airplane had passed overhead. When he gave us the all clear, Michael asked me the interview question again. Before I'd spoken many more sentences, the sound man said, "Wait!" While Michael and I chatted quietly, he bounded over the stone wall to the neighbors' house to ask the carpenter who was repairing the roof to kindly stop hammering for a short while! We began filming again as soon as the sound man returned. But as I launched into my answer once again, another voice piped up, saying, "Wait!" Michael and I turned to see the cameraman pointing excitedly at a bedraggled opossum that had wandered out of the woods by our pine tree and was now waddling across the grass behind us. The film crew, it turned out, had never seen an opossum before; there are no marsupials in England. They spent some time taking a few pictures of it, and then we finally proceeded. When we'd finished the filming in the garden and in my kitchen, we had a quick lunch and they were off to do filming in Old Lyme. They were a nice group of people to work with.

ONGOING RESEARCH

I continued to have the researchers at the Connecticut Agricultural Experiment Station use my property for various studies of Lyme disease. Over the years they had used different kinds of traps to attract bugs for study. In 1987 they concentrated on mosquitoes and deerflies, because Dr. Louis Magnarelli was studying them to see if they were capable of transmitting the spirochete. (Over the years there had been anecdotal reports of Lyme disease acquired from the bite of a deerfly.) Dr. Kirby Stafford worked on tick studies. One trap that the researchers used that summer looked like a suspended black witch's cauldron steaming some strange brew. In reality it held dry ice, which attracts deerflies.

MEETINGS WITH DR. STEERE

Following the Yale conference in 1983, I did not correspond with Dr. Steere as often as I had before. As I have mentioned, he went on sabbatical to California in 1984–1985. In May 1986, I did meet with him at the hospital cafeteria. We hadn't talked in a long while, and we took time to catch up on his research and my activities. I also brought him up-to-date on the symptoms some of the family had recently experienced, telling him that David had been found to have mitral valve prolapse and a heart arrhythmia. His condition had improved over a year's time and one of his doctors had wondered if it had been caused by an infection. I wondered if cardiologists were sufficiently aware of the heart complications of Lyme disease. Were people in endemic areas who were suddenly afflicted with heart symptoms being questioned about possible Lyme infection? If people with a history of Lyme disease were having surgery, and tissue had to be removed, couldn't pathologists examine the tissue for *Borrelia burgdorferi* spirochetes? Such research could further our knowledge of the presence of Lyme disease spirochetes in the various organs of the body.

I told Dr. Steere that I was puzzled by some recurrent symptoms among people in our area who had had Lyme disease, including elbow, wrist, and jaw problems, stiff necks, and numbness. In listening to patients' reports of peculiar rashes that accompanied their Lyme disease and typical ECM rash, and I wondered whether the spirochete might trigger skin problems other than ECM. I recalled the work of C. Lennhoff, who in a 1948 paper entitled "Spirochaetes in Aetiologically Obscure Diseases" reported that he had found spirochetes in specimens of psoriasis, pityriasis rosea, seborrheic eczema, and erythema migrans, as well as in other skin problems he had investigated. He had even found spirochetes in heart tissue.[7] Other investigators had not been able to reproduce Lennhoff's work. But now researchers had found that he was correct in attributing erythema migrans to a spirochete. A few of the Lyme patients I talked to said that they had had acne as teenagers, and that the Lyme infection had triggered a recurrence. Perhaps other skin diseases might also be spirochetal in origin. Certainly our family had been afflicted by some of these skin problems.

I told Dr. Steere that I thought that people who were constantly exposed in endemic areas could have late-stage symptoms of the disease and then get bitten again and have early-stage symptoms along with their late-stage symptoms. He replied that the complex ways in which the disease manifests itself were not yet clearly understood, and encouraged me to keep questioning and expressing my views and to keep working on my book.

I again met with Dr. Steere for lunch at the hospital in September 1986. We discussed the problem of negative test results sometimes being caused by lab error, or by testing too early in the disease, before there was an antibody response. I told him that it seemed that people in endemic areas, exposed to tick bites every year, manifested a cumulative effect of the disease which made them feel malaise and develop rashes within hours of the bite. I raised the possibility that there were different strains of the spirochete that may cause variations in the severity of the disease symptoms as well as possibly throw off the reliability of the tests. I asked him whether urinary problems, thyroid irregularities, appendicitis, and epididymitis might be triggered by the spirochete. I had heard from a number of people who told of these problems following Lyme infection or relapsing fever, another *Borrelia* infection.[8]

Toward the end of our conversation, Dr. Steere told me that during the next year he would be moving to Massachusetts to take a position as chief of the Rheumatology and Immunology Division of New England Medical Center at the Tufts University medical school. There he would continue his research; my friend Elise Taylor would work with him. This news was difficult to hear, because Dr. Steere and Elise had worked so hard uncovering the mysteries of Lyme disease in their years at Yale, and had connected with so many, many patients. I wondered how they would all be followed up. There was so much to learn from a group of patients followed for a long period of time, from studying those who seemed cured, those who relapsed after treatment, those who were re-infected, and those who did not respond to treatment at all. It seemed to me that it was a lot to ask patients to travel two and a half hours to Boston. Dr. Steere said that research on Lyme disease would be continued at Yale, where they would have the Lyme disease clinic. A positive factor, I felt, was that the change would mean that some research work on the disease would now be moved to another large metropolitan center, from where, I was sure, awareness would then spread to new populations.

CHANGING ATTITUDES

In 1986, I met Dr. Steven Luger, a general practitioner in Old Lyme who had treated many Lyme disease patients and who was dedicated to finding out all that he could about the illness. In his practice he carefully documented rashes with slides; he also attended conferences, gave lectures, and raised consciousness about the disease. In conversing with him I felt that he was seeing the disease from a close perspective and was as puzzled by certain aspects of it as some of his patients were. He saw the difficulty and unreliability of tests for the disease, the re-infections, and the recurrences despite antibiotic treatment. There was a widening gulf between what the patients were experiencing and what most of the medical literature was reporting that Lyme disease should be like. Patients were becoming confused and frustrated by the dilemmas in diagnosis. Dr. Steere seemed to be less receptive to what patients were describing, and I felt it more difficult to understand his position on diagnosis, treatment, re-infection, and seronegative patients.

In 1989, while traveling in Kentucky, I read the June 16 *Cincinnati Enquirer* and was shocked to read that at the annual meeting in Cincinnati of the American College of Rheumatology, Dr. Ilona S. Szer, who worked with Dr. Steere in Boston, was quoted by reporter Elizabeth Neus as saying, "But even in the absence of antibiotic treatment, children with Lyme do great. . . . If [a child] has had antibiotics, it's like having a strep throat. It's gone." Todd and David read the article too, and we were all troubled by the message that this description of Lyme disease sent out to the world. I knew too many children who had had a difficult time following Lyme infection to accept Dr. Szer's statement as accurate. It disturbed me very much. From my perspective, I believed that long-term follow-up of patients was not always being done by physicians, and that when it was done, perhaps not enough questions about the person's general health were being asked. Patients who do not understand the full spectrum of the illness would not volunteer information about symptoms they might think were irrelevant to Lyme disease. For example, a patient who goes on to experience insomnia, carpal tunnel syndrome, depression, memory difficulties, jaw problems, eye and ear irregularities, or behavior changes might not connect these symptoms with Lyme disease and therefore wouldn't think to mention them to a doctor as possibly related to it. The problem of long-term chronic patients had not yet been fully investigated, and many of these patients were continuing to suffer.

In 1991, I met with Dr. Steere in Boston to discuss with him his ideas about Lyme disease; at that meeting we agreed to disagree over a number of points. In the fall of the same year he came to Old Lyme for the first time in many years to meet with former patients and to inform them of what the researchers now knew about the long-term consequences of the disease. He told them: "It's an incredible thing for me to be here tonight. You are very special people to me. You're the people that taught me about what Lyme disease is like, and for that matter, are still teaching me about what Lyme disease is like." He went on to say that "the epidemic goes on here; my impression is that it really hasn't dampened down at all. We know something more about how to deal with the symptoms and treatment of the disease, but the tick is as prevalent as ever and spreading. It's also become clear that there can be long-term effects of this disease and that the organism can survive latently for long periods of time and then cause active disease again. Usually in a different form than was the case previously, and this is a cause for concern and really the reason that I wanted to meet tonight." Later in his talk he admitted: "We still do not know all of the long-term effects of the disease." Dr. Steere went on to discuss the long-term effects that were now documented worldwide. He had a chance to meet with many of his former patients following the meeting.

From 1983 on, there developed an increasingly divisive atmosphere in the Lyme disease community, and issues related to Lyme

CHAPTER FIFTEEN

THE POLITICS OF LYME DISEASE

It would be a serious mistake for the physician to allow his superior knowledge of health care in general to lead him to believe that there are no particulars in which laymen may be better informed. . . .

I teach my students to listen very carefully to their patients and to concerned and informed laymen. Good medical practice begins with good listening.

NORMAN COUSINS, *ANATOMY OF AN ILLNESS*[1]

By the mid-1980s, many patients began to feel that while they perceived Lyme disease as a public health threat, the local, state, and federal governments, as well as many in the medical community, were giving it inadequate attention, describing it as a simple and easily treated illness. As more and more patients failed to fit the simple model of Lyme disease, either because they did not quite match the accepted diagnostic criteria, or were not cured by prescribed treatment regimens, the gulf continued to widen between many patients' experience of Lyme disease and the model as described by the medical "experts."

Patients were speaking out, voluntarily helping to educate the public, and joining together to share ideas. Some contacted politicians in different states with their concerns, and several politicians became involved and educated about the disease.

My first contact with people out of state who were concerned with public awareness and getting governmental action on Lyme disease came in May 1986, when I received a letter from a woman named Barbara Le Sauvage in Chappaqua, New York, who was interested in working on Lyme disease awareness programs. She was in contact with Dr. Durland Fish in Armonk, New York. Dr. Fish, an entomologist, was studying the tick. I started to keep in touch with awareness efforts in their area, and later in the year I met in Armonk with a group of volunteers there, including Barbara, Gloria Wenk, and Susan Weiss. The group in New York had corresponded with politicians, and their progress seemed to me to far outpace the efforts on funding and awareness thus far in Connecticut. I left Westchester County hoping that Connecticut could emulate some of the things that were being accomplished there.

The summer of 1986 was proving to be a bad tick season, and it seemed that suddenly people were very much more aware and alarmed at the mounting number of cases of Lyme disease. Pfizer was distributing 35,000 copies of its excellent new brochure. Michael Cray, a writer for *The Day,* had reported on July 17 that according to the results of state surveillance, "in 1985, the number of cases of Lyme disease reported to the state Department of Health totaled 863, up about 70 percent from 1984." In May 1986, the State Health Department had decided that the state laboratory would no longer accept patients' blood for testing for Lyme disease. Instead, the antigen would be provided to three laboratories in the state, which would take over the testing program. As a result, the state lost its former counting system. According to Dr. Lyle Petersen, interviewed in *The Hartford Courant* on July 16, 1986, the state was trying to put into effect a Lyme disease surveillance system to begin in the 1987 season. I had numerous calls from frustrated patients who felt that not enough was being done by the medical profession and the state officials. Lyme disease was becoming a political issue in Connecticut.

Jane DeWolf, owner of the H. L. Reynolds Company, a general store that has provided for many generations of Lyme residents and is diagonally across from the Grange Hall and the Congregational church in the center of town, observed an increase in the number of people discussing Lyme disease in her store. Thomas Farragher, a reporter for *The Day,* wrote on August 13, "In a spiral notebook tucked under the cash register, the proprietor of this town's unofficial meeting place—its general store—records by word of mouth what has become her customers' paramount concern." Jane DeWolf said, "In one day, I got 47 names of people who have it or have a relative with" Lyme disease.

One of the forty-seven was Marilyn Reynolds, a nurse who had left her career to raise her family. Marilyn had been very ill, and so had other members of her family. Her situation reminded me of the time our family had been stricken in the summer of 1975. She called newspapers, state health officials, local health directors, TV and radio stations, and elected officials, including the governor, to make them aware of the concerns of frustrated patients in our area.

I talked at great length to Dr. Matthew Cartter and Dr. Lyle Petersen at the Department of Health Services about our concerns. I told Dr. Cartter that I felt that one of the most important areas to address was that of educating physicians to recognize the illness in all of its complicated stages.

The patients with whom I was now working felt strongly that the standard tests were not accurate and yet were being taken as the most important diagnostic criteria for the disease, especially by the medical centers doing research, which used positive test results as an entry requirement for many of their studies. Those whose blood tests turned out to be negative, it seemed, were just being ignored. Living in an area with such a great number of cases, we knew personally a large group of people with the same symptoms and clear history of tick bite and rash, who always tested negative, or who had been positive at one time and later tested negative. Many were chronic Lyme sufferers. We knew that antibiotics could abort the antibody response so that the patient would test negative. In some cases the negatives would convert to positive later, and then back to negative. The picture was extremely confusing and frustrating to the patients, who were often told they did not have the disease. Many had been treated and had improved with medication, only to relapse or be re-infected later.

We felt that we must somehow lobby for what we wanted to achieve. A group of us were talking daily about the problem, and Sylvia Harding, whose family goes back for generations in Lyme, suggested we write up a petition and put it in Jane's store to see

how much support we could get. We thought that was a great idea.
I went home and wrote up the following petition and put a copy in
the store:

> *We, the undersigned, petition that the Governor of the State
> of Connecticut and the Connecticut State Legislature should
> raise funds for Education in Prevention, Recognition, and
> Treatment of Lyme Disease. Programs should reach: Residents,
> including school age children, out of state visitors, and all
> physicians and health care workers. Information could be
> distributed via pamphlets, media coverage, documentaries, and
> warning posters in public areas known to be highly infested with
> ticks. Other points to consider: 1. Make Lyme Disease a
> "Reportable Disease." 2. Fund a Lyme Disease Clinic in the
> Endemic Area for up-to-date treatment and research into the
> disease with affiliation with a major medical center. 3. Improve
> diagnostic tests. 4. Establish a 24 hour "Hotline" with referrals
> to prompt treatment. 5. Continue research into possible methods
> of environmental control of the disease.*

It was several days before the annual Hamburg Fair held in the
center of the town of Lyme, which would open Friday night and
close Sunday night. The fair attracted thousands of people to its
agricultural exhibits, horse and oxen pulling contests, country
music, and amusement rides. Nineteen eighty-six was a guber-
natorial and state senatorial and representative election year, and
we heard that the town Democratic Party would host a "meet the
candidates" reception at the nearby home of a Columbia University professor named Roger Hilsman. A rumor began to circulate
that Governor William O'Neill, U.S. Senator Christopher Dodd,
and State Senator Richard Schneller would be attending, and
would come to the Hamburg Fair on Saturday.

On Thursday our small group of concerned citizens decided to
seize the moment and take our petition to the fair. Because Marilyn was feeling so sick, she stayed home and made last-minute arrangements to set up an educational booth next to the booths of
the politicians. My son David was to arrive home for a visit, and

after I met his train in Saybrook, we ran to the copy center and had great numbers of copies of the petition run off. In addition to the petition, we also had a sheet for people to sign up if they had had symptoms of the disease but had not received a definite diagnosis because their test results were negative.

Over the past few months I had talked to several people about the possibility of the formation of a Lyme disease foundation, which I envisioned as fostering education of health professionals and the general public, and supporting research into the best methods of diagnosis, treatment, and prevention on a local, state, and national level. The foundation would also bring together people afflicted by the disease into a supportive group, with a newsletter to communicate information on the disease. We decided to put out a sheet that people could sign if they were interested in supporting such a foundation.

David helped me with some of the labor of setting up the booth and transporting brochures and educational material to the fairground. We had the displays of actual ticks, maps, and a large tick warning sign used in New York State; we enlisted volunteers to run the booth. Linda Courtney and Mary Tisdale were a great help to us and have continued to contribute their time in the work of Lyme disease awareness.

During those three days of the fair we reached a tremendous number of people and obtained many hundreds of signatures on the petition. The Lyme disease stories told us by visitors to the booth reinforced our feeling that it was critical that more education and funding be made available. One man was able to identify the undiagnosed illness of his small child after seeing our pictures of the rash and a swollen knee.

On Saturday afternoon the politicians arrived at the fairground. We showed them our exhibition and the tick specimens. The governor studied our maps of Lyme disease distribution and seemed surprised that it was endemic in so many areas of the Northeast. He said he had not realized the scope of the problem, and would look into it. I voiced our concern to Senator Dodd as well.

The following week I participated in a radio program on Lyme disease from a station near Hartford. During the month we got a lot of media coverage as we spread copies of the petition everywhere we could think of throughout the lower Connecticut River Valley. On August 29, Dr. Matthew Cartter was quoted by Colin Poitras in *The Hartford Courant* as saying that "greater funding would certainly help research and education efforts. . . . I encourage people to contact the legislature." On September 2, our petition was mentioned in *The New York Times.* U.S. Representative Sam Gejdenson expressed support.

I wrote to Gloria Wenk about our petition efforts in Connecticut. The group in New York petitioned Governor Mario Cuomo and the New York State Legislature for "an in-depth research program with respect to Lyme disease" and for tick research and control.[2]

Our group of concerned citizens decided that we would present our petition to State Senator Schneller, who would represent Governor O'Neill at a meeting of the Lower Connecticut Valley Selectmen's Association (representing nine towns) to be held in Old Saybrook in the middle of October. We invited other Connecticut politicians to attend. We also arranged for Dr. Steven Luger to talk to the selectmen from area towns about the clinical aspects of the disease, and for Dr. Anderson and Dr. Magnarelli to talk on research and control.

At the meeting, Dr. Luger showed some excellent slides of rashes, joint swellings, and Bell's palsy, and gave an extensive talk. Dr. Luger has a gift for speaking, filling his talks with a number of funny asides. He has a very human approach and audiences respond well to him. I spoke on the many issues that our group felt were important, including a request for a simple method by which all doctors would report all treated cases, not just those that showed positive serology, to the state and the CDC. Because of the blood test's unreliability in early Lyme disease, a *clinical* early diagnosis ought to be reportable. A study should be made of the long-term success of antibiotic treatment in these patients. We urged the selectmen to write to the governor supporting our petition. I presented the petition, with over two thousand signatures, to Senator Schneller to deliver to the governor.

I received a letter from the governor on October 31, 1986; some of its contents were published in the local papers:

> *I will immediately request that two additional positions be created in the Connecticut Agricultural Experiment Station to assist in the further research, study, and control of the disease. I will also request that the Department of Environmental Protection begin to erect informational signs in state parks to alert the public to the disease.*
>
> *In addition, I have asked the State Department of Health Services and the Office of Policy and Management to study and develop a program of further assistance to affected parties and the general public along the lines of the recommendations in your petition.*

In early January 1987, I met with Dr. Luger to put together a proposal for further work on Lyme disease in Connecticut. I wrote up suggestions for public awareness and research programs for the state to consider. My hope was for a study that would include long-term follow-up of cases, evaluate the results of treatments, study the possibility that a single tick bite might transmit more than one infection, and study re-infection rates and chronic Lyme disease. The study could also track patients who had symptoms of the disease following a tick bite, but who test negative.

Shortly after my meeting with Dr. Luger, he and I met with State Senator Mark H. Powers of East Lyme to talk about the kinds of programs that should be developed if the state passed funding that provided for the disease. We discussed the possibility of appointing a Lyme disease coordinator for the state.

After consulting with those working on Lyme disease in recent weeks, I had written a plan for the composition of a task force "to advise, to make recommendations and to coordinate the efforts of various agencies in dealing with the problem of Lyme disease." The task force would include researchers from the Department of Health Services and the Connecticut Agricultural Experiment Station, the office of the governor, and the Department of Environmental Management; medical researchers from the University of

Connecticut and Yale University; private physicians; legislators; and representatives of patient-concerned citizen groups. I gave Senator Powers a copy of this proposal.

One wintry day, Gloria Wenk, Susan Weiss, Barbara Le Sauvage, Betty Gross, and I gathered for lunch. I had talked on the phone to Betty, a patient from Irvington-on-Hudson, New York, but had not met her until that day. We had an interesting time comparing levels of Lyme disease awareness among physicians and the public in our different locales. Betty later formed a support group in Westchester. She had had a severe case of Lyme disease several years before, and was finally properly diagnosed and treated after months of incapacitating illness, so she knew full well the devastating nature of the disease. A very organized, active, and civic-minded person who possesses an ease with people, Betty skillfully encouraged patients in her community to work together. Other patients in other areas would follow her lead, forming or joining support groups in order to educate the public about the disease and secure emotional support for themselves or stricken family members.

On Wednesday, February 4, 1987, Governor O'Neill announced his budget for fiscal year 1988; it included $24,000 for control of ticks carrying Lyme disease.

On June 9, the papers announced that the Public Health Committee of the Connecticut General Assembly had put together an interim study committee on Lyme disease. As reported by Sam Libby of *The Hartford Courant*, Barbara Salthouse, a legislative clerk for the Public Health Committee, said, "The committee will complete a report evaluating the public health threat posed by the disease by October and propose state legislation to combat the disease for next year's legislative session." From the Lyme area, Dr. Steven Luger and I were chosen to serve on this interim study committee.

Our local citizens' group was still interested in making the disease reportable, and Senator Powers said that he would write a letter to the governor in support of this idea. (Our group convinced quite a few people to write.) In *The Day* on June 27, 1987, Marcel Dufresne wrote that Frederick G. Adams, the Connecticut health commissioner, had declared a new policy making reporting of the disease mandatory. According to *The Day*, Adams "took the step now after conferring with Gov. William A. O'Neill. The Governor had been under continuing pressure from a group of politicians, physicians, and private citizens from southeastern Connecticut who have urged the reporting requirement and other state initiatives to battle the disease."

In September 1987, the state public health committee and health department sponsored a meeting at Old Lyme High School. Dr. Luger spoke in favor of increased state funding, and Dr. Matthew Cartter outlined the Department of Health Services proposals. It was suggested that we as citizens write to legislators and the governor making our wishes known. Marilyn Reynolds pointed out that we had already phoned, written letters, and submitted a petition. Nevertheless, State Representative Beatrice Murdoch requested that Dr. Luger and I get together on a letter, and that we encourage others to write soon, because the budget was being formulated. A few of us decided to place a form letter in local newspapers which could be clipped out, signed, and mailed to the governor. I also distributed copies of the letter for people to send, and did a radio public service announcement. Dr. Luger wrote a letter to the governor spelling out our concerns, and I co-signed it.

On November 13, 1987, I received a letter from the governor outlining the steps that had already been taken by the state and saying that $100,000 for Lyme disease was included in the proposed budget for the Department of Health Services. He encouraged me in my work to educate people about the disease.

The legislature's Lyme disease interim study committee, which had been formed during the past summer, met about every two weeks in Hartford or New Haven. It was a very busy fall for me. Through the support groups, patients were coming forward with their stories. The more media attention there was, the more phone calls I received from people all over the country wanting further information.

Members of our committee and the public health committee made recommendations, which were included in a larger state bill entitled "An Act Concerning Health Promotion and Disease Prevention."

We all worked hard on telephoning for support of the bill, and through the newspapers urged citizens to write letters to the state legislature's Public Health Committee. In January 1988, a group of us testified at a Hartford hearing conducted by the committee. The group included a number of physicians, among them Dr. Luger, who gave a powerful, graphic description of the disease. Nancy Considine, Timothy Hertwick (a patient advocate), Marge Anderson, Karen Forschner, eleven-year-old Joshua Puhlick (whose younger brother, Justin, had contracted the disease), and I also testified. I emphasized the need for public awareness, saying that it "works best if it is accompanied by the awareness of all physicians in all specialties as well as health care workers in any given community. It does not make sense to have a fully knowledgeable patient if the doctors that they go to are not able to recognize and treat the disease in all of its manifestations and stages. Frankly, I say this because in my personal experience I have come across or have heard of too many instances where doctors seem sadly in the dark about this disease."

In addition to our oral testimony we presented written testimony, and I gave the committee many signatures gathered in our area in support of the bill. We later learned that the Public Health Committee approved the bill by a fifteen-to-zero vote. Now the Appropriations Committee would have to endorse the legislation by the third week in March before it could be put into law. With letters to Connecticut newspapers, we then urged people to write to the Appropriations Committee in favor of the bill.

What happened next was summed up to me in personal correspondence from Dr. Matthew Cartter: "Eventually, the Lyme disease section was stripped from the bill, and a $100,000 line item for a 'Lyme disease clinical center' was added to the state health department's budget by the appropriations committee. . . . Later we learned that the state health department would have to find the $100,000 in its operating budget, which meant that the money would be taken from other programs."

The outcome was discouraging in that more money had not

been allotted; but at least we had raised consciousness about the disease in the political arena, and in the future we would continue to receive some state funding for Lyme disease. The need for such funding had been discussed in the newspapers, and more and more people in our state were made aware of the problem. One very positive result of the whole initiative was that a number of us who had worked together for so many months had decided to form a Lyme Disease Awareness Task Force in Connecticut, which would be part of the Arthritis Foundation's Connecticut chapter. This group continues to work on education and awareness programs.

In April of 1988, I received a call from Barbara Matia of Arizona, who had been testifying in Washington, D.C., for five years for NIH funding for infectious arthritis. She wanted me to join her in Washington in early May to testify, because she knew that Lyme disease was a newly recognized infectious arthritis. I planned to go; however, just before I was to leave a health problem forced me to cancel the trip.

Early the following year, Barbara Matia called to ask me again if I could testify in Washington. She told me that if I wanted to testify in support of newly proposed legislation for Lyme disease, I should write U.S. Senator Tom Harkin. I did so on February 8, 1989, requesting to be scheduled to testify before the Senate Appropriations Subcommittee on Labor, Health and Human Services, Education and Related Agencies in the spring of 1989.

Representatives Sam Gejdenson of Connecticut and George Hochbrueckner of New York sponsored a bill that would provide $2.5 million annually for three years for work on prevention and treatment of Lyme disease, and $1 million annually for three years for public education. Connecticut's Christopher Dodd and Joseph Lieberman sponsored an identical bill in the Senate, to be introduced by New Yorker Daniel Patrick Moynihan. Grants for funding would be applied for by state and local governments, nonprofit organizations, and private groups. Many in the Lyme disease community were working toward the passage of the bill.

I met Representative Gejdenson at a meeting in East Lyme. When I had time I worked on my testimony for the hearing, scheduled for May 8 in Washington. I had been asked to send in ten copies of the testimony ahead of time.

I took a train to Washington and stayed at a friend's. At breakfast on that Monday morning she timed my oral testimony, making sure that it came in at the required length of less than three minutes. I found my way to the designated room in the Dirksen Senate Office Building that beautiful spring day, where I met Barbara Matia for the first time. After I testified, I visited the offices of Sam Gejdenson and Christopher Dodd.

The Lyme Disease Awareness Task Force and the Connecticut Department of Health Services executed a program in spring of 1990 to train fifty Connecticut public health professionals, physicians, and veterinarians to give educational talks on Lyme disease and to form a speakers' bureau. Participants would be supplied with slides and a model talk. The task force continued to distribute posters, fact sheets, tapes, brochures, and educational displays. A poster in Spanish was in the works, and for the fall, we planned a conference along with the state health department and Pfizer on the public health response to Lyme disease. During 1990 Congress granted the CDC $1 million annually for Lyme disease for 1991, 1992, and 1993, and researchers all over the country were applying for CDC funding to study all aspects of the disease. Others sought support for awareness programs. The Connecticut State Health Department was awarded $142,101 in June 1991 and they were now able to have an integrated public health response to the disease. The NIH also increased their funding with grants to key research projects around the country.

On August 5, 1993, an oversight hearing, "Lyme Disease: A Diagnostic and Treatment Dilemma," was held in Washington before the Senate Committee on Labor and Human Resources, chaired by Edward M. Kennedy of Massachusetts. There was a great deal of response from across the country: Hundreds of doctors and Lyme patients wrote letters, over fifty people sent testimony and statements, and a number of patients and experts testified at the hearing.

Thus the politics of numbers has had an impact on the direction of research and legislation concerning this disease. My voice alone, back in the early seventies, was not taken seriously. In 1975, with more people having similar symptoms, the medical profession finally became interested in the problem. From 1975 on, more and more patients in a growing number of states had joined to share information and to become a political force in order to make their concerns known.

CHAPTER SIXTEEN

REPORTING

Men are naturally most impressed by diseases which have obvious manifestations, yet some of their worst enemies creep on them unobtrusively.
RENÉ DUBOS, *MIRAGE OF HEALTH: UTOPIAS, PROGRESS, AND BIOLOGICAL CHANGE*[1]

Because of the relapsing episodes of Lyme disease and its multisystem involvement, conscientious reporting and monitoring could significantly aid in describing the way the disease manifests itself. With a central pool of information, the CDC and physicians throughout the country could find out how many reported cases were early infections, re-infections, relapses, or late-stage disease.

However, all patients are not being counted. The full scope of the disease has not been accurately realized because doctors are failing to report the disease. There are several reasons for this. Physicians may not be educated to recognize Lyme disease, or they may not report cases that they do recognize and diagnose because of the work involved in reporting. Another reason why Lyme disease may not be recognized and reported is the use of tests whose reliability is questionable. (I shall discuss these tests in a later chapter.) The reliance on positive test results also may result in underreporting of the disease, as patients may have Lyme disease but test negative for antibodies to the spirochetes and thus not be reported.

Carl Brenner, a Lyme disease patient and New York Coalition member, wonders about the seronegative patient, who is not included in clinical studies and often finds it difficult to find treatment. In a letter to the magazine *Science*, Brenner wrote, "Arbitrarily withholding antibiotic therapy from all seronegative patients guarantees that an unacceptably high percentage of them will go on to develop incurable late stage Lyme disease. Such a policy also can lead to the underreporting of the real incidence of Lyme disease."[2]

According to an article by Dr. Stephen B. Thacker and his colleagues, "The Surveillance of Infectious Diseases," disease reports can be passive—initiated by providers—or active—solicited by health departments. "Whatever the method of collection, surveillance data are necessary to portray the ongoing pattern of disease occurrence, which will allow detection of unusual disease patterns and subsequently trigger disease-control and prevention efforts. In addition, these data can be used for resource allocation in public health planning and to evaluate control and prevention measures." As the authors pointed out, "The practicing physician is the key to effective surveillance of infectious disease."[3]

Without accurate assessment of the magnitude of the problem, Lyme disease researchers are hindered in their ability to obtain government research grants. Government officials look at the inaccurately low number of reported cases and surmise that the disease is not a big enough problem to warrant substantial funding.

As far as I was concerned, doctors who are not properly reporting the disease are not only thwarting Lyme disease researchers, but in effect disenfranchising their Lyme disease patients. Holding the reins of disease reporting, doctors can tremendously affect the political and social impact of disease. Patients who may want to be counted as part of the process are being disempowered by this underreporting. Perhaps doctors should be given a simple, quick method of reporting. It is vital to track patients over the long term. Without a clear picture of where the disease is endemic and how many cases there are to indicate the magnitude of the problem, it is difficult to settle on a proper level of research funding. One would hope that all doctors would report cases conscientiously.

In the other extreme of the dilemma of reporting, I have heard of an instance where a medical group in an endemic area did scrupulously report the cases in their practice, only to be told that they had overreported and could not possibly have diagnosed that many patients with Lyme disease. This group of doctors had actively pursued information about Lyme disease, taking special physician education courses, and had kept up with current research on the disease. These extremes in reporting seem to reflect the old saying "You're damned if you do, and damned if you don't."

When Dr. Allen Steere moved to California on sabbatical in 1984, the Connecticut Department of Health Services took over the job of tracking Lyme disease cases. They sent out a letter to physicians informing them of the blood-testing program in Connecticut and urged them to use it. At that time positive tests were an important criterion for counting cases.

In 1984, Dr. Anita Curran, health director of New York's Westchester County, declared that there was an epidemic of Lyme disease in the county and urged doctors to report cases to the County Health Department. The department would actively pursue reporting of cases; if doctors were too busy to fully report cases at the height of the tick season, then follow-up review was recommended for complete information on reported cases.

By 1987, cases of the disease in Connecticut had increased tremendously. On February 19, 1987, Dr. Louis Magnarelli gave a talk at the Thames Science Center in New London; according to the February 20 issue of *The Day*, he "found it incredible that despite the rapid spread of Lyme Disease into northern Connecticut, there is no requirement to report cases to state officials." (As I recounted in the preceding chapter, on June 23, 1987, Connecticut made such reporting mandatory.)

On July 1, 1990, *The Milwaukee Journal* published a special report on Lyme disease. In discussing the status of reporting, Neil D. Rosenberg wrote that "Lyme cases are vastly underreported, public health officials agree. At a Lyme disease meeting in Boston this spring, [a well-known Lyme disease researcher] acknowledged with chagrin that he had never reported any of his hundreds of Lyme patients to public health authorities in Massachusetts as is required by state regulation. He said he just wasn't familiar with the process and thought it would be too time-consuming. It turned out that a simple telephone call was all that was needed."

According to a report by Robert Hamilton in *The Day* of September 23, 1991, Connecticut could expect a large number of cases of Lyme disease in 1991. Dr. Matthew Cartter said, "It looks like we'll at least go over 1,000 cases this year, which will be the highest we've ever gone." A full-time Lyme disease research assistant had been hired to do surveillance. Cartter said, "We're trying to improve reporting so we can have a better feeling for the actual incidence of the disease in Connecticut. What we're uncovering is a serious problem with underreporting."

On October 29, 1991, *The Pictorial Gazette,* a Valley Shore newspaper, carried a story by Liz Michalski about a new two-year, twelve-town study (Old Lyme, Lyme, East Haddam, Old Saybrook, Essex, Deep River, Chester, Haddam, Westbrook, Clinton, Killingworth, and Madison) by the Department of Health Services, designed to evaluate reporting of the disease. Pat Mshar of the State Health Department explained that "under the new study, the department will be requesting a monthly report from physicians and following that up with a phone call." According to the report, "Old Lyme Health Director Frank Kneen is one official who was happy with the idea of the study. 'I'm concerned with the lack of reporting, and I've been complaining for years,' Kneen said, adding that he receives reports of around 17 cases a year. 'Try 500 cases as a more realistic number,' he said."

As of 1990, the Council of State and Territorial Epidemiologists approved a resolution urging that the disease be reportable nationally. Surveillance of Lyme disease had been initiated by the CDC in 1982. "Forty-nine states and the District of Columbia require reporting of Lyme disease."[4]

At the Fifth International Conference on Lyme Borreliosis, in May 1992, it was announced that in the United States, 40,000 cases of the disease had been reported since 1982 in every state except Montana, and it was widely accepted that the disease was grossly underreported.

In June 1993, at the Sixth Annual Rheumatology Symposium at Yale University, Pat Mshar reported for Dr. Matthew Cartter that Connecticut's "54 cases per 100,000 population in 1992 was the highest [rate] reported in the United States." Health department researchers found that only 7 percent of a selected group of 4,570 primary-care physicians (internists, pediatricians, general practitioners, and dermatologists) reported cases in 1991 and 1992. Thus the problem of underreporting has not improved very much. Active surveillance probably helps, as it has in a few endemic areas so far.

The 1994 figures show dramatic increases in the reported cases in Connecticut and New York. In Connecticut, 3,473 cases were reported to the health department in 1994, as compared with 2,536 cases in 1993. Of these, 2,030 were confirmed cases. New York had 5,131 confirmed cases reported to the State Health Department in 1994, an increase of 86 percent over 1993's reported confirmed cases.

Early in 1995, Betty Gross told me of a tremendous increase in the number of phone calls that she received about Lyme disease during the last month of 1994 and the first months of 1995. The heavy snow cover of the winter of 1994, combined with the unusually warm weather during the fall of 1994 and early winter of 1995 have most likely been a factor in these increases.

The case counts nationally climbed strikingly in 1994, totaling 13,083 for the year, an increase of 58 percent over the 1993 national figures. Connecticut had the highest infection rate, at 62.2 per 100,000 population; then came Rhode Island with 47.2 per 100,000, then New York at 29.2 cases per 100,000, and then New Jersey at 19.6 per 100,000. Children in the five- to nine-year-old age group were infected most often.[5] Due to the lack of proper reporting, these numbers reflect only a portion of the number of Lyme disease victims annually. I hope that in the future, with better reporting, a more accurate assessment of the magnitude of Lyme disease will emerge. Ideally, if more doctors report their cases, governmental and private funding will be increased to help to combat this rising health problem.

CHAPTER SEVENTEEN

THE DIAGNOSIS

Failure of existing rules is the prelude to a search for new ones.
THOMAS S. KUHN, *THE STRUCTURE OF SCIENTIFIC REVOLUTIONS*[1]

HISTORY

The way in which the story of Lyme disease unfolded is typical in the history of science. As my son Todd wrote in a paper during his first year of medical school in 1990:

> *One obvious lesson that physicians might learn from the [Lyme disease] story is that medical knowledge is limited, and is constantly changing. Just because the information gleaned about a patient does not fit neatly into today's set of possible diagnoses does not mean that the symptoms are not real. Physicians must keep in mind the nature of scientific discovery and advancement, which is well described by Thomas Kuhn in* The Structure of Scientific Revolutions. *Science, Kuhn postulates, is not a gradual, linear increase in knowledge, but rather is marked by quantum leaps ahead. The period between each jump ahead is always marked by increasing knowledge of data that are anomalous to the present understanding, data which are often marginalized by some scientists in a conscious or unconscious desire to maintain the viability of the current paradigm that explains reality. Eventually somebody develops a new paradigm that explains the previously anomalous data, and the new paradigm replaces the old as that which truly explains reality.*

In the case of Lyme disease, the paradigm explaining the disease has clearly shifted over the years. Prior to 1975 in the United States, there was no concept of Lyme disease, and patients were made to fit the existing diagnostic classifications of that time—for example, summer flu, rheumatic fever, rheumatoid arthritis, spider bite, ringworm, juvenile rheumatoid arthritis, idiopathic Bell's palsy, multiple sclerosis–like illness, trauma, or hypochondriasis. With the initial scientific reports of Lyme arthritis in 1976, the primary focus of the model was on the arthritis, along with mention of the primary ECM and some related symptoms. At this point the disease was believed to be viral, and although trials of antibiotics were initiated and evaluated every other year by Yale researchers, interestingly they were not found by Yale researchers to be effective in preventing progression of the disease until 1979–1980. From then on antibiotics were recommended for the treatment of Lyme disease. Gradually the clinical description of Lyme disease has expanded to incorporate myriad manifestations, including central nervous system, ophthalmic, cardiac, muscular, and psychiatric symptoms; the list is still growing. In 1981–1982 the disease was proven to be bacterial. Soon a serologic test was developed for it, and many doctors felt that it could now be easily diagnosed and treated.

More recently, cracks in this paradigm have appeared as patients have been proven by isolation and culture of the spirochete to have Lyme disease even though the results of diagnostic blood tests were negative. Additionally, patients treated at length with antibiotics have failed to improve, and again the spirochete has been found in the patient despite lengthy treatment. As Dr. Kenneth B. Liegner (also referring to Kuhn's model of scientific discovery) told the Fifth International Conference on Lyme Borreliosis in 1992, "These anomalous observations have revealed the deficiencies of the existing paradigm for Lyme disease, and until it is modified to accurately reflect the biologic reality of *B. burgdorferi* infection, things will seem 'out of joint.' "

There is ample evidence that Lyme disease was around for many years before 1975, when the concept of Lyme disease first developed. It is interesting to look back to earlier years in our country's history for clues as to when Lyme disease was first here. Scientists Andrew Spielman and Sam R. Telford III believe that similar vector-borne infections go back to a pre-Pleistocene time.[2] For as yet unknown reasons, Lyme disease has been increasing its range since the mid-1970s. At the beginning of the study of Lyme disease in the United States, researchers had speculated that the disease might have been brought to this country from other continents recently, but now studies have shown that it has been here for many years. One report stated that evidence of spirochetal DNA was found in ear skin samples from two 1894 museum specimens of mice in Dennis, Massachusetts, on Cape Cod.[3]

David Persing of Yale reported at the Fourth International Conference on Lyme Borreliosis in 1990 that a number of ticks collected in the Long Island town of Montauk in the 1940s had been tested and were found to be positive for specific *Borrelia* proteins—which suggests that infected ticks had been in that region at least since that time.[4]

In my own research and experience I have found anecdotal evidence that Lyme disease has been afflicting people in this area for many years prior to 1975. I have informally interviewed lifelong residents of our area for memories of illnesses that might have been Lyme disease. Many noted that during the first thirty years of this century the first ticks they were aware of were found on sheep. Later they started seeing wood ticks and dog ticks, especially when in the woods or raking leaves. The town of Lyme had much more pastureland then; many roads were dirt, and their edges were mowed. Fields and brush were burned regularly. Only since the early 1970s, several years before Lyme disease was recognized as a clinical entity, did people distinguish the tiny deer tick from the other ticks and note that it was becoming increasingly plentiful. The deer population has steadily increased since the turn of the century, to the point now of overpopulation and real concern over the damage inflicted by deer. The increased risk of Lyme disease, as associated with the proximity of deer, is of concern to many.

During the fall of 1987, the problem of the burgeoning deer population really hit home. I had all my large, overgrown yew bushes taken out from in front of my house to let in more light and air. The bushes were piled in an enormous heap in the middle of my front lawn, ready to be taken to the town dump the following day. The weather turned cold, and when I awakened in the middle of the night to close the window, I looked out and couldn't believe my eyes. In the moonlight it looked as if my lawn was moving around a center of green. The mountain of yew had been eaten down to almost nothing, and a huge wreath of twenty or more deer was vying for position to finish off the feast. The next morning the landscaper who was working for me couldn't believe the yew bushes were nearly gone, but was pleased that most of his job had been done for him. (For years my garden plantings have been eaten. As defensive measures one now has to plant species that the deer don't like to eat [which are very few] or cover one's garden with plastic netting. Now some neighbors are building electric fences to protect their properties, and researchers are studying the effect of this on tick populations.)

Town reports that I read at the Lyme town hall comment on malarial diseases (especially during the 1890s and early 1900s), on influenza in 1920, on fifty-five cases of German measles in 1964, and in 1966–1967 on quite a few cases of conjunctivitis and strep throat. Otherwise, no unusual health problems were noted until 1976, when public health nurse Florence Christian reported that "the town of Lyme has received the dubious distinction of having a strain of arthritis named for the geographic area in which this peculiar viral disease is being studied. Dr. Steere, from Yale, is following clients very closely and hopefully, may soon be able to tell us the cause of the arthritis-like symptoms, and perhaps the preventive agent."

Several older residents I have talked to now think that certain of their early illnesses were probably due to Lyme disease. One man remembered that he had had ringworm back in 1928 or 1929. Although medicated, the rash would not get better and lasted a long time. Afterward he had extreme swelling of one knee and was unable to get around for months. He had no injury. Dr. Josiah Griffin Ely of Lyme had him consult a specialist in Middletown; his knee was drained of fluid, but no one could diagnose his problem. He has had intermittent problems with the knee ever since.

A hunter from Old Lyme had many tick bites over the years and had a history of water on the knee years ago. He has had a huge ECM-like rash and disseminated infection and treatment four times in the last few years. In 1993 the rash was photographically documented by his doctor. (This shows how people in an endemic area can be re-infected repeatedly. On May 8, 1994, Ellen Liberman, staff writer for the *The Day*, reported on a house painter in Old Lyme who claimed to have had Lyme disease "10 times since 1978." On December 12, 1994, John Foley reported that Edward F. McGovern, Jr., of Block Island, and his wife had both had Lyme disease. Furthermore, Foley wrote, "the manager of the island's Nature Conservatory has had it at least five times, and the former chairwoman of the Conservation Committee has also been stricken five times. Apparently, it has hit at least 20 percent of the residents.")

An elderly man whom I interviewed first came to Lyme in about 1922 and later moved to Old Lyme. About 1927, when he was eight years old, he had an ECM-like rash and "was violently sick and it was terrible." Dr. Josiah Griffin Ely "saddled up and came all the way down to Old Lyme with a horse and surrey from up in Lyme" to see him during the illness. Because the boy's family had goats, the doctor thought that he might have undulant fever (brucellosis), an infection transmitted by several kinds of farm animals; however, a specialist who was consulted did not think so. Whatever his illness was, he recovered eventually and then went for a long time without having another ECM-like rash. Now he gets such a rash at least once a year because he is so often exposed to ticks. Back in the 1930s, he had a job removing ticks from sheep with his bare hands. He remembered that back in the 1950s everybody he knew seemed to be getting water on the knee and hobbling around. Later there were a number of cases of tic douloureux in town. (Tic douloureux is an extremely painful condition involving the trigeminal nerve, or fifth cranial nerve, in the head. This nerve can also be affected by Lyme disease.) Recently this man has had the rash break out as many as three times in one summer and has been treated with antibiotics. He gets Lyme disease symptoms nearly every summer, and now reacts very quickly to tick bites. His wife starts to feel terrible when she is bitten by a tick, although she does not have the swelling or rash that her husband and son have had. Their son had a huge knee swelling in the 1970s and was treated by Dr. Steere at Yale.

Another person in Old Lyme around 1937 had a large red rash on his abdomen and went to see Dr. Julian Ely who was stumped as to what the rash might be. Dr. Julian Ely, whose father and grandfather had preceded him in caring for the people of Lyme, took out every medical book with pictures and descriptions of rashes that he had in his Lyme office, and together they sat on the floor and went through them trying to identify the mysterious rash. They had no success and the patient was sent home with the hope that the rash would improve. Dr. Ely consulted state experts, but no one knew what the rash was. Over time it gradually faded.

Members of our family saw Dr. Ely on a number of occasions over the years, and he treated infections with penicillin or tetracycline. It is likely that in his practice he treated people infected by the Lyme spirochete before the disease was identified. He treated reactions to a tick bite with tetracycline.

One former Lyme resident told me that back in 1954 her husband had consulted a doctor from Old Lyme with a terribly stiff neck and headache during the summer and was treated with antibiotics. The doctor told him that year after year the symptoms were a regular summer complaint in the area. He didn't know what caused the illness. Years later, in the early 1970s, her husband had the ECM rash, which formed a bib around his neck; he also suffered from high fever, stiff neck, and extreme malaise. Several days into the infection he was again treated with antibiotics, but went on to develop joint problems and uncontrolled muscle twitching.

In an article in *Science,* "Detection of *Borrelia burgdorfer* DNA in Museum Specimens of *Ixodes dammini* Ticks," David Persing et al. reported information given to them by R. Semlear, Jr.: "Reports from senior medical practitioners in eastern Long Island indicate that 'Montauk knee' and 'Montauk spider bite' have been in the vernacular of the local residents for many years."[5] In Nantucket, there was a summer fever labeled Nantucket fever.

Some go back even further in New England history to locate what might have been Lyme disease. In an account by Mary Nelson of the Long Island newspaper *Newsday* on November 9, 1988, she reported that:

> *On July 15, 1783, a young man on Shelter Island wrote to an aunt in Nova Scotia, describing conditions just after the Revolutionary War: "You will find by the date of this letter that we have removed from Connecticut and are returned again to our farm on this Island . . . now 8 weeks, 7 of which my Papa has been very ill and still continues very weak and low. He was first taken with a Colon Morbus which brought on a fever that reduced him so low that we almost despaired of his recovery. His complaints now are mostly nervous, chiefly a violent pain in his head and the back of his neck which throws him into spasms, of which he hardly escapes a day. He desires me to acknowledge to you the receipt of your letter, to present you his love and to inform you that if he ever gets well enough to write (which he has very little expectation of, as he feels himself sitting on the side of the grave just ready to fall in) he will answer your letter."*

The reporter wondered whether Lyme disease might go as far back as the 1700s. (Shelter Island and the eastern end of Long Island are endemic areas for Lyme disease.)

We will probably not find certain answers to our questions about the possibility of early cases of Lyme disease; however, it is interesting to continue to look for any such evidence.[6]

People ask me what the reaction has been in the town of Lyme to the evolving story of Lyme disease. On January 15, 1985, an editorial in *The Day* had said, "What a pity for Lyme that its most famous resident turned out to be a tick, that its name, which should flow from the mouths of poets, instead has entered the vocabulary of epidemiologists." But not everyone seems to be sorry about the town's identification with an illness. In an April 18, 1989, story in *The New York Times*, townspeople were interviewed about their feelings:

" 'It's an honor,' said William Beebe, the unofficial town historian.

" 'Made us famous,' said another resident, Dinah Mulligan.

" 'We sort of chuckle over it,' said Town Clerk Ruth Perry. . . .

"Many here hope the disease scares off developers and newcomers." As Mr. Beebe put it, "We don't want to get the town overrun."

This expression of love for the town and desire for it to stay just the way it has been—simple and idyllic—seemed an accurate reflection of what I'd heard from townspeople. I remembered being told several years back that the Lyme disease scare was like "instant zoning" for our beautiful town. On the other hand—as has been the case since the first media reports emerged in the spring of 1976—there were those who were not happy that the town's name was forever linked to a nasty disease. As the *Times*'s William Safire remarked in the June 2, 1991, installment of his "On Language" column, "Citizens of Lyme in New Hampshire—where Lyme disease is rare—are still wondering why they were hit by the name."

PROBLEMS IN DIAGNOSIS

Despite the more detailed characterization of Lyme disease over the years and the media attention given to it, patients with Lyme disease continue to be misdiagnosed. I have heard countless stories of patients going from physician to physician before an accurate diagnosis is made. But thanks to publicity about the disease, a number of patients have been diagnosed because they or their doctors realized that their puzzling illness matched the description of Lyme disease. Sometimes public awareness efforts really pay off.

It is not only laypeople who have trouble with proper diagnosis. Even a doctor can be misunderstood. To me, one of the most dramatic and impressive reports of the international conference in Stockholm was that of Ingrid Gamstorp, a sixty-five-year-old retired pediatric neurologist from the University Hospital in Uppsala,

Sweden. Dr. Gamstorp had begun having progressive symptoms in 1973—sleep difficulty, aches, stiffness, tender muscles, and fatigue. Later, she suffered neurological problems which especially affected her hands, making her pediatric work difficult. She began to lose sensation in her hands. Surgery for carpal tunnel syndrome did not help. Next, her feet and sense of balance became impaired. She lost weight. After consulting a number of colleagues and undergoing many diagnostic tests, which came back negative, she was sent from doctor to doctor. Dr. Gamstorp said, "I assure you that I did not feel at all better because the tests were negative." She wondered if she might have fibromyalgia, a disorder characterized by musculoskeletal pain and stiffness, fatigue, and distortions of physical sensation. By late summer 1986 she was depressed and suicidal and put herself under the care of a psychiatrist, who sought a physical cause for her distress. By then Dr. Gamstorp's hands, feet, and knees were blue. One colleague looked only at her hands and suggested Raynaud's phenomenon—insufficient circulation to the fingers, caused by arterial spasms—which gets worse with age. The response of some doctors was a pat on the shoulder and a "You know, women of your age, they have some ailments, and you have to learn to live with it."

Finally, in January 1988, a co-worker of fifteen years who was sitting next to her at a conference noticed how blue her hands were. He said, "The way your hands look, should you have the *Borrelia* test done?" No one had ever suggested *Borrelia* infection before. The result was highly positive—or, as Dr. Gamstorp put it, "underlined in red ink."

She was treated with antibiotics: intravenous penicillin for two weeks, oral penicillin for two weeks, oral tetracycline for three weeks, and intravenous cephalosporin for two weeks, and the progression of her symptoms was stopped. Many symptoms disappeared, but Dr. Gamstorp still has some residual problems—namely, fatigue, sleep difficulties, and some neurological symptoms, which are at least no worse than they were before treatment.

No one had ever asked her about tick bites. Of this, Dr. Gamstorp said that "the history that a physician gets is never better than the questions he asks." She remembered no one tick bite or

ECM rash, but recalled that "For 25 years I have spent my summer vacations on the little Danish island which to me is the paradise on this earth, but I must admit that there are ticks, and for at least 20 years I have every summer removed at least 4 ticks from my legs. . . . To get a tick bite has become as natural as getting a mosquito bite, nothing one tells a physician about—unless asked for."

The doctor urged physicians to ask the right questions and carefully rule out infection in their diagnoses; to believe the patient; to examine all the symptoms; and especially to remember to "never pat elderly women on the shoulder saying: 'Well, you know, women of your age . . .' " Her presentation was very powerful.[7]

There are several reasons for misdiagnosis. One is that a physician may simply be poorly informed about Lyme disease. In this age of increased travel, Lyme disease may be picked up on vacation in an endemic area; the patient then returns to his or her home in a nonendemic area, where physicians are often unaware of the disease. Over and over again I have heard from frustrated patients that in other parts of the country, doctors may be inclined to think you can get Lyme disease only around Lyme, Connecticut. A sketchy view of the disease seems to stick in the minds of physicians unfamiliar with its complicated presentation. Heart, eye, ear, neurological, and arthritic troubles, rather than the tick bite or diagnostic rash, may be the first symptoms noticed. Lyme disease can be a diagnostic nightmare, and some doctors deny the disease's importance rather than deal with the problem or be curious about the disease's complexity.

Many doctors have latched on to the idea that a tick bite followed by a circular expanding rash is the telltale sign of the disease; they are unaware that sometimes atypical rashes follow the tick bite. Sometimes there is no memory of the tick bite; approximately 30 percent to 40 percent of Lyme disease patients don't remember a rash. There is also difficulty in diagnosing the ECM on dark-skinned people. In 1985, *The New York Medical Quarterly* dedicated an entire issue to the proceedings of the October 1984 Lyme Disease Symposium in Valhalla, New York. Several papers focused on the difficulty of diagnosing the disease in children. Dr. Stuart Beeber wrote, "Sometimes the rash is not as characteristic [as the classic ECM] and differential diagnosis is a problem. The rash may not be the typical circle. Frequently one does not see the bite mark or obtain a history of a tick bite. Some rashes are warm; others itch. Some patients have a small circle that can be confused with ringworm. Also, the skin lesion occurs at a time of the year when pediatricians see a large number of dermatological problems—poison ivy, impetigo, hives, mosquito bites. All of these can mimic the Lyme disease rash."[8]

During my meetings with Dr. Luger from 1986 on, I learned of the more atypical symptoms he was seeing in his Lyme disease patients. Some of his patients had rashes that he was sure were associated with the disease though they were not part of the typical description. Dr. Luger was documenting the rashes with slides. Later, in a public talk on Lyme disease, he described his findings this way: "If you look for big red rings with white centers, you'll find textbook medicine but you'll miss a lot of erythema migrans." (After 1986, physicians increasingly dropped the "chronicum" from erythema chronicum migrans when referring to the rash.) The classic ring rash, he explained, was only 10 to 15 percent of what doctors actually see in Lyme disease. Rashes may be blistering, or a red oval, or purple, or blue. They come in many shapes— sometimes blotchy, sometimes like a bull's-eye, sometimes even triangular.

In the early 1980s, I learned that Dr. Bernard Berger of Long Island was also documenting the rashes he was seeing in his practice, and had written a number of articles on the dermatological aspects of Lyme disease. It was encouraging to hear of these studies; such "in the field" research was very important, because it helped attest to many of the suspicious symptoms that patients had suffered with and suspected were part of Lyme disease. Hearing about Dr. Luger's and Dr. Berger's research reinforced my belief that listening to the patient and closely observing all of his or her symptoms remains extremely important in the diagnosis of patients. In an age when overburdened doctors have come to rely perhaps too heavily on tests, a patient's intuitions about his or her body and the connections between symptoms are a valuable diagnostic tool that often gets lost in the shuffle. A patient's hunches are especially important when dealing with a disease such as Lyme disease that is still being described.

IDENTIFICATION OF THE DISEASE IN NEW AREAS OF THE COUNTRY

Another realm in which the dominant model needed to be challenged or proven inadequate was the understanding of Lyme disease's geographic distribution. At first the focus was, of course, on the area around Lyme. From 1975 on, the northeastern coastal states, the mid-Atlantic states, Wisconsin, Minnesota, and northern California were added to the list. Others continue to be added. The disease has been reported from almost all of the United States. I believe that the possibility that Lyme disease exists throughout the country should determine prevailing policy and should be carefully scrutinized in each state with help from the federal government. Every medical school should teach a comprehensive course on this complicated disease.

Doctors in certain areas of the United States that are not as yet considered endemic by the Centers for Disease Control are having trouble establishing that they are seeing Lyme disease. In some areas rats, not mice, are a chief source of the infection. The tick transmitting the infection is not always *Ixodes pacificus* (western United States) or *Ixodes scapularis**. Where there is debate among health professionals about whether Lyme disease exists in a given state, patients with Lyme-like symptoms often have a difficult time obtaining a diagnosis. While their illness might not be Lyme disease, doctors should be open to the possibility that it could be Lyme disease appearing for the first time in their area, or that the patient might have contracted the infection while traveling out of state.

For the past six or seven years, there has been controversy over the diagnosis of Lyme disease in Missouri. Dr. Edwin Masters, a

---

*In 1993 *Ixodes dammini* was subsumed into *Ixodes scapularis* because the two were found to be one and the same.[9]

family physician in Cape Girardeau, had reported a number of cases of EM (a total of 180 cases in southeast Missouri were reported during 1989, 1990, and 1991) and an illness that he believed fit the CDC criteria for Lyme disease, even though *Ixodes dammini* ticks were not found in Missouri. Dr. Masters felt strongly that the Lone Star tick *(Amblyomma americanum)* was the vector in his Missouri cases, but the CDC would not classify the Missouri illness as true Lyme disease until more studies were undertaken. As Dr. Masters told Elisabeth Rosenthal of *The New York Times* on March 21, 1991, "It walks like, quacks like, looks like Lyme, and I don't have an alternative diagnosis." His colleagues Dr. Dorothy Feir, an entomologist at St. Louis University, and Julie Rawlings, a scientist at the Texas Department of Health, were collecting and testing Lone Star ticks and found evidence of Lyme disease spirochetes, supporting Dr. Masters's assertion. He persevered with his care and research, reporting all cases that he deemed fit the CDC national surveillance criteria for Lyme disease. But the CDC maintained that they had not been able to identify and grow *Borrelia burgdorferi* from Missouri. So far, researchers have been unsuccessful in culturing the Lyme spirochetes out of blood and tissue samples from patients with Missouri "Lyme-like illness," as the CDC and state health departments called it.

Dr. Masters did not think that his patients with Lyme-like illness were hypochondriacs: "Suffice it to say that do you really believe hypochondriasis arises de novo in a previously healthy person in middle age with no identifiable external stresses, etc.? When was the last time you saw a patient that suddenly became a hypochondriac Labor Day weekend of 1991?" He went on to say, "I'm a country doc in a small town and I have to see these patients, and I can't give them two weeks of whatever treatment and say you are cured, don't bug me anymore, or I'll send you to a psychiatrist. I have to live with these people, and they come back—and we just have to call it like we see it. . . . These people are sick and they need to be treated."[10]

Another Missouri physician, Dr. Cal Greenlaw of Chillicothe, who was also seeing Lyme disease cases, said, "I try very hard to find a different diagnosis, believe me. Lyme disease is just too frustrating. And I do find other diagnoses on patients who have been referred to me. I'd rather not see a Lyme disease case. There are too many unanswered questions, but you don't give up. You get into a situation where if you don't treat them, who does? . . . There's no doubt we're dealing with two types of patients suffering from the disease: patients who are easy to diagnose and are positive on all tests, and patients with classical symptoms and presentations identical to Lyme disease but who don't respond as readily to treatment. Make no mistake, these are solid people who aren't hypochondriacs. I have five to six people in this category."[11]

Chuck Lay, editor, in an article entitled "As Lyme Disease Debate Rages, More and More People Are Diagnosed," wrote, "Len Peery, who is diagnosed with Lyme disease, had probably the most insightful comment on the debate. He said he doesn't care what the disease is called, he just wants to be rid of it. And in the final analysis, that's what's really important."[12]

In January 1994, I received the following letter from Dr. Masters: "I thought you might be interested that we have finally isolated *Borrelia burgdorferi* [from ticks] in southeast Missouri. Once in a while, when one encounters something that looks like a duck, quacks like a duck, and flies like a duck—it's a duck." Officially however, because the spirochete has not been isolated from patients, Missouri cases that meet the strict surveillance criteria for reporting Lyme disease to the CDC are presently still considered by that agency to be "tick-associated Lyme-like illnesses" which have not yet been shown to be caused by infection with the Lyme disease spirochete.[13] So debate continues. The roles of the American dog tick and the Lone Star tick in transmitting Lyme disease in this area of the country are presently being investigated.[14]

THE TESTS

A second reason patients may not be diagnosed with Lyme disease is the unreliability of tests for the disease. In one study by Dr. Steven Luger, blood samples were taken from nine patients with major manifestations of Lyme disease, including facial palsy, swollen knee, and erythema migrans rash, as well as positive antibody tests. Each patients's blood serum sample was divided into halves. The first half of each patient's sample was then divided into nine parts and one part was sent to each of nine different laboratories doing Lyme serology. Two weeks later the identical second half of each patient's sample was divided into nine parts and one part was sent back to each of the same nine labs for testing. In all each lab received eighteen specimens. The results varied widely from lab to lab. Some labs missed as many as 50 percent of cases, giving the samples a negative reading. Some patients positive at one lab were negative at the same lab two weeks later with the identical half of the original blood sample. Because of these inaccurate and variable results, the study's authors pointed out the urgent need for standardization of testing.[15]

At present new tests are being evaluated. In 1994, a PCR (polymerase chain reaction) test for the presence of the spirochete in the synovial fluid of joints of patients with Lyme arthritis was developed, which should help to identify those with persistent infection.[16] The Lyme disease PCR is a sensitive diagnostic test that seeks to detect portions of the DNA of the *B. burgdorferi* spirochete by testing samples of urine, blood, or cerebrospinal fluid from a Lyme disease patient. It is a time-consuming (a week to obtain results), complicated process that at this point is used only in a Lyme disease research setting. The major problem in laboratory work with this test has been contamination of the sample, which is so sensitive that temperature, dust, and contamination from other outside sources can skew the results.

Not only are problems caused by faulty testing but some patients may not be serologically positive simply because they are not mounting a good immune response to the bacterium. This can be the case with patients treated early in infection with doses of antibiotic that abort the immune response without curing the disease.

The imprecision of Lyme disease tests remains a source of conflict among physicians who treat Lyme patients. The development of a quick and reliable diagnostic test, one based on the presence of the spirochete rather than on antibodies to it, is under way; if researchers are successful, such a test would make a tremendous difference in the problems of diagnosing Lyme disease. Until then, some doctors rely heavily on present tests and believe that seronegative Lyme disease exists only very rarely; others will diagnose Lyme disease if a patient has a spectrum of symptoms and a history consistent with the disease, even if the tests are negative. Debate over this issue has recently grown more heated with the publication (in *The Journal of the American Medical Association*) of a study reporting that Lyme disease is commonly *over*diagnosed, and that only 23 percent of 788 patients who thought they had Lyme disease and came to Dr. Allen Steere's clinic actually had active disease. Dr. Steere and his colleagues wrote: "Of the patients who did not have Lyme disease, 45% had had positive serological test results for Lyme disease in other laboratories, but all were seronegative in our laboratory."[17]

A number of physicians and Lyme patients wrote to the editor of *The Journal of the American Medical Association* reacting to this report. Dr. Joseph J. Burrascano, Jr., of East Hampton, New York, wrote: "My experience in a practice that serves as a referral center for thousands of patients with chronic Lyme disease from all over this country and other countries is that the predominant problem with these patients is underdiagnosis and undertreatment."[18]

Martha Kramer of the Lyme Disease Coalition of New York wrote: "We struggle with the debilitating symptoms of the disease and its accompanying emotional and financial burdens while academicians in the name of good science semanticize the disease out of existence. Call it persistent infection, call it fibromyalgia, call it chronic fatigue, but ask why these diagnoses are multiplying in endemic areas. Acknowledge that we are here by the score and please do not trivialize the disease by publishing a study that relies on unreliable tests and, in the light of an ever-growing body of scientific research to the contrary, uses failure to respond to treatment as a criterion for the elimination of Lyme disease as a diagnosis."[19]

In September 1993, Douglas S. Dodge, a retired businessman who with his wife and a child and grandchild of hers has had Lyme disease, wrote in *The Vineyard Gazette,* a Martha's Vineyard, Massachusetts, newspaper: "The pronouncements of those who claim that Lyme disease is overdiagnosed continue to disseminate

through clinics, hospitals, government agencies, insurance compa-
nies, medical cooperatives, and organizations, and tens of thousands of doctors' offices. Prestigious scientific presses parrot their
findings and jeopardize the health and happiness—the life—of
those they mislead.''
        Deborah Amdur, M.D., of Livingston, New Jersey, the mother
of a Lyme disease patient, wrote to the editor of *The New York Times*
(July 1, 1993): "As a physician trained in an academic institution, I
find the defensiveness, denial and refusal of Dr. Steere and his colleagues to recognize what is, rather than what fits their disease paradigm, both frightening and destructive.''

NEUROLOGICAL SYMPTOMS

    What is known about the manifestations of Lyme disease con-
tinues to expand. Over the years I have either experienced myself
(or heard described by others afflicted with Lyme disease) of many
manifestations before they were "discovered" officially and written up in the medical literature. Thus, it is clear to me that among
those living with a disease there may be knowledge of the disease
which goes beyond present medical understanding; what is "discovered" eventually by physician researchers may have been
known to the patients for some time. For example, for many years
I felt, on the basis of my own experience, that of my family, and
many anecdotes recounted by other patients, that Lyme disease
causes neuropsychiatric symptoms, and gradually this has been increasingly well documented by the medical community.
    Over the years I had talked to Dr. Steere about these symptoms
of Lyme disease, and had read relevant papers by neurologists Dr.
Louis Reik and Dr. Andrew Pachner, both of Connecticut. By 1985
I knew that Dr. Reik had reported the neuropsychiatric symptoms
of Lyme disease in eighteen patients. These symptoms included
"aseptic meningitis, encephalitis, chorea, cerebellar ataxia, cranial
neuropathy (including bilateral facial palsy), motor and sensory
radiculoneuropathy, mononeuritis multiplex, and myelopathy.''
The authors of the study also described patients with headaches,

stiff neck, sensory disturbance, nausea and vomiting, photophobia (intolerance of light), somnolence and lethargy, emotional lability and irritability, poor memory and concentration, blurred vision, and depression.[20]

In early 1985, Dr. Pachner, who was at Yale University, telephoned and asked me whether we could get together to discuss my observations on neurological and psychological Lyme symptoms. I had earlier expressed an interest in discussing these with him, and he knew that over the years I had talked to a great number of people afflicted with Lyme disease.

At our meeting I told Dr. Pachner that I thought behavior changes and depression were caused by the effect the spirochete was having on the brain and nervous system and not, as I had heard many doctors had told patients, an emotional reaction to living with a chronic illness. Similarly, I was convinced that the extreme fatigue experienced by Lyme disease patients was not an emotional response, but a physical one. People who had not experienced the disease could not imagine the depth of that fatigue. Seizures, optic neuritis, depression, appetite changes and cravings, anxieties, learning problems, withdrawal, dizziness, agitation, insomnia, and memory loss were being described to me by people who called me or talked to me in the supermarket.

A good number of these people had consulted specialists, a few had been hospitalized, and many of them were being diagnosed with ailments other than Lyme disease. In some cases they and their doctors did not associate their earlier history of tick-related illness with the later stage symptoms they were having now. Although some had a clear history of a bite and serologically positive Lyme disease, others had a history of a bite but were testing negative to the spirochete, and therefore were difficult to pin down absolutely from a clinical standpoint.

Dr. Pachner and I had a good discussion and agreed to keep in touch.

Each year brought more research. In 1985, Dr. Pachner reported that in a Yale study of a group of patients with chronic central nervous system (CNS) symptoms he found neuropsychiatric problems including focal CNS lesions (definite, localized lesions that can be observed by tests such as a CAT scan) with multiple-sclerosis-like attacks, psychiatric symptoms, and fatigue.[21] In July 1986, Dr. Reik reported on neuropsychiatric symptoms in eight patients who had not had the diagnostic ECM rash.[22]

In a letter to *The Journal of the American Medical Association* (October 31, 1986), Dr. Alan MacDonald, a pathologist at Southampton Hospital on Long Island, wrote of finding *Borrelia burgdorferi* in the brains of two autopsied patients with dementia. He suggested that some patients with dementia might have had a Lyme disease infection that triggered their problem: "If *Borrelia* infection can be linked to cases of dementia by serology or by culture, a group of patients will be candidates for intensive parenteral antimicrobial therapy analogous to the treatment now used for neurosyphilis."[23]

At the Second International Symposium on Lyme Disease and Related Disorders in Vienna in September 1985, Dr. Andrew Pachner presented a paper on thirteen "third-stage" Lyme disease patients. "All five patients [in the group with neuropsychiatric symptoms] . . . presented with personality changes during childhood. Examples of their symptoms included difficulties with concentration and interacting with peers, wide mood swings, loss of friends, and a drop in grades. One patient had an 'anorexia nervosa'–like syndrome lasting for many months, leading to weight drop from 59 to 45 kilograms and hospitalization in a psychiatric institute. A number of neuroleptic drugs were of no benefit. The patient responded dramatically to a two-week course of intravenous penicillin: he regained weight back to greater than his previous weight, he stopped obsessive dieting and exercising, and returned to school within a month after treatment."[24]

In 1987, at the Third International Conference on Lyme Borreliosis, Dr. Göran Stiernstedt and his colleagues powerfully described the ways in which neuroborreliosis (neurological problems resulting from borreliosis) presents to the physician in Sweden, and the diagnostic problem it frequently poses: "Another way of showing the broad clinical spectrum of neuroborreliosis is by examples of how the symptoms and signs listed were interpreted by the patients and physicians before the diagnosis of neuroborreliosis was set. In our experience, patients with neuroborreliosis might appear within all medical disciplines." Dr. Stiernstedt described how the radicular pain (nerve root pain) of Lyme disease can be confused with abdominal pain, gastric ulcer, gallbladder disease, and kidney stone. The lumbar pain of Lyme disease can be confused with a herniated disc. The disease can imitate stroke, heart problems, brain tumor, viral meningitis, cancer, and fever of unknown origin. Dr. Stiernstedt also mentioned that 12 percent of the neuroborreliosis patients in his study had been negative in both blood and spinal fluid tests.[25] This summary by Dr. Stiernstedt clearly spelled out how easily this illness can be misdiagnosed.

Several follow-up studies on patients with Lyme disease were done at the New England Medical Center in Boston. In November 1990, Eric L. Logigian, M.D., and his colleagues reported that "the most common form of chronic central nervous system involvement in our patients was subacute encephalopathy affecting memory, mood and sleep, sometimes with subtle disturbances in language." They went on, "In addition to encephalopathy, most of our patients had peripheral sensory symptoms, either distal parasthesias or spinal or radicular pain." One patient had leukoencephalitis, a brain inflammation. Associated symptoms were fatigue, headache, unilateral hearing loss, tinnitus, and fibromyalgia.[26]

Nineteen ninety-one saw a second follow-up study, "The Long-Term Course of Lyme Arthritis in Children," by Ilona Szer, Elise Taylor, and Allen Steere. The report served as the conclusion to the study of "46 children in whom the onset of the disease occurred between 1976 and 1979 and who received no antibiotic therapy for at least the first four years of the illness." The researchers discovered that "the course of initially untreated Lyme disease in children may include acute infection followed by attacks of arthritis and then by keratitis [inflammation of the cornea of the eye], subtle joint pain, or chronic encephalopathy."[27]

Thus the symptomatology of the neurological aspects of Lyme disease was constantly expanding as doctors discovered the many ways the Lyme spirochete can affect the nervous system.

PSYCHIATRIC SYMPTOMS

At the First International Symposium on Lyme Disease at Yale University in 1983 I had spoken of the great need to study the psychiatric consequences of Lyme disease. Thus, at a conference at Yale in the spring of 1988, I was very interested to hear what was, to my knowledge, the first discussion by a psychiatrist of the psychiatric manifestations. Dr. Anita Lopkar of Yale gave a riveting presentation, describing the many psychiatric symptoms that were part of the clinical picture, including problems with memory and concentration, depression, social adjustment, personality and behavior changes, profound fatigue, impulsiveness, eating problems, irritability, and withdrawal. I found it very encouraging to learn that research was under way in this area.

During August 1990, I heard several accounts of people having psychiatric problems following Lyme disease infection—some manifestations were quite severe—and I decided to pursue the idea of finding others in the psychiatric profession to do research into this area and publish their findings. I heard of two young psychiatrists who were interested in the subject, and I spoke by phone with both of them and encouraged them to do a study. I also told them that I would be more than happy to talk with them about what I had observed over the years.

In the time that I had been talking to victims of the disease, I had often heard that some doctors would react to patients who were agitated, irritated, and angry by saying that they did not have Lyme disease, even if they had the symptoms. Instead such patients were told that they had an emotional problem and should see a psychiatrist. I disagreed. I encouraged these patients to seek a doctor who understood Lyme disease. After treatment these people would return to their previous emotional well-being, often to tell me that they had felt "off the wall" with sickness when they were trying to get treated. I'd heard that some doctors referred to patients trying to get treated as "antibiotic junkies," exhibiting "antibiotic-seeking behavior." Doctors who are not trained beyond medical school psychiatry often back off from a patient who is unpredictable, argumentative, angry, teary, withdrawn, irritable, hyperactive, or depressed and take the easy route of referral. Perhaps doctors refer patients quickly because they feel unequipped to handle such intense emotional states. Lyme disease can certainly affect the brain and nervous system, but in addition, patients often have a further emotional reaction to a doctor's lack of knowledge and understanding. Patients want a doctor who is an ally working with them to solve their problems.

Suppose the patient is sent on to a psychiatrist or psychologist; how many mental health professionals are schooled in the effects of Lyme disease? *Very few.* There must be improvement in the education of psychiatrists, who are historically aware of the devastation of the mind and nervous system by syphilis, but who are not yet fully aware of this cousin of syphilis, Lyme disease.

On July 29, 1991, the two psychiatrists I had contacted about research into Lyme disease and mental health, Dr. Brian A. Fallon of the New York Psychiatric Institute and Dr. Jenifer A. Nields of Fairfield, Connecticut, came to my house for a visit. We talked most of the day about possible neuropsychiatric symptoms resulting from Lyme disease. The doctors said that they had sent out a questionnaire to Lyme support groups throughout the country and were now evaluating the resulting data. They planned to publish the research at the completion of the studies. I felt reassured as we talked that warm July day that the process of finding out about these life-altering symptoms had begun.

A year later, at a Stamford, Connecticut, conference on Lyme disease, Dr. Fallon gave a talk on the psychiatric presentations of Lyme borreliosis. He said, "Because Lyme borreliosis, like syphilis, has neuropsychiatric manifestations, psychiatrists are being asked to see these patients often before the diagnosis of Lyme disease has been made. Incorrectly labeling these patients as having a functional illness, such as depression, hypochondriasis or a somatization disorder, may result in a delay in the initiation of antibiotic treatment. Such delay may lead to further dissemination of the infection, and in some cases severe disability and possibly chronic neurologic damage." He went on to describe several Lyme disease patients; one had developed an agitated depression, and another had developed a manic-depressive disorder. Both improved with antibiotic treatment.

Dr. Fallon reviewed the scant existing medical literature on the psychiatric manifestations of Lyme disease, and then he described how Lyme patients feel in dealing with their illness. He said that many patients face disbelief from their doctors and those close to them. Because of the transient episodes of illness, they can't predict how they will be feeling in the future; thus, they hesitate to plan ahead. Their diagnosis is often uncertain, and treatment plans vary from doctor to doctor. Their normal life is threatened; they worry about jobs, insurance coverage, and strained relationships with those around them. Dr. Fallon went on to say, "And primarily I think that the feeling of the patient with Lyme borreliosis is a loss of control. You lose control of your bodily feelings and you lose control of the ability to anticipate and predict the future."

In his evaluation of seropositive patients, Dr. Fallon found that only 4 percent were diagnosed by the first doctor they consulted, and many went without a proper diagnosis for years. Forty-seven percent said that before their Lyme diagnosis they were thought to have rheumatologic or neurologic illness, and 46 percent said they were thought to have a psychiatric illness. They were referred to mental health professionals either because they were thought not to have a serious medical problem, or because they were thought to need help in dealing with a serious medical illness. Dr. Fallon said these people described "deep depressions, suicidal thoughts, anxiety, panic attacks, feeling of being in a fog, violent thoughts, rage, personality change, uncontrollable mood swings, low self-esteem, 'I doubted my sanity,' memory problems and depersonalization." Patients told of disorientation and sleep disturbances. Some were helped by medications used in psychiatric illnesses, others by antibiotics.

Dr. Fallon ended his talk with a description of the psychiatric problems of children with Lyme disease. Some chronically ill children had been unable to attend school for long periods of time. Dr. Fallon said, "A great deal of work needs to be done with these kids, and, as far as I know, nothing really has been done."[28]

At the Fifth International Conference on Lyme Borreliosis, in

1992, Dr. Fallon reported that "mental health professionals need to include LB [Lyme borreliosis] in the differential diagnosis of major depression." Dr. Nields reported on anxiety disorders and Lyme disease.[29]

The following fall Drs. Fallon and Nields and their colleagues published an excellent report, "The Neuropsychiatric Manifestations of Lyme Borreliosis." The article gave a comprehensive and clear description of the disease and reviewed the psychiatric literature. Dr. Fallon wrote, "The course and severity of illness can vary. In most cases, Lyme disease if treated early is a transient illness with mild symptoms and no long-term sequelae. In a smaller portion of patients, the course may be chronic and severe. . . . Patients given antibiotics early in illness tend not to have major late complications, although an unknown percentage of patients treated early still develop late complications."

Dr. Nields described the psychiatric manifestations of late-stage Lyme disease that she found in her research, based on clinical interviews with a number of patients and on seropositive Lyme patients' responses to the questionnaire. The symptoms she found included fatigue (94 percent) and memory loss (83 percent); photophobia (70 percent); sound sensitivity (48 percent); sensory hyperacusus (hypersensitivity to sound, touch, taste, and smell; taste 30 percent, smell 25 percent); extreme irritability and/or emotional lability (84 percent); word reversals when speaking and/or letter reversals when writing (69 percent); spatial disorientation (57 percent); fluctuations in symptoms; worsening of symptoms during antibiotic treatment; and uncertainty as to diagnosis and treatment. Dr. Nields summed up the patient's dilemma this way:

Many patients have felt abandoned by their medical doctors when the diagnosis was uncertain or the treatment not fully curative. Others have had to see many different doctors before one was able to put together the diversity of their symptoms and come up with a diagnosis. Several patients have said that the hardest thing to bear—even more than the pain and disability—had been the feeling that they were somehow inexplicably altered, in their emotions and personality and ability to function, without hope of finding a cause or a cure, and without a doctor who could honor their difficulty, whether or not he or she could solve it. For some patients, then, the ambiguities surrounding diagnosis and treatment and the consequent sense of abandonment by medical professionals were among the most distressing aspects of the illness experience. The psychiatrist can be of help by lending respectful support to such patients; by listening and by helping them to clarify their options.

Finally, Dr. Nields stated, "in cases of known Lyme disease, it is important for psychiatrists to take a comprehensive approach to treatment as so many aspects of the patient's life—physical, emotional, cognitive, sexual, social, and occupational—may be significantly affected by the illness."[30]

After reading this paper, I was reassured that psychiatrists now had a fine reference on Lyme disease in the medical literature.

LYME DISEASE IN PREGNANCY

This is an area that needs continued attention by the research and medical community. There clearly have been cases where Lyme disease spirochetes contracted during pregnancy have been transmitted to the fetus; such transmission is associated with congenital problems.[31] Spirochetes have been identified in multiple organs in stillborn infants of mothers who had Lyme disease; in one case, the stillborn infant had multiple congenital cardiovascular abnormalities. (However, these anomalies were not necessarily caused by the Lyme disease.)[32] In another study, five of nineteen pregnancies during which Lyme disease occurred had adverse outcomes, including death of the fetus and prematurity with cortical blindness.[33] The possibility that infected mothers may pass the spirochete to their baby through breast feeding should also be evaluated. Adequate, early treatment is crucial, and it is important to state that when early diagnosis is made and adequate medication initiated, the result most often is a normal pregnancy outcome.

In 1990, Dr. Steven Luger reported on six patients who had had varying stages of Lyme disease infection during their pregnancy; he had treated them with antibiotics and followed them in his practice. "All six pregnancies resulted in healthy babies; one mother was infected prior to pregnancy but was not diagnosed until two years later, one during late first trimester, two during second trimester, and two during third trimester. Two placentas showed inflammatory changes, two mothers had premature labor, and one had a Cesarean section. Five mothers are well, one has persistent joint symptoms, and one mother failed IV penicillin therapy and was successfully retreated with IV ceftriaxone." Dr. Luger went on to state his treatment guidelines for Lyme disease in pregnancy: "All pregnant women bitten by *Ixodes* ticks [should] be treated with oral antibiotics, amoxicillin being my drug of choice. Since we know that *B. burgdorferi* can cross the placenta, I would recommend parenteral [intravenous] therapy for any woman with erythema migrans during pregnancy, with ceftriaxone being my drug of choice. The only exception I might make for this would be to those women with erythema migrans if the physician believes that erythema migrans is really a local disease without systemic involvement. I think oral antibiotic therapy may be appropriate for this group of patients. The only caveat I have for that is Dr. Weber's reported case of a woman treated with oral penicillin in low doses who did go on to disseminate despite the lack of systemic symptoms. And finally for disseminated or late stage disease in pregnancy I think parenteral ceftriaxone would again be my therapy of choice."[34] In December 1994, Dr. Luger told me that he had now treated a total of sixteen pregnant patients, with normal outcomes for mothers and babies in every case. He had followed up these patients for one to five years.

Continued reporting, investigation, and documentation of any new cases with an adverse outcome is important. Epidemiologists and researchers are interested in cases of Lyme disease in pregnancy. The CDC runs a national Lyme Disease in Pregnancy registry, which began in 1985. The Lyme Disease Foundation also has a pregnancy registry.

SURGERY FOR UNDIAGNOSED LYME DISEASE

Over the years I have heard of a number of people having surgery for problems later found to be caused by Lyme disease. Two papers deal with symptoms which may be seen by surgeons; in these cases, the patients were evaluated for Lyme disease. In their paper "Meningoradiculoneuritis Mimicking Vertebral Disc Herniation: A 'Neurosurgical' Complication of Lyme Borreliosis," the Swiss neurologist C. Meier and colleagues reported three cases of meningoradiculoneuritis (inflammation of the membranes of the brain and spinal cord and of the nerves and nerve roots of the spinal cord) due to Lyme disease that had been confused with disc herniation. Two of the patients had been unsuccessfully operated on for herniated disc, one of them twice. After extensive tests, the doctors properly diagnosed Lyme borreliosis in the three patients and treated them with antibiotics. The patients were rapidly helped to recover from their pain.[35]

At the 1990 international Lyme disease conference, doctors from Austria presented data showing that five of fifty-eight patients with disc herniation were found to have positive Lyme tests.[36]

On August 2, 1993, writer Michael W. Miller told the story of Richard Gerstner, a former top IBM executive, in *The Wall Street Journal*. Gerstner's four-year search for a diagnosis for his threatening physical symptoms began in 1987. In 1989 his illness caused him to leave his job. Gerstner saw many doctors and therapists, and had two unsuccessful back surgeries. "In February of 1992, Mary Joette Gerstner ran into another IBM employee's wife and recounted her husband's ordeal. The other woman's eyes widened—she herself had suffered many of the same symptoms and finally found an accurate diagnosis. 'It's Lyme disease,' she told Mrs. Gerstner." Richard Gerstner was finally treated for Lyme disease and his health has improved.

Carpal tunnel syndrome of the wrist, jaw difficulties, and neck problems should be evaluated for underlying Lyme disease before surgery.

One Lyme disease patient told me she was having serious problems with her foot along with symptoms of Lyme disease, and I remembered my years of hobbling around with foot pain. I found in the literature a paper by a group of doctors in New York, "Foot and Ankle Disorders Resulting from Lyme Disease," which described Lyme disease patients' multiple joint and muscle problems of the forefoot, midfoot, and heel. In ten people with Lyme disease, "painful joints included tibiotalar, subtalar, talonavicular, and metatarsophalangeal. Synovitis was not palpable in most cases. Heel pain, plantar fasciitis, Achilles tendinitis, posterior tibial tendinitis, and dorsal foot swelling were all seen. Unusual dysesthesias were also noted." Most patients underwent months of unsuccessful physical therapy and medication until they were diagnosed properly and treated with antibiotics, which were successful in most cases.[37] In my friend's case, surgery had been suggested for her incapacitating foot symptoms. Instead, she was treated with antibiotics for her Lyme disease and her foot problem improved tremendously.

At an oversight hearing on Lyme disease before the U.S. Senate Committee on Labor and Human Resources on August 5, 1993, Carl Brenner, a scientist and chronic Lyme patient, testified that he had undergone sinus surgery to alleviate persistent headaches before he was properly diagnosed two years into his Lyme disease infection. The surgery was not successful.[38]

Because Lyme disease can affect so many parts of the body in so many ways, people with a history of a tick bite and Lyme disease should investigate whether their condition is related to Lyme disease before having surgery.

(In some cases of chronic, long-term Lyme disease, surgery is necessary to correct joints that have been damaged by the disease.)

PROBLEMS THAT MAY BE RELATED TO INFECTION WITH LYME DISEASE

Irregular Uterine Bleeding

Because of my contact with so many people with Lyme disease, I have been something of a clearinghouse for patients' experiences and therefore have been able to see connections that otherwise might not be easily apparent.

One symptom that I have been seeking information on is the irregular uterine bleeding experienced by some Lyme patients. At the Stamford, Connecticut, conference on Lyme disease in 1992, a well-attended public forum was held, and I was glad to hear a woman get up and ask the panel of experts, "Would someone please address the issue of hormonal upheavals in women who are diagnosed . . . with Lyme disease?" The questioner went on to say, "My only hope is that there will be some literature available on the subject. I haven't seen it discussed very much and I think it's an issue that is affecting a lot of people. I mean we [women] are about fifty-two percent of the population."

Menstrual problems and irregular bleeding are associated with Lyme disease by a number of patients, including me.

Dr. Kenneth Liegner, an internist from Armonk, New York, responded that his female patients reported an exacerbation of their Lyme symptoms at the time of menstruation. He had not done any formal studies, but recently had urged those patients to keep a diary of their illness in order to detect changes related to their menstrual cycle.

Other doctors have noted irregular bleeding patterns and changes in Lyme disease symptoms related to menstrual cycles, although no formal research has been done.

The discussion reminded me of a case presented by Dr. Paul Lavoie, a San Francisco rheumatologist, at the 1986 international meeting. In describing the case of a woman who had had Lyme infection since 1976, and had later developed acrodermatitis chronica atrophicans and was treated with antibiotics in 1985, Dr. Lavoie wrote that in September of 1976, one month into her infection, she "developed inappropriate intermittent vaginal bleeding which persisted for a month."[39] As far as I know, this symptom had never before been mentioned in the Lyme disease medical literature.

In his 1971 book *Borrelia: Strains, Vectors, Human and Animal Borreliosis*, Dr. Oscar Felsenfeld reported a number of hematologic changes in relapsing fever. He noted irregular uterine bleeding and nosebleeds in other borrelial infections in some parts of the world.[40] I had, as I have mentioned, heard of women with irregular-bleeding problems. I had always wondered about other bleeding problems in some Lyme disease patients, such as bruising and nosebleeds. Could they have anything to do with the presence of the spirochete? Some of our family had experienced these symptoms in the years when we had active Lyme disease.

A very interesting article, "Radical New View of Role of Menstruation," appeared in *The New York Times* on September 21, 1993. The reporter, Natalie Angier, wrote that scientist Margie Profet of the University of California–Berkeley believes that the function of menstruation is to help prevent infection of the uterus and the Fallopian tubes and that "inexplicable uterine bleeding should be viewed as a possible early sign of infection, a symptom that the body is struggling to thwart disease." I wondered whether this theory might explain the bleeding that some women associate with Lyme infection.

Perhaps now that more and more women were connecting such problems with Lyme disease, researchers will feel more compelled to find some answers.

Appendicitis

Another illness that may be triggered by *Borrelia burgdorferi* is appendicitis. I have been aware of a number of cases of appendicitis following Lyme disease infection. One of these cases was a person in her sixties. (Appendicitis is most common in adolescents and young adults.) Two children, several of whose family members and pets were afflicted with Lyme disease, had appendicitis within a year of each other. In our family, Gil and David had appendicitis. I knew of two boys in our area of Connecticut who had had appendicitis following Lyme infection. I have been told about a child who was diagnosed with Lyme disease in the summer of 1992 and who had an appendectomy in early 1993. Denise Lang's book *Coping with Lyme Disease* describes a patient named Lynn Latchford, who had a flulike illness due to an infected tick bite in 1983. She was not diagnosed or treated at the time for Lyme disease, and within six months she had surgery for appendicitis. "Four months later, another doctor said she had thyroid problems, depression, and menstrual irregularities."[41] Whether there is any connection between Lyme disease and the development of appendicitis is unknown, but this might be an area worth investigating. Are appendectomies performed at a higher rate in areas where there are significant numbers of Lyme disease cases?

CONFUSION IN DIAGNOSIS

Over the years the confusion over diagnosis became a very complicated problem. I continued to hear of cases of multiple sclerosis, lupus, chronic fatigue syndrome, amyotrophic lateral sclerosis (ALS), fibromyalgia, and even dementia, that also mirrored some of the symptoms of Lyme disease. In some people the development of these diseases followed a history of Lyme disease infection in an endemic area. These diseases are considered in the differential diagnosis for Lyme disease. Is one sometimes being diagnosed as another? Yes. Could the spirochete infection possibly trigger the development of any of these diseases? I think that this should be carefully studied and not totally ruled out.

We should all ask why are there so many people with these often "nonspecific" symptoms, who have been healthy, vibrant, and productive until they had a rash or flulike illness, after which their health deteriorated as they went from doctor to doctor seeking a diagnosis and the restoration of their health. Dr. Anthony Komaroff, an expert on chronic fatigue syndrome at the Division of General Medicine, Brigham and Women's Hospital in Boston, says that people suffering with "minor" illnesses—as distinguished from "major" illnesses such as cancer, stroke, AIDS, or heart disease—are often wrongly diagnosed with psychiatric disturbances. Writes Dr. Komaroff: "Before a pathophysiologic basis was established for systemic lupus erythematosus, Lyme disease, or multiple sclerosis, for example, patients with these illnesses who presented with fatigue, headaches, myalgias [muscle pains], arthralgias [joint pains], blurred vision, numbness, tingling, and related symptoms were frequently given psychiatric diagnoses. Indeed, in our experience, the same error is still made today in some patients with these illnesses.''[42]

In addition to patients often being given erroneous psychiatric diagnoses, it seems that patients suffering from diseases such as Lyme disease and chronic fatigue syndrome are sometimes dismissed as having a bad case of ''the flu.''

Indeed, Lyme disease and chronic fatigue syndrome patients themselves often think that they are just coming down with a flu-like illness at the onset of their disease.

In a letter to the editor of *The New York Times* (September 10, 1989), Dr. Komaroff described a few of his chronic fatigue patients this way: ''A 17-year-old girl, previously at the top of her class and the captain of her school's basketball team, who was stricken with a 'flu' in 1984 and has not yet been able to return to school; a 52-year-old lawyer and competitive athlete who came down with a strange 'flu' in 1983 and has been unable to work more than 10 hours a week since then; a 65-year-old woman, in perfect health all her life, a leader in her town's civic organizations and an avid gardener, who became suddenly ill with a 'flu' in 1986 and has never recovered. She spends most of the day resting.''

I believe that research should be done on the epidemiology of these diseases that often begin with flulike illness and that have overlapping, chronic symptoms. Neurologists, internists, rheumatologists, and infectious-disease experts might share information so that a broader perspective is gained. Clues as to the cause of the episode of ''flu'' that reportedly triggered so many of these long-term illnesses might be discovered. Perhaps there could be a geographic mapping of cases of all these diseases that mimic each other. We have the technology to do this. Are there clusters of cases? Are there seasonal variations? Are these mutually similar diseases coinciding with areas where the risk of Lyme disease is high? Does one disease later lead or predispose to the development of another? I will discuss a few of these diseases.

ALS (Amyotrophic Lateral Sclerosis)

In August 1987, Burton A. Waisbren and his colleagues at the Clinical Cell Biology Laboratory in Milwaukee wrote to the *Lancet* describing a possible link between Lyme disease and the nervous system disorder amyotrophic lateral sclerosis (ALS), otherwise known as Lou Gehrig's disease. Waisbren had tested the blood of fifty-four people with Lou Gehrig's disease and found that four of them had antibody levels consistent with Lyme disease infection. One of these patients developed ALS six months after having a generalized rash while on vacation in Wisconsin. She died of respiratory failure three years later. Another patient had also vacationed in Wisconsin and developed ALS. Her blood tests for Lyme disease became more positive as her illness progressed. She was then treated with intravenous ceftriaxone for Lyme disease and her condition stabilized.[43]

According to Dr. Louis Reik, "It does appear that Lyme disease can mimic ALS . . . but how often it does so is not clear. If it does so frequently, then the incidence of ALS should be higher in endemic areas."[44] I think that another possibility might be that Lyme disease may actually trigger ALS in some people. Further evaluation of the possible link between the two diseases should be made.

Lupus (SLE)

In August 1990, Betsy Lehman of *The Boston Globe*, reported a cluster of forty lupus cases in Gardner, Massachusetts.[45] In the past decade I had heard references to other possible clusters. I believed that these should be evaluated for the possibility of Lyme disease infection, given the similarity between some of the symptoms of Lyme disease and those of lupus.

In 1993, *Lupus News* reported a study of the Gardner cluster. The researchers were assessing the possibility of an environmental cause. Of the sixty-six individuals reported to have lupus, they could confirm the diagnosis in only five; many patients had died or moved away, or their records were unavailable. After evaluation of all available records by the rheumatology staff at the University of Massachusetts, eleven people were not thought to have had lupus after all. The researchers noted that there is no state or national registry or coordinated reporting system for SLE. Although they found no environmental cause, the investigators said: "It must be stressed, however, that missing case information may have inhibited the ability to detect an environmental association. For this reason the researchers believe that more study is warranted in a larger population of lupus patients (perhaps on a national level) that would allow for more meaningful statistical analyses."[46]

At a 1992 conference on Lyme disease, Dr. Paul Lavoie summarized his findings concerning a possible connection between Lyme disease infection and lupus: "Four lupus patients who amply fulfilled the diagnostic criteria for lupus (1982 Revised Criteria for Classification of SLE) were tested by the novel Rosa and Schwan probe for *Borrelia burgdorferi* DNA by PCR (polymerase chain reaction). Three showed the DNA in one or two of the three heparinized blood fractions." Dr. Lavoie concluded, "These observations suggest a spirochete might contribute to the immunopathogenesis of lupus. Larger trials might be indicated."[47]

I was reminded by this report that John H. Talbott, a contributor to Dr. Edmund L. Dubois's book *Lupus Erythematosus*, suspected that infection played a role in the etiology of lupus. Talbott wrote: "The current concepts of the pathogenesis of SLE include autoimmunity, hypersensitivity, and infection." Dr. Dubois's book also described what sounded like an ECM rash of Lyme disease in a patient diagnosed with lupus. "One patient had annular [circular] lesions with erythematous scaling, elevated borders, and central clearing. We have observed similar lesions."[48] Might these be misdiagnosed Lyme disease lesions? Can Lyme disease possibly trigger some cases of lupus? I know of a Connecticut patient who had Lyme disease and later additionally was diagnosed with Reiter's syndrome (a combination of urethral inflammation, conjunctivitis, and arthritis, whose cause is unknown) and lupus; another person on the West Coast was diagnosed with both lupus and Lyme disease.

Another intriguing bit of evidence is that the drug Vibramycin (doxycycline), which is commonly used to treat Lyme disease, can have the side effect of exacerbating SLE.[49] Some patients with Lyme disease experience a so-called Jarisch-Herxheimer reaction to antibiotics: Their symptoms actually get worse. Could some of the SLE patients who react badly to doxycycline actually be Lyme disease patients having a Jarisch-Herxheimer reaction?

The similarities and epidemiology of both of these diseases should be carefully studied. Confusion in diagnosis may on the one hand mean a lack of necessary antibiotic treatment for a Lyme disease patient misdiagnosed with lupus, while on the other hand the steroids used in the treatment of lupus would be contraindicated for use in Lyme disease.

Relapsing Fever, Chronic Epstein-Barr Virus (CEBV), and Chronic Fatigue Syndrome (CFS)

In chronic fatigue syndrome individuals become overwhelmed by fatigue and other symptoms without an obvious organic basis. The cause is unknown and has been the subject of much speculation. It is interesting that other diseases such as relapsing fever, mononucleosis (which is caused by Epstein-Barr virus), and Lyme disease can also be marked by symptoms of chronic fatigue. Is there an infectious etiology for CFS? Do some patients with CFS have Lyme disease?

In November 1984, I received a phone call from a Scottsdale, Arizona, woman named Bonnie Bennett. Her husband, Dick, had been afflicted with a recurrent illness that had required several hospitalizations. He had sporadic attacks of high fever, internal bleeding, and other life-threatening symptoms. Initially, doctors thought he had acute leukemia. Bone marrow tests for the disease, however, were negative.

Doctors at several hospitals were baffled. Bonnie became frustrated, so she pursued a diagnosis on her own, consulting medical books at the Phoenix library. She remembered that Dick had been bothered by what they thought was an insect bite while on vacation in Lake Tahoe. Relapsing fever, caused by the spirochete *Borrelia hermsii*, is carried by a soft tick common in the high altitudes of the Rocky Mountain states. Bonnie deduced that Dick's illness was relapsing fever.

She talked to her husband's doctors about her hunch. They refused to do the tests, dismissing her theory as amateur and unfounded. Finally, she managed to locate an infectious-disease expert at the University of California–Irvine who was willing to test her husband. The test was positive. Dick was treated with antibiotics and recovered his health.

Bonnie and I had a very interesting time comparing our stories. We were struck by how many similarities there were between relapsing fever and Lyme disease. She was very eager to find out what was happening in Lyme disease research, and told me that she was coming East in a few days to help a friend who was seeking treatment for symptoms similar to infection with *Borrelia*. The following Saturday, Bonnie and her friend came to Lyme.

Bonnie filled me in on her findings. She found that two other people who had been in Lake Tahoe had had mysterious fever illnesses. At Bonnie's suggestion they were tested, and were positive. She found seventy more similar cases of undiagnosed fever illnesses from the West; after appropriate testing, forty-seven were confirmed to have had a *Borrelia* infection. Dr. Willy Burgdorfer, with whom she consulted about the cases, praised her for her contributions.[50]

On August 1, 1986, I heard from a number of Lyme disease patients who had seen a story on ABC's *20/20* the night before, discussing chronic infection with the Epstein-Barr virus (CEBV) as a cause of a strange array of symptoms, including fatigue. My callers said that they noticed a great similarity to Lyme disease; so had I.

The following year I heard a news report on CEBV telling of an outbreak of two hundred cases among the 20,000 people living in Lake Tahoe from 1984 to 1986. Later, 105 people were ill with a similar illness in Yerington, Nevada, which is about fifty miles from Lake Tahoe.

CEBV's presentation sounded comparable to that of *Borrelia* infection. I remembered Bonnie Bennett's story of uncovering a cluster of relapsing-fever cases in the Tahoe area. In the Nevada outbreaks, once-healthy, active people described having a flulike illness followed by a debilitating long-term syndrome of extreme fatigue, low-grade fever, swollen glands, muscle aches, sore throat, headaches, and sleep problems, which drastically altered their lives. The 1986 20/20 show interviewed Dr. Anthony Komaroff, who had gone to Tahoe and Yerington in February of 1986 with a team of epidemiologists to study the outbreaks and take blood samples of those afflicted.

Over the years, people in Connecticut had reported to me that several members of the same family had been suddenly stricken in early summer with an illness; some were diagnosed with Lyme disease, others with infectious mononucleosis. Many of the symptoms The Merck Manual described as those of Lyme disease seemed to overlap with the symptoms of this strange fatigue syndrome, including enlarged spleen, chest pain, cough, meningoencephalitis (inflammation of the brain and the membranes enveloping it), Bell's palsy, and swelling of the eyelid and the area around the eye.

Descriptions of CEBV in various magazine articles written about the disease also sounded very much like Lyme disease. CEBV symptoms included memory loss, difficulty concentrating, dizziness, shooting pains, headaches, anxiety, and depression. (To my knowledge, an ECM-like rash and arthritis were not associated with chronic EBV disease.) In the many accounts I'd heard and read, a number of CEBV patients said they'd been told their illnesses were psychosomatic. Dr. Komaroff had studied a group of patients in Boston; he did not feel that their problems were due to psychological factors. Rather, he believed CEBV to be an organic illness, most probably triggered by some kind of infection.

In February 1987, I wrote to Dr. Komaroff about the 20/20 segment on the outbreak of CEBV in Tahoe, saying that I had been haunted by the many similarities of CEBV and Lyme disease. I asked if he had tested his blood samples for Borrelia, because I was concerned that if patients with Lyme disease or other Borrelia infections were misdiagnosed with CEBV and not treated with antibiot-

ics in the infection's early stages, they might have chronic problems later. I wrote that there obviously might be no connection at
all between his group of CEBV patients and borreliosis, but I felt
that I must raise the question.

Dr. Komaroff called me shortly thereafter; during our long
conversation I referred him to Bonnie Bennett, who, I was sure,
would be happy to share her information about the Tahoe outbreak. I told Dr. Komaroff how some patients with Lyme disease,
despite treatment, go on to have a chronic, debilitating illness that
sometimes lasts for years; according to Bonnie Bennett, relapsing
fever seemed to cause the same reaction in some people. Dr. Komaroff wrote to Bonnie Bennett, who sent him a comprehensive
report of her findings.

On February 29, I wrote to him again with some further information, and mentioned a February 26, 1987, *Hartford Courant* article reporting the rising CEBV epidemic since 1977. According to
Courant writer David Jacobsen, "One survey of illness onset in 185
CEBV patients in 35 states found 'a rising epidemic began about
1977.' " (I knew that Lyme disease cases had also escalated during
this decade.) Dr. Komaroff, who was interviewed for the article,
described CEBV patients: "Typically they were high-energy, successful, happy, very physically active people. Then one day, and
they can usually tell you the day—the last week of July in 1982 or
the middle of March of 1984—one day they got what seems to be a
virus, the flu—and they never recovered." I had read that similar
inexplicable outbreaks had been reported in the past under many
names such as Royal Free disease (named for an outbreak at Royal
Free Hospital in England in 1955), Icelandic disease, neurasthe-
nia, myalgic encephalitis, glandular fever, epidemic neuromyas-
thenia, vegetative neuritis, benign myalgic encephalomyelitis, and
postviral fatigue syndrome. A new name for it was "Yuppie disease."[51]

In early March, Dr. Komaroff responded, telling me that he
planned to get together with Dr. Allen Steere to discuss the possibility of a link between the diseases. I never heard what came of
their meeting. I wondered whether one illness might be misdiag-

nosed as the other, and hoped that people suffering from chronic fatigue syndrome would be aware of the possibility of Lyme disease and get a blood test.

In January 1992, several chronic fatigue syndrome investigators, among them Dr. Komaroff, published a paper in the *Annals of Internal Medicine,* reporting research on groups of people from the vicinity of Lake Tahoe and people from urban Nevada and California who had a severe fatigue syndrome and some neurologic disorders that followed a "flulike syndrome." These groups were compared with an epidemiologic control population. The researchers found that Epstein-Barr virus and HHV-6 (human herpes virus type 6, another virus) may be associated with chronic fatigue syndrome, but their role is as yet unclear. Describing the illness as a "chronic, immunologically mediated inflammatory process of the central nervous system," the authors stated their belief that chronic fatigue syndrome "probably is a heterogenous illness that can be triggered by multiple different genetic and environmental factors (including stress, toxins, and exogenous infectious agents), all of which can lead to immune dysfunction and the consequent reactivation of latent viruses. Several different exogenous and endogenous infectious agents may be involved in this illness, acting singly in some cases and collaboratively in others. In addition to HHV-6 and Epstein-Barr virus, the enteroviruses [certain viruses that dwell in the intestines], *Borrelia burgdorferi,* and other infectious agents may be involved in some cases."[52] The link between Lyme disease and CFS had been made in 1990 by two Long Island neurologists, P. K. Coyle and Lauren Krupp. They wrote, "*B. burgdorferi* may act as a trigger in susceptible hosts to precipitate" chronic fatigue syndrome.[53]

Multiple Sclerosis (MS)

Lyme disease can mimic multiple sclerosis, and the possibility that *Borrelia burgdorferi* triggers some cases of MS has been studied. Researchers have found that it is difficult to differentiate Lyme disease from MS on the basis of magnetic resonance imaging (MRI); findings are the same in both. In 1990, Dr. Kenneth Liegner brought up the possibility that the Lyme spirochete had caused MS in twelve patients whom he had studied; previously diagnosed with MS, they were also found by Dr. Liegner to have evidence of Lyme disease infection. He was studying the patients further to learn whether they did indeed have Lyme disease and, if so, whether it had caused their MS or was a coincidence.[54] Other studies have tested MS patients for Lyme disease; however, as I have mentioned, recent research shows that Lyme disease can exist despite negative test results, so using serology as a basis for excluding it may not be valid. I personally have heard of several patients who have had a Lyme-like rash and illness in a highly endemic area before being diagnosed with MS; I also know of people diagnosed with Lyme disease who later developed MS. Multiple sclerosis has been associated with temperate climates, where Lyme disease is also most prevalent. It has also been associated with proximity to animals. Future research, I am sure, will clarify the puzzling aspects of many of these diseases.

It is interesting that diseases such as SLE, MS, and ALS are all thought to invove immunologic mechanisms. SLE has typically been considered an autoimmune disease, meaning that its symptoms are caused by the body's immune system attacking the body. The question with such immunologically mediated diseases always has been: "Why does this occur?" One explanation for such phenomena has been that an infection may trigger an autoimmune process in some genetically predisposed individuals. Indeed, the arthritic effects of Lyme disease were interesting to immunologists because they were a clear-cut case of an infectious agent setting off self-attack in the joints. Thus the distinction between infectious diseases and autoimmune ones may begin to blur. Diabetes mellitus of childhood onset is now thought to be a self-attack on insulin-producing cells triggered by a virus. In the future, an infectious onset of other autoimmune phenomena may be discovered. Infectious triggers for diseases such as SLE and ALS may be identified, and the Lyme spirochete may be one of them. Careful studies of disease incidence patterns and of individual histories of those afflicted with these diseases, as well as further investigation into accurate diagnostic criteria and testing methods, will perhaps shed further light on the cause of these mysterious ailments. If infectious triggers are identified and eradicated by medication, will the auto-immune phenomenon vanish?

CHAPTER EIGHTEEN

TREATMENT, CURRENT
CONTROVERSIES

To become a true doctor, the candidate must have passed through all the
illnesses that he wants to cure, and all the accidents and circumstances
that he is to diagnose. Truly I should trust such a man. For the others
guide us like the man who paints seas, reefs, and ports while sitting at
his table, and sails the model of a ship there in complete safety. Throw
him into the real thing, and he does not know how to go at it.
MICHEL DE MONTAIGNE (1533–1592)[1]

Before "Lyme arthritis" was described, people who had the arthritis were thought to have a number of other ailments, including juvenile rheumatoid arthritis, rheumatoid arthritis, water on the knee, rheumatic fever, joint infection, or trauma. The patients thought to have rheumatic fever or a joint infection were most likely treated with antibiotic, the others probably not.

In the beginning of the research into "Lyme arthritis" by the doctors at Yale University in 1975–1977, there was debate over whether antibiotics were helpful. On one hand, when doctors at the Navy's Submarine Medical Center in Groton studied ten cases of the ECM skin rash in 1975 and 1976, they found that the penicillin or erythromycin that they gave to these patients had promising results. Only two patients went on to develop arthritis.[2] On the other hand, the Yale researchers prescribed treatments for the arthritis which included aspirin, draining of the fluid from the knee, corticosteroid injection into the joint, nonsteroidal anti-inflammatory drugs, hydroxychloroquine, the resting of swollen joints, and the use of crutches. Antibiotics were tried but were not found to be clearly helpful.

In a 1980 paper, "Antibiotic Therapy in Lyme Disease," Dr. Steere and his colleagues wrote that "we were initially skeptical of the role of antibiotics because of the frequent short duration of untreated erythema chronicum migrans, the clinical resemblance of associated complaints to certain viral illnesses and the negative results of cultural and serological attempts to demonstrate a bacterial pathogen." The researchers gave antibiotics to patients with active erythema chronicum migrans during the summers of 1977 and 1979. When comparing the results of the first two years, 1976 and 1977, they did not see any difference between the untreated and the antibiotic-treated groups in the duration of the rash or the development of later symptoms. In 1978, Yale patients were again not treated with antibiotics; however, the patients in this group seemed to develop arthritis at a significant rate, so after combining the data on the three years, 1976, 1977, and 1978, the Yale group decided to use antibiotics to treat patients with active ECM again in 1979. With respect to the development of neurological symptoms and cardiac problems, the treated and untreated groups were found to be similar. The researchers concluded: "In our experience, neurologic involvement may develop even if penicillin is given early in the course of erythema chronicum migrans. . . . We believe that the later manifestations of Lyme disease—neurologic, cardiac, and joint—are immune mediated."[3]

After the discovery of the *Borrelia burgdorferi* bacterium in 1981, the model of how to treat Lyme disease changed, and a sufficient course of antibiotics was thought to be curative. By 1985, however, there was some controversy about treatment. Dr. Peter Welch, a private practitioner, wrote, "One of the major problems confronting the practitioner who diagnoses and treats Lyme disease is the fact that many remain chronically incapacitated for months after the disease even though they initially were treated appropriately according to the literature."[4]

In a 1985 article in *Physicians' Weekly*, Dr. Sidney Gellis, Tufts's emeritus pediatrics chairman, was quoted as saying that "doctors are taking the disease too lightly" and "the ideal chance to wipe out every spirochete is when it's first diagnosed." He believed that "the standard initial therapy—an oral antibiotic—makes as little sense as it would for syphilis." Oral doses, he said, raise questions of absorption and compliance; thus, even stretching oral therapy to a month would not be sufficient. He favored "at least one initial IM [intramuscular] wallop of penicillin."[5]

During the past ten years, many different antibiotics have been used, alone or in combination, intramuscularly, orally, and intravenously, with varying results. The groups of drugs used have been the penicillins, the tetracyclines, the macrolides, and the cephalosporins. At present some doctors are using weekly intramuscular shots of penicillin. The search for better treatment is an ongoing process. Long-term treatment should be carefully studied and evaluated.

Since 1976, I have seen the climate change with respect to notions of the length of the illness, the length of appropriate treatment, and the relative importance of test results. The recommended duration of antibiotic treatment, both oral and intravenous, has been extended, as doctors have found that the *Borrelia* spirochete can be difficult to eradicate.

I think that the use of antibiotics for other ailments may change the presentation of Lyme disease. Say a child is exposed every year to tick bites. Some children also are treated with antibiotics for sore throats, earaches, injuries, and so on. The Lyme disease infection in these children may be kept in check by the antibiotics given for other ailments. It may smolder, only to be triggered again by further infected bites. Many adolescents are put on long-term antibiotics for acne, and this may also alter the presentation of the disease in that group. I also believe that when one is bitten repeatedly year after year in an endemic area, the response to the infection may be cumulative. Each bite may cause a more intense and faster reaction. Individual immune responses are also involved. I don't believe that this subject is well understood at this point.

Some doctors I have encountered think that Lyme disease is easily treated by a single course of oral antibiotics in its early stages; if patients fail to overcome the infection after one treatment, their future complaints are considered to be not associated with Lyme disease. These doctors believe that once a patient is treated, he or she no longer has Lyme disease.

In 1987–1988, tremendous media attention was given to the disease; I think this was generally beneficial. Correct information must prevail over ignorance. However, when the public saw the grave outcomes suffered by the patients who appeared on TV, an increased fear of the disease developed, with the result that many were scared that if they were bitten by a tick, they would have devastating illness. While a number of people do not respond to treatment or have not had treatment and have had severe complications, a proportionately far greater number are treated and seem to do well. (It is true, however, that some may relapse or enter another stage of the disease, sometimes many years later.)

Some doctors during this period of media attention were inundated by people worried that they might have the disease; they called this anxiety Lyme hysteria and Lyme paranoia. Some patients, as I have mentioned, were told they were "antibiotic junkies." There seemed to be many extremes in attitude, some physicians being unwilling to diagnose Lyme disease even with a classic presentation, and others willing to treat anyone with any vague symptom for Lyme disease. The unreliability of Lyme tests, as we shall see, did not help matters.

A number of physicians continued to say that media hype was distorting the true profile of Lyme disease and was scaring people unnecessarily. True, the adverse outcomes were proportionately rare; however, to the rare patient with a devastating outcome, statistics are irrelevant. The fact remains that the more proper information citizens and physicians are armed with, the more likely they will be to protect themselves from Lyme infection and to detect and treat Lyme disease early so that devastating outcomes will be less likely.

As the number of cases continued to rise, some physicians in endemic areas began to see great numbers of patients with Lyme disease. With their growing experience, many of these physicians became convinced that suggested treatment regimens were insufficient to combat the disease in some cases and were calling for longer and more aggressive treatment. They began to encounter patients who clinically seemed to have Lyme yet tested negative, while a number of patients continued to have persistent symptoms and remained chronically ill for years despite treatment. This area of chronic complications is the most controversial and the most disheartening part of the Lyme disease story.

Evidence has been found for the persistence of the spirochete in various parts of the body, despite antibiotic treatment and negative tests. A 1990 paper by V. Preac-Mursic and colleagues reported studies of patients who had originally been seropositive, had been treated with antibiotics, and then had become seronegative. However, spirochetes could be cultured from skin specimens and spinal fluid from these patients, showing a persistence of the infection. In her summary, Dr. Preac-Mursic said, "We conclude that early stage of the disease as well as chronic Lyme disease with persistence of *B. burgdorferi* after antibiotic therapy cannot be excluded when the serum is negative for antibodies against *B. burgdorferi.* . . . The isolation of *B. burgdorferi* from CSF [cerebrospinal fluid] and skin biopsy in our patients after antibiotic therapy with normal CSF-values and negative serological tests for *B. burgdorferi* raises important considerations in the treatment of Lyme borreliosis."[6] Indeed, this study raises important questions as to both the adequacy of antibiotics in treating the disease and the reliability of the tests in detecting the disease.

Other doctors involved in the controversy over caring for chronic Lyme disease also believe that the spirochete persists in the body. They believe in treating the patient with antibiotics until all symptoms are gone, even if that means keeping the patient on antibiotics for extended periods of time. According to these physicians, many people have been helped by prolonged antibiotic therapy. I have heard of many people with recurrent or chronic Lyme disease who have been successfully treated or made functional again by having long-term or repeated antibiotic treatments.

Over the years I have heard the stories of several physicians who have contracted Lyme disease; a number of them have treated themselves aggressively with antibiotics. Are they exhibiting "antibiotic-seeking behavior" just because they sought treatment until their symptoms were eradicated in order to have a normal life? It also seems that doctors who have experienced Lyme disease have a different perspective than those who have not, especially if they have had a protracted course of the disease. As Henrietta Aladjem said in *The Sun Is My Enemy,* "Perhaps it takes a sentimentalist or a physician who has experienced illness to make an ideal clinician, and though sentimentality is hardly a virtue, it is still more appealing than the callousness and indifference exhibited by so many physicians."[7]

In a 1987 book entitled *When Doctors Get Sick,* Dr. David Bingham, an obstetrician-gynecologist who lives in a town neighboring Lyme, describes his encounter with Lyme disease. In April 1979, he had two tick bites, and over the following days developed the typical early presentation of the disease, including a rash around each bite that resembled streptococcal cellulitis (tissue inflammation). "Although I had lived in the area all my life, I had never seen ticks this small before," he said. A week later he developed aches and a flulike feverish illness. He had read newspaper accounts of Lyme disease; now he consulted the medical literature. At the time, the literature "indicated that antibiotics did not seem to prevent the symptoms from occurring, and that the only treatment recommended was to use aspirin or other anti-inflammatory agents." Some of Dr. Bingham's neighbors had had serious complications with Lyme disease; however, they had all recovered over two or three years' time. Dr. Bingham had a bout with arthritis symptoms six months after his initial illness; at the same time he had severe problems with his jaw joint on the left side, so he had to resort to "liquids or semiliquid foods put through the blender."

After a thorough workup and consultation with Dr. Allen Steere at Yale, who confirmed that he had Lyme disease, Dr. Bingham was prescribed high doses of aspirin. During the following two and a half years he took aspirin for his joint problems, but periodically he had difficulty walking and had to use crutches. He had three injections of cortisone into his knee, which helped only for a while, and later developed a Baker's cyst, which ruptured. "While making rounds in the hospital in the morning, hobbling around on crutches, I felt a sharp increase in pain in the calf of my leg. By late morning the whole leg was swollen as large as my knee and tender throughout.'' After a visit to Dr. Steere and a cortisone injection with the suggestion that heat and elevation would help, he recovered. Dr. Bingham was ''less mobile than before'' and missed participating in certain sports, but kept up a positive attitude in coping with the disease.

Meanwhile, the results of antibiotic treatment were being evaluated at Yale; although antibiotics were now thought to be of benefit for the early stage of the illness, the therapy was unproven for illnesses of several years' duration. Dr. Steere informed Dr. Bingham that Yale was initiating a study on antibiotics that would be injected into the patient rather than taken orally in the treatment of chronic cases. In his account of his illness, Dr. Bingham said, ''At about this time, I had an elbow swollen the size of a grapefruit and had difficulty tying a necktie. Fortunately, I was able to deliver babies at arm's length and do surgical procedures, but I could not brush my teeth or button my shirt except with my left hand, because I simply could not bend the elbow beyond a right angle.''

For the sake of scientific accuracy, the antibiotic study was to be double-blinded: Some patients would be given the antibiotics and the others would be given a placebo; the two groups would be chosen at random. ''Although I believe strongly in double-blind studies,'' said Dr. Bingham, ''I was getting concerned that I might not be able to operate if things got any worse. I therefore decided to go ahead and take penicillin on my own, in relatively large amounts (500 mg Q.I.D. [four times daily] for a month), even though there was no medical literature to support the efficacy of my self-medication.'' After this treatment, Dr. Bingham's health gradually improved to the point that he was able to resume his normal activities.[8]

Dr. Steven Luger, who acquired his Lyme disease infection on August 12, 1986, noticed no rash. ''I woke up at about two o'clock on a Thursday morning with a fever of 103, muscle aches, headaches, and joint aches, and I thought I was dying, I felt terrible.'' Dr. Luger stayed home from work for only the second time in eight years. His doctor told him that he had either early Lyme disease or a ''summer virus''; in the absence of a rash it was difficult to tell, and even a blood test would not give meaningful results so early. "I think you may have early Lyme disease," his doctor told him, "I'm starting you on antibiotics." "I took my antibiotics for two days, my fever went away, I felt great, but I got sick to my stomach from the antibiotics and I did what all bad patients do, I stopped my antibiotics and didn't call my doctor. Two days later the fever came back and I did what all good patients do, I called my doctor back." After fourteen days of taking a different antibiotic, Dr. Luger again felt well, but a few months later he began to have back pain, bursitis, and pain in his left wrist and elbow. "I was . . . getting very close to forty years old, and I thought that this was what getting old was all about." However, follow-up blood tests for Lyme disease were very strongly positive. "So I went on antibiotics for about a month and a half and felt perfectly fine after that."[9] (Dr. Luger's account points up the fact that additional long courses of antibiotics are often needed to treat this illness.)

Dr. Joseph Burrascano from Long Island had Lyme disease many times: "I had Lyme disease when I was approximately thirteen years old, and I didn't know what I had—in fact, I didn't know I was sick; I thought everybody was that way. I remember times when I could not pull my pants on because my knees were so swollen." But he believed that everyone felt ill "whenever they did things too much and I thought everyone would sleep sixteen hours three or four days a week." Finally, in the early 1980s, a patient of Dr. Burrascano described her son's "weird illness," whose symptoms exactly matched Dr. Burrascano's own. "She pointed her finger at me and said, 'You have it too.' It showed up with the antibody test which at the time was basically experimental, it wasn't commercially available, but I knew the people who were doing it. I tested extremely reactive. A course of antibiotics modified the illness to the point where the major symptoms seemed to go away. Approximately a year and a half later I was rebitten, didn't recognize it at the time because the bite and rash occurred on the back of my head and I got severely ill. I was on antibiotics for twenty-six months continuously before the whole thing went away." After that, "I felt the best I had felt in years."[10]

For his Lyme infections over the years, Dr. Burrascano had

taken a number of oral and intraveneous antibiotics. Later he got another infection and needed further treatment. Dr. Burrascano's experience also supports the need for extended retreatment and provides further evidence that re-infection can occur. (Surprisingly, it is still not accepted by some doctors that re-infection with Lyme disease can occur.) All three of the physicians' accounts show that doctors seek treatment when symptoms return. They, like the rest of Lyme disease patients, just want to feel well again.

At the time of the Fifth International Conference on Lyme Disease in 1992, the controversy over treatment continued. As more and more patients had troubling experiences with Lyme disease—having to see a number of physicians before finding one knowledgeable about Lyme disease, not receiving antibiotic therapy, continuing to have symptoms despite antibiotics, or testing negative and being disenfranchised from Lyme treatment—many became increasingly dissatisfied with the status quo. They began forming support groups. By the time of the 1992 conference there were over a hundred support groups nationwide, and a second foundation, the American Lyme Disease Foundation, had been formed. Support group representatives from all over the country attended the conference and began to voice their concerns. (Since 1992 more support groups, networks and coalitions, and associations have been formed.)

A number of papers submitted by physicians in endemic areas had been rejected by the conference's program committee. After protests from support groups and patients concerned that important new information on the disease was being excluded, the committee reversed its decision.

As *Science* magazine reported, "Most Lyme researchers say the spirochete is wiped out in nearly all patients after 2 to 4 weeks of antibiotic therapy. Symptoms of late Lyme, they say, occur in some patients even after the spirochete is gone, and those symptoms don't respond to antibiotics." The reporter pointed out that doctors who specialize in treating Lyme disease in endemic areas disagreed with this point of view, instead holding that the continued presence of the spirochete is what causes symptoms.[11]

I believe that in some cases the spirochetes are persistent and cause long-term symptoms that do respond to further antibiotic treatment. Dr. Joseph Burrascano from Long Island, New York, was quoted as saying, "There are people out there who are really sick, who go back on medicine and get better again."

It was my feeling that the patients who attended the conference primarily wanted better research and information on treatment evaluation and the development of more effective therapies and techniques of prevention. They were obviously interested in a cure. Many had found that the prescribed four-week treatment with antibiotics was not sufficient, and that they relapsed if not treated for a long enough period of time. They questioned commonly accepted paradigms of the illness and believed that important questions were not being investigated. As Carl Brenner, scientist and chronic Lyme patient, wrote in a letter to *Science* magazine following the conference, "Good science is as much about asking the right questions as it is the sensible pursuit of answers, and many Lyme disease patients do not feel that the mainstream Lyme disease researchers are asking the right questions. The existing theories need to be reevaluated in light of the emerging evidence on chronic infection in late Lyme disease."[12]

After the conference a number of patient representatives wrote to its heads, citing six papers presented at the meeting that endorsed the theory that the spirochete persisted even after treatment and that a patient could be seronegative and yet have Lyme disease. They "asked for more research on pathogenesis, long-term antibiotics and innovative drug delivery systems" and "offered their services as participants in an NIH-sponsored effort to find a cure for chronic Lyme disease."[13]

The debate over the status of the chronic Lyme disease patient continues. On August 5, 1993, the U.S. Senate Committee on Labor and Human Resources held an oversight hearing on Lyme disease.

Prior to the hearing, after chronically ill patients voiced their concerns to the committee, the originally planned list of people testifying was extended to include those representing patients with chronic Lyme disease. Among those who testified were Andrea Keane-Myers of Maryland, who, it is to be hoped, has recovered from Lyme disease after two treatments; Karen Forschner of Connecticut, who told the story of her son Jamie, who died at the age of five from complications of Lyme disease acquired in utero; and Ruchana White of New York and her son, Evan. Evan, fourteen years old, is in a wheelchair and unable to speak due to the disease. Also testifying was Carl Brenner of Pennsylvania. Brenner, a formerly active, healthy marine geologist at Columbia University, was bitten by ticks while vacationing in the Pocono Mountains in 1989 and then was misdiagnosed for three years. He is now a chronic and disabled Lyme disease patient; unable to care for himself, he lives with his parents. Brenner said: "I am a scientist by vocation and a skeptic by nature, but I am here today to tell you that this is happening, that we *are* real, and that I am not some rare anomalous case that slipped through the cracks. Lyme disease has already destroyed the lives of thousands of productive Americans, with untold thousands more persistently infected and standing on a precipice."[14]

Ohio Senator Howard Metzenbaum said at the completion of the patients' testimony, "I think that you've sounded a clarion call. We ought to get off our butts and do something about this, and I think frankly it's an illness that has been swept under the carpet and not many people have paid attention to it."[15]

The statements given by the two clinical physicians who testified pointed up the opposing attitudes toward Lyme disease held by the medical profession. Dr. Joseph Burrascano spoke about the problems of underdiagnosis, undertreatment, and underreporting of Lyme disease; he called for "decades" of follow-up of Lyme disease cases. He addressed the issue of inadequate tests and spoke of a 20 percent to 30 percent incidence of seronegative Lyme disease.[16] On the other hand, Dr. Allen Steere said that Lyme disease can be clinically diagnosed and the diagnosis supported by positive testing. He rarely sees seronegative patients, only one or two a year. He considers chronic Lyme disease to be an unusual illness and finds that oral or intravenous antibiotic treatment of up to a month's duration usually cures Lyme disease. In a small number of patients, a second month of treatment might be necessary. Dr. Steere believes that Lyme disease triggers other "puzzling syndromes," such as fibromyalgia and chronic fatigue syndrome, and that Lyme disease has now become a "catch-all" diagnosis for other conditions.[17] The senators understood the controversy over chronic persistent infection and wanted to find the optimum methods to deal with the problems in diagnosis. When Dr. Burrascano said, "The blood test is not reliable to use as a diagnostic tool,"[18] Senator Metzenbaum interrupted him: "This gentleman [Dr. Steere] says exactly the opposite."[19] The dilemma facing many Lyme disease patients was clarified for the people attending the hearing.

Further testimony was given by Dr. Kenneth Platt, a veterinary epidemiologist from Iowa; by Dr. Matthew Cartter, by Joseph McDade, M.D., of the CDC; and by John R. LaMontagne, Ph.D., of the National Institutes of Health. Their emphasis was on surveillance (especially in targeting local disease hot spots), reporting, prevention, and the education of our country's physicians about Lyme disease.

As a result of the hearing, in early February 1994, the NIH invited a number of experts to review knowledge about and address the problems of the chronic or late-stage Lyme disease patient. Meeting participants discussed research into better ways to evaluate, diagnose, and treat this group of patients. At a second, similar meeting in October, a number of patient representatives observed. Presentations and discussions continued toward the goal of designing a study of these long-term patients; some doctors referred to them as having "post–Lyme disease syndrome," while others felt they were persistently infected with the Lyme spirochete. Thus the wheels are in motion to give attention to the long-term Lyme disease patient, and to further understand this very complicated disease.

In August 1994, Dr. Harold Varmus, director of the National Institutes of Health, was kind enough to meet with patient representatives and organizations to discuss the problems of the long-term Lyme disease patient.

In 1994, human trials of a new vaccine (developed by Smith-Kline Beecham) for Lyme disease were announced by the media. The double-blind trials would take place throughout the United

States and in Europe, with vaccine or placebo administration succeeded by follow-up evaluation. In 1993, another human vaccine,
developed by Connaught Labs of Swiftwater, Pennsylvania, began
human trials. In 1995, important new research into the role of
outer surface protein C (OspC) of the spirochete was published in
The Proceedings of the National Academy of Sciences.

Many dedicated scientists have worked for years on the development of vaccines for this menacing disease that shows no signs
of doing anything but yearly claiming more and more victims. Let
us all hope that the vaccines are successful.

CHAPTER NINETEEN

THE MURRAYS

[The Convalescent Home patients] were all much wiser than the doctors who treated them! There is among doctors, in acute hospitals at least, a presumption of stupidity, in their patients. And no one was "stupid," no one is stupid, except the fools who take them as stupid. Working in a chronic hospital, with the same patients, one gains a greater respect for them—for their elemental human wisdom, and the special "wisdom of the heart." But at that first breakfast with my "brothers"—not my colleagues in expertise, but my fellow-patients, fellow-creatures—and throughout my stay in the Convalescent Home, I saw that one must oneself be a patient, and a patient among patients, that one must enter both the solitude and the community of patienthood, to have any real idea of what "being a patient" means, to understand the immense complexity and depth of feelings, the resonances of the soul in every key— anguish, rage, courage, whatever—and the thoughts evoked, even in the simplest practical minds, because as a patient one's experience forces one to think.

OLIVER SACKS describing his stay in a convalescent home in England while recovering from a leg injury, from his book
A LEG TO STAND ON[1]

With the rest of the family now living in urban environments and away from Connecticut, their Lyme disease symptoms improved, although they did have some relapses. Once one has been afflicted with the disease, whenever odd symptoms appear there is a natural urge to wonder whether they might be related to Lyme. As a family we have generally been lucky. Those of us who had Lyme disease have sought further antibiotic treatment, which, when given for long enough, alleviated most symptoms. I would again like to emphasize that what our family experienced is minimal compared with what I know a growing number of patients who have had prolonged symptoms due to this illness have suffered.

The years after 1983 were a hectic time of life for me. I was very busy arranging for the care of my elderly relatives in New York and New Jersey and I made regular trips to be with them. It was wonderful to see all of the children pursuing their individual lives, and I was trying to adjust to not seeing them as much as I had. The time of bringing up children moves so very swiftly. Elise Taylor and I had a successful show of our work in 1985 and since then I have kept up my art and doll work whenever I have had time. Over the past few years I have begun to exhibit my paintings again.

In 1985, Gil and I were legally separated, and in 1986 we were divorced. Although the divorce had been in the making for many years, the finality was an adjustment for our whole family. Gil was remarried in 1988. He recently told me that through the years he has had episodes of Lyme disease–like symptoms. He has a heart arrhythmia. Otherwise he is doing well.

I have not been as lucky in avoiding Lyme disease. Despite precautions, I was re-infected nearly every spring or summer and had to be treated each time. Following EMs, my symptoms returned, at different times including subconjunctival hemorrhages, irregular bleeding, foot problems, multiple joint symptoms, bruising, and two bouts of incapacitating lower back pain. A CT scan of my back showed bulging discs with a possible herniation. In addition, at times when symptoms flared up, my balance seemed off and I developed transitory short-term memory and concentration problems. Gradually my medication was strengthened and prescribed for extended periods of time and my symptoms were controlled. My chronic foot problems disappeared.

Over the years my children and I debated the pros and cons of my moving to an area where Lyme disease is less prevalent; we invariably ended up deciding that our roots were here and that our house was too full of good memories to give up. After my divorce I had again decided that I wanted to stay in Lyme. I didn't want to give up the sense of stability that remaining in the house gave to all of us. However, the old days of playing and walking with abandon in the fields and woods were gone. Now I look fearfully at anyone I see lying in the grass, oblivious of ticks. But with education and caution about Lyme disease, life must go on. This disease mustn't take over everyone's lives; we must learn to deal with it. I keep the lawn cut short and the brush cleared. I dress protectively and spray my clothes if I go near the brush or woods. In the heat of the summer, however, it is unreasonable to cover all exposed parts of the body in the immediate environs of one's house. I check myself for ticks, and I no longer have pets.

I have found that my body now usually tells me if a tick is on me. Once, over graduation weekend at Todd's university, I had slight nausea and insomnia, but didn't think of a tick as the cause. As I drove home to Lyme, my upper leg began having severe pains and spasms, making driving difficult, and suddenly I realized that I might have a tick bite. I checked as soon as possible, and sure enough I discovered a nymphal tick deeply embedded in my upper right leg even though I had carefully checked myself for ticks just before I left Lyme. The tick had been on for two or three days. I removed the tick and got treatment. Over the years I have learned that if I start to feel feverish and achy, get insomnia, have shooting pains, or get a headache, I should look for a tick.

I certainly wasn't the only one having Lyme problems year after year. A friend of mine with a long history of tick bites, infection, and treatments for Lyme disease informed me that she also reacted quickly to tick bites now. One day recently when she took her usual morning walk she had an excruciating headache and shooting pains in various parts of her body. Finally she felt so dreadful that she sat down by the side of the road to rest awhile, wondering what was happening to her. Her physician husband was with her; they went directly home, checked her for ticks, and found an *Ixodes dammini* tick embedded in her neck. Her husband removed it, she went on medication, and her condition improved. This story made me wonder whether in endemic areas, and after numerous tick bites, one's immune system may react quite differently than to an initial exposure. I believe this phenomenon should be scientifically studied. Certainly our family had had such reactions, and the friend just mentioned has since found that she should look for a tick when she starts having symptoms such as sore throat, headache, stiff neck, rashes, or strange migratory aches and pains. According to the medical literature, the tick bite is supposed to be painless, and this is true for most people; however, people frequently bitten may develop different reactions.

The year 1988 was especially difficult for me because four months after my first mammogram (which was normal), I found a small lump in my breast where I had noticed a fleeting pain. It was found to be a cancerous tumor and I had a lumpectomy. I found out as much information about my disease as I could, and looked into programs for further treatment. I decided on a mastectomy and follow-up adjuvant chemotherapy. My chemotherapy was complicated because I had a re-infection of Lyme disease at the same time and was treated for that as well. Within hours of each chemotherapy treatment, rashes would appear on my cheeks and neck and around the area of the surgery; tender nodes also appeared. I felt very ill and had other complications. My doctors were puzzled and my surgeon was troubled by my condition. Chemotherapy suppresses immune function, which might explain a resurgence of infection. I was given antibiotics, and I consulted with Lyme disease experts. None had encountered my difficulties before. After three chemotherapy treatments it was decided to not continue my therapy. Later I had a slight fever and jaw problems; also, other rashes appeared. I was given more antibiotic. (In late October 1993, I had a checkup with oncologists at Yale, during which I asked whether in my doctor's experience he had seen anyone with skin manifestations such as mine directly following chemotherapy treatments. He said no, that any reactions as a result of chemotherapy were quite different. I still feel that underlying Lyme disease infection was involved. Perhaps oncologists will be aware of the possibility of resurgent Lyme complicating chemotherapy.)

Gradually in 1989 I regained my health; however, Lyme disease symptoms returned. This time I took a different antibiotic, Minocin. Following this medication my rashes, joint pain, and swellings disappeared.

The year 1993 was a good one for me. I had only one tick bite; the tick was on me very briefly and I had no Lyme disease symptoms with the exception of a subconjunctival hemorrhage. In 1994 and 1995, I was successfully treated with amoxicillin for Lyme disease symptoms.

Sandy is living in Boston and is the sales marketing manager for a wine-importing company. He has become fluent in French and Italian, has gained an impressive expertise in wine, and enjoys visiting vineyards worldwide for his business. He has had to favor one knee, which becomes painful and swollen if he stresses it too much. Otherwise, he has been healthy over the years.

David finished up his premed courses at the Columbia School for General Studies and taught science for a year in a private school in Brooklyn. In December 1984, during a routine physical, he was found to have a heart arrhythmia. Further examination revealed a mitral valve prolapse. He entered Case Western Medical School in Cleveland, Ohio, the summer of 1985. A doctor there later said that his mitral valve prolapse was gone, and wondered if it had been due to an infection.

After graduating from medical school in 1989, David entered a residency in general surgery at Saint Luke's–Roosevelt Hospital in New York City. One evening during the summer of 1991, in his second year of residency, he had a sudden episode of atrial fibrillation and was admitted to the hospital and put on medication to normalize his heart. It adjusted to a normal rhythm by the following morning. He has had no problems since. When he finished his residency in 1994, he went on to a fellowship in trauma surgery.

Wendy's career brought her to New York City once she graduated from Vassar College in 1983. She worked for a number of years for a women's magazine, first as an assistant fiction editor, then as associate health editor. Now she is a senior editor of an education magazine. Over the last decade her health has been good, by and large, and she hasn't experienced any Lyme disease symptoms. But in 1995 she was found to have a heart arrhythmia during a routine physical. Whether the family's incidence of heart arrhythmia is related to Lyme disease infection is unknown.

Todd has had repeated episodes of symptoms over the years. I think his symptoms are not triggered by further bites; instead, he has an underlying infection, which flares up periodically and has to be treated. In 1984 and 1985, his junior and senior years at

Brown University, he had some chronic Lyme-like symptoms, including rashes that were brought out by heat or the sun, hyperesthesia, insomnia, and joint aches. His Lyme IGM test for antibodies was still positive, showing active infection. He had a course of doxycycline.

After graduation Todd moved to New York; he worked long hours as a legal assistant for a large law firm and considered becoming an environmental lawyer. But by 1986 he was taking premed courses at the Columbia School of General Studies, and working for the university as well. He had occasional bouts of fatigue, insomnia, fleeting pains, joint aches, headaches, and skin rashes. He was treated with tetracycline in October. It was noticed that he now had mitral valve prolapse. Over his Christmas holiday in 1988, Todd was seen by Dr. Luger for his ongoing symptoms and was treated again with doxycycline for two months.

Todd's Lyme disease symptoms continued; in April 1989 he had an MIR scan of the brain and a lumbar puncture. The MIR was normal, but the lumbar puncture showed signs of ongoing infection, as did serum antibody tests. He was given four weeks of intravenous ceftriaxone followed by oral doxycycline. In June he had an evaluation with Dr. Steere. It was an intense and demanding time for Todd because he was working full-time in research while taking courses at Columbia, and taking his MCAT exam toward applying to medical school.

On a very hot Thursday afternoon in late July I got a phone call from a doctor at Columbia Presbyterian Hospital saying that Todd had had a sudden heart irregularity (atrial fibrillation with right bundle branch block), and had been admitted to the hospital so that his heart rate could be regulated and tests run. After five or six hours of intravenous medication Todd's heart returned back to normal. He was soon discharged from the hospital, but was kept on heart medicine for a while. He was told he no longer had mitral valve prolapse. His echocardiogram was normal.

During the few weeks prior to his arrhythmia, Todd had noted that he had intermittent pains in his chest and joints, felt very fatigued, had numerous twitches in his arms and legs, and had a few dry, itchy lesions on his torso and upper arms.

In the years following this episode Todd has been feeling well, with the exception of periods of insomnia, recurrent uncontrollable muscle twitching, occasional joint pain, and a sun rash he has had intermittently since he first developed Lyme disease. He entered medical school at Columbia in August 1990.

In December 1992, Todd came home for the holidays and told me of an experience he had in medical school, which made him feel that he had come full circle with Lyme disease. I suggested that he write down his experience for me to include in the book. This is what he wrote:

"In September of 1992, as part of my clerkship in pediatrics during my third year of medical school, I was assigned to spend three weeks at a suburban hospital in New Jersey. In driving through the countryside on the outskirts of the town, I was surprised at how many deer I saw—most open spaces seemed to have at least a few deer on them, and in some fields I saw veritable herds of ten to twenty deer. And indeed, there was lots of Lyme disease out there. As the wife of one of my teachers described it, practically every child in the neighborhood, including one of her own, had come down with Lyme. She said that many of the mothers were anxious that not enough was being done about the disease, and that the attitude of many physicians that Lyme was a simple curable illness did not seem to fit the reality of the disease.

"In my last week of my clerkship, I went with some of the pediatricians from the hospital to perform school physical examinations on the children at a local junior high school; the children were being screened en masse so they could be allowed to play sports. My third patient was a twelve-year-old boy who wanted to play soccer. He had a heparin lock in his left forearm for intravenous therapy. 'What's that for?' I asked, though I already had a more than sneaking suspicion what the answer was. 'I'm being treated for Lyme disease,' the boy said, explaining that he had become sick a few months before and had been started on intravenous antibiotics. The boy was very polite and wore glasses, and reminded me of the way I had probably seemed at that age. I could not help but break from my professional persona for a moment. 'When I was your age I had Lyme disease too,' I said. 'I had it when nobody knew what it was, when it was just being discovered.' We spoke for a minute about the various symptoms that we had each experienced. The boy was fit to play soccer, and I was glad to be able to approve him to play, as I remembered how I had not been able to; I was on and off crutches a lot back then. The boy had been treated early, and hopefully he was cured.''

Todd graduated from Columbia in May 1994 and is now doing his residency in emergency medicine.

EPILOGUE

One of the biggest needs in medical education today is to attract stu-
dents who are well-rounded human beings; who will be interested in peo-
ple and not just in the disease that affect them; who can comprehend the
reality of suffering and not just its symptoms; whose prescription pad
will not exclude the human touch and who will take into account not
just malevolent microorganisms but all the forces that exercise a down-
ward pull on the health of their patients.

NORMAN COUSINS, *HUMAN OPTIONS*[1]

Throughout the years I've been working on this book, I've constantly asked myself whether telling the story of Lyme disease is
worth the effort. Would anyone be interested in reading about my
own lonely journey with the illness? After all, Lyme disease is not a
potentially fatal disease like cancer or a fatal one like AIDS. The
reasons I pushed on with the book are many, but perhaps the thing
that compelled me most was the number of phone calls I received
over the years from people struggling with Lyme disease or other
undiagnosed illnesses. Whether they were calling on behalf of
their children or their spouses or themselves, they were desperate
to regain the normal routines of their lives. I could hear in their
voices the strain of living with chronic illness, and I suppose I
relived my own difficult search during these calls. Many were grateful to have someone listen to their story. If this book helps these
people and others like them to push for a diagnosis, or to feel less
alone, then it has been worth the effort.

The other audience I've hoped to reach with this book are
those who are living with someone who has a chronic illness, or
who are treating people who have undiagnosed illnesses. I want to
say to them: Be patient, try to see beyond the intensity of the person who is debilitated. People whose lives are disrupted by illness
are on a single-minded mission to regain their healthy bodies, as a
means to restoring their very selves. With their body in trouble,

their heart and soul and selfhood are thrown off kilter. The physician Richard J. Baron writes: "Illness obliges a loss of the taken-for-grantedness of things. . . . It is one's embodiment, one's capability of interacting with the universe, that is damaged in the event of illness. . . . When the effortless experiencing of embodiment is compromised, one is obliged to deal with one's body as obstacle. Illness is then understood as a loss of the integrity of body and self."[2]

I sympathize with the patient who acts anxious and sounds strident in the effort to feel well again. I have been there—frantic and exhausted. Just as I regained a calmer demeanor once I restored my health, many of these patients, once properly treated with antibiotics, again become their normal selves.

One thing I know for sure is that the scope of this disease is not fixed; it will be decades before a complete picture is established. Having talked with many, many victims over the years, I am struck by how Lyme disease never seems to act exactly the way it is supposed to, how each individual seems to respond differently to the spirochete. This idiosyncratic presentation challenges clinicians and researchers. Yet, against these odds, many dedicated, imaginative, and compassionate doctors have brought their expertise to bear on Lyme disease for many years. The amount that these doctors have learned about Lyme borreliosis represents an enormous feat given the relatively short time involved. During the last five years, ophthalmologists have written about the numerous eye problems of the disease. The heart complications have been more extensively described. Veterinarians have done a great deal of research on Lyme disease in horses, cattle, dogs, and cats. The Lyme disease research effort has been furthered not only by medical clinicians but also by workers in other disciplines, including entomology, epidemiology, public health, and microbiology. Dedicated scientists already have a vaccine for dogs and are working on further vaccines for other animals and humans. And, of course, many laypeople have contributed to Lyme disease awareness.

In some respects, though, the wheels of research seem to move surprisingly slowly. Some of the problems that were described to doctors by Lyme patients in the 1970s and 1980s are just now being studied or reported in the medical literature of the 1990s. Rashes other than the classic EM lesion, for example, were not fully acknowledged as part of the disease until practitioners in the field and other researchers described them, photographed them, and published their findings in the medical literature.

Similarly, in the early days of Lyme disease research, when patients described terrible fatigue and depression as part of the syndrome, they were often told by their physicians that these were by-products of living with chronic illness. Now, years later, many researchers agree with the patients' hunches, and think the fatigue and depression are due either to the persistence of the spirochete and its effect on the brain, or to an immune response triggered by the spirochete.

When I talked to various researchers in the late 1970s and early 1980s about psychiatric disturbances I felt were part of the disease—peculiar food cravings, anorexia, behavior changes, anxiety attacks, insomnia, irritability, and so on—no one seemed to be interested in pursuing research into these areas. A number of patients with such symptoms were even dismissed as neurotic and referred to psychiatric counselors. More than a few marriages and families broke apart under the strain of these misunderstood manifestations. Now these symptoms are acknowledged to be part of the clinical picture of Lyme disease in some cases.

I am particularly encouraged by the work of Dr. Fallon and Dr. Nields, who were the first in this country to publish research on the psychiatric symptoms of Lyme disease. Dr. Fallon is in the midst of conducting a study on the psychiatric complications of Lyme disease in children. His research could unlock a lot of mysteries about behavior changes in children that have eluded the mental health profession thus far. I have a hunch that some children in areas where Lyme disease is common who suddenly have medical, social, or academic trouble may well be helped by this research.

Pathologist Dr. Paul Duray has also helped to further our understanding of the complexity of the disease. By locating the spirochete in various body tissues, Dr. Duray has unequivocally documented that the spirochete can migrate to diverse parts of the body. In time, researchers will come to understand exactly what occurs in the human body after the spirochetes first enter the skin at the site of the tick bite. They will learn more about the damage that the spirochetes can inflict, and the immune reaction to the process.

The time lag between a patient's intuitions concerning a particular symptom and the symptom's entrance into the medical literature on Lyme disease is inevitable, and in some respects advisable, if stringent standards of scientific research are to be upheld. Still, the sluggishness of scientific publication has some adverse effects. As patients become more educated and aware, they become more frustrated by this time lag between the "street knowledge" and the published research becoming known by doctors all over the country.

While the dispute among physicians about treatment continues, a great number of the patients who are chronically afflicted, some with serious complications, find it difficult to cope with the unknowns of the disease. They are scared by their experience—and, as Dr. Gerald Weissmann of New York University School of Medicine puts it, "When we become more afraid of Lyme disease, we may be moved to greater action."[3] For these patients, the support groups that have sprung up all over the country are lifelines. They provide a forum for patients to meet with others and share their concerns; many groups publish newsletters that include articles by doctors, case histories, news of current research and conferences, and information on where to seek help. I feel that support groups play a vital role. They keep patients up-to-date about the disease and they give them hope. In fact, I now believe in the politics of numbers: Research progress will accelerate as more and more patients band together for increased attention, compassion, funding, and research.

As Dr. Anthony Komaroff, in speaking of patients with chronic fatigue syndrome, said in 1990: "There is no doubt that patients themselves have done more than any other group to change the medical world's perception and understanding of this illness. Four years ago they were alone. Today they can look forward to increasing help from doctors, researchers and their own support groups."[4]

Indeed, as the researchers Alan G. Barbour and Durland Fish have pointed out, one of the significant things about Lyme disease is that it "shows that a newly recognized disease may be defined as much by individuals and groups outside of academic and governmental institutions as by those within them." As a result of this, "a mix of opinion has formed about what Lyme disease is and how it should be managed."[5]

The preponderance of support groups and of patients acting individually as their own advocates is symptomatic of a health care profession that has become so stressed and fractured that the opportunity for a successful doctor-patient relationship has been compromised. In doing research for this book, I have read many accounts of doctors who question the direction in which medicine is heading. These physicians feel that the technology introduced in recent decades, while offering tremendous benefits, has eroded the art of medicine, sapping the profession of some of its humanity. In his book *Doctors, Patients and Placebos,* Dr. Howard M. Spiro explains the modern dilemma of physicians this way: "The more medical science advances, the more the art of medicine seems to decline. . . . The more medical practice does for disease, the less physicians seem to do for patients. . . . Truth in medicine has moved from what the patient says to what the physician finds."[6] The dialogue between the doctor and the patient often focuses on the interpretation of diagnostic technology, leaving little time for discussing how the patient feels. As Dr. Richard J. Baron wrote, "We must learn to hear our patients as well as their breath sounds; after all, what are we listening for?"[7]

Eric Cassell, M.D., in an article entitled "The Nature of Suffering and the Goals of Medicine," also reminds doctors of the importance of empathy in the treatment process: "The relief of suffering and the cure of disease must be seen as twin obligations of a medical profession that is truly dedicated to the care of the sick. Physicians' failure to understand the nature of suffering can result in medical intervention that (though technically adequate) not only fails to relieve suffering but becomes a source of suffering itself."[8]

Doctors learn to verbally reduce a patient to the most basic possible description when writing case histories. In his book *The Man Who Mistook His Wife for a Hat,* Dr. Oliver Sacks tells of this tendency to distance and dehumanize patients: "There is no 'subject' in a narrow case history; modern case histories allude to the subject in a cursory phrase ('a trisomic albino female of 21'), which could as well apply to a rat as a human being. To restore the human subject at the centre—the suffering, afflicted, fighting, human subject—we must deepen a case history to a narrative or tale; only then do we have a 'who' as well as a 'what,' a real person, a patient, in relation to disease—in relation to the physical."[9]

The mobility of modern civilization has contributed to the depersonalization of medicine. A few generations ago, people were apt to have a single general practitioner for the greater part of their lifetime. Today, both doctors and patients are less likely to stay in one locale for a long time. As a result there is less continuity of care, and doctors and patients are less able to form a healthy, trusting relationship.

Thirty years ago Dr. Selig Greenberg wrote, "Specialization has greatly improved the quality of medical care, but it also has made it enormously more costly and has tended to disperse responsibility for the patient."[10] Specialization may hinder doctors from seeing the full scope of Lyme disease. A rheumatologist, for example, might know a great deal about joint complications, but not be as knowledgeable about or open to discussing the psychological or ophthalmological aspects of the disease.

There are still many unanswered questions about the disease caused by the *Borrelia burgdorferi* spirochete, and an all-out offensive against the illness must be waged. The sooner we understand the mechanisms of Lyme disease and how to diagnose and effectively treat it, the lower the costs will be of helping those afflicted with it to regain their health. The number of misdiagnosed patients who must move from doctor to doctor to find help will then be diminished considerably.

If inadequate antibiotics given early in the disease abort the antibody response, then might there be an accumulating number of patients out there who test negative and are excluded from the diagnosis and treatment of Lyme disease when they have chronic symptoms triggered by their inadequately treated infection?

What role do concurrent infections with other *Ixodes* tick–borne infections—for example, babesiosis and ehrlichiosis—have on the symptoms and tests for Lyme disease?

A combination of preventive measures against the tick should be undertaken. These include personal protective measures: knowing how to identify the tick, protectively dressing when in endemic areas, frequently checking for ticks on family and pets, carefully using repellents and (in some situations, and with precise targeting) pesticides, controlling rodents around houses, and mowing grass and clearing leaves and brush. Strategic fencing for deer control is being tried by some homeowners and may prove to be effective.

Patients suffering from Lyme disease should be studied over the span of many years, ideally for a lifetime. Doctors in endemic areas should publish any new findings about Lyme disease symptomatology and treatment. At the 1994 Lyme Disease Conference in Stamford, Dr. Martina Ziska, medical director of the Lyme Disease Foundation, discussed the death of Dr. Paul Lavoie, which saddened the Lyme disease community. Dr. Ziska remarked that it was regrettable that Dr. Lavoie had not been able to publish his knowledge and insight about his Lyme patients. "During almost twenty years of practice, seeing virtually hundreds of Lyme patients, he has gathered the invaluable information about the clinical course, diagnosis, and treatment response to the disease, which will never be tested by others, because, unless published, this information cannot be shared with the medical community." She told the researchers and clinicians in the audience: "This is the first step which has to be done: carefully, but truthfully, document what you see. . . . Knowledge, however partial, should replace controversies."[11]

Major medical centers throughout the country, which see patients from a large geographic pool, have a great capacity to track overall trends in this disease. But these research centers might perhaps do more long-term, comprehensive studies in communities where the disease is endemic. I think such studies will yield many answers about Lyme disease. Whether highly focused or worldwide, they might also reveal that the spirochete is the culprit (or a triggering factor) in other illnesses that we have not yet fully explained.

I've been asking questions about Lyme disease for years now, and I imagine I always will. I pose them to myself; I share hunches with friends in the Lyme disease community and with my children. People ask questions of me; I continue to ask my doctors questions. There are those within the medical community who would prefer it if laypeople such as myself would stop second-guessing, would stop saying, What if . . . ? How about . . . ? Do you think there's a connection between . . . ? Have you studied . . . ? But until more is known about Lyme disease, the questions are going to keep coming. That's human nature.

I may have been one of the first to start asking questions back in the mid-1970s, but since then I've been joined by a chorus of voices from the field, most of them belonging to women. The vast majority of phone calls and letters I've received about Lyme disease are from women. A number of women have started support groups and newsletters. I think the women's role in Lyme disease is part of a broader trend in our culture; more women are becoming whistle-blowers and patient advocates about health issues. And these women have tremendous power, for they are often driven by a primal instinct to protect their young.

Perhaps the intuition traditionally associated with woman plays a role in her sensitivity to the condition of those around her; women are intuitively responsive to the health of their families. In fact, over their lifetimes women are often communicators and caregivers for three generations. A woman cares for herself and her spouse, her children, her aging parents, and sometimes her grandchildren. I wonder if sometimes just the sheer number of medical concerns that women discuss with their doctors on others' behalf makes some doctors consider them neurotic or anxious.

But woman's role as advocate for her spouse and family may be starting to change, as the popular culture begins to encourage a greater degree of emotional expressiveness in men. For example, in the 1990s, I've noticed more and more media stories that look at the different ways in which men and women approach their health problems. These reports touch upon how men in our culture tend to have been raised to have a stiff upper lip, not to show emotion. Men tend to deny illness and put off getting medical attention, seeing illness—whether physical or psychological—as a sign of weakness. This is unfortunate, because often seeking outside help when you are in a situation that you feel is more than you can handle alone is the reasonable thing to do.

Seeking outside help was very important to me. A competent, impartial professional can be a lifesaver. In my own experience I have encountered people who are unwilling to reach out for a helping hand for their problems, and as a consequence, they have had a very difficult time.

I have learned through my involvement with Lyme disease that there are many ill people in this country who live in a difficult limbo because their conditions have not been definitely diagnosed. These can be people in the early stages of multiple sclerosis, lupus, ALS, Alzheimer's, and so on, or sick with illnesses that the medical profession has not yet described. These difficult-to-diagnose patients should be evaluated carefully, not written off as hypochondriacal.

In addition, patients with difficult-to-diagnose symptoms who think that they might have Lyme disease should be carefully worked up by their physicians to make sure that all other possibilities are ruled out. It would be a tragedy if a cancer or other serious illness was overlooked in a patient who was attributing too many of his or her symptoms to Lyme disease.

It seems to me that there must be a sensible balance between the needs of the patient and the needs of the medical profession in caring for those patients. Of course scientific standards must not be compromised in the process. Medical protocols are there for the protection of the doctor and the patient. Checks and balances must be the order. Drugs, tests, and vaccines must be evaluated carefully.

But perhaps above all, as the story of Lyme disease has taught us, the most important thing is for doctors and patients to simply *listen* to each other.

AFTERWORD

In any effort to understand what lies ahead, as much as what lies behind, the role of infectious disease cannot properly be left out of consideration. Ingenuity, knowledge, and organization alter but cannot cancel humanity's vulnerability to invasion by parasitic forms of life. Infectious disease, which antedated the emergence of humankind, will last as long as humanity itself, and will surely remain, as it has been hitherto, one of the fundamental parameters and determinants of human history.

WILLIAM H. MCNEILL, *PLAGUES AND PEOPLES*[1]

The Widening Circle reports the triumph of one woman's uphill battle to find a diagnosis for the multiplicity of puzzling signs and symptoms that afflicted her family and neighbors. Despite sickness with unexplained debilitating symptoms and despite the glib dismissals of doctors who accused her of being a hypochondriac, Polly Murray persisted. After telling her to stop searching for a diagnosis, one doctor quipped, "I suppose you think this is some new disease!" Another doctor advised, "Forget this fruitless search for a label . . . for a disease that exists most likely only in your mind." Patients throughout the world are benefiting from the fact that Polly Murray did not listen to these doctors. By means of her carefully recorded observations and clear, convincing epidemiologic arguments, Polly Murray succeeded in finally galvanizing a medical community to action.

The Widening Circle documents how one quiet, reserved woman shaped medical history. This contemplative woman—artist, mother, and nature lover—would certainly not have chosen to be the initiator of a medical controversy had she not been called upon by circumstances to do so. Through compelling personal tales of her own detective work and her interactions with doctors, Polly Murray has written an absorbing account of medicine at its worst and at its best. Her book not only reflects her probing mind, her persistent inquisitiveness, and her mastery of a complex medical field but also conveys important larger messages. This invaluable document will educate students, historians, patients, doctors, and scientists about a key period in the annals of medicine. While *The Widening Circle* raises unsettling questions about the fragmented state of contemporary medical care, it also points toward the future by raising intriguing questions about the relationship between Lyme disease and other neurologic and medical illnesses. Furthermore, this book provides a model for how a collaborative and respectful relationship between doctor and patient can not only create the context for healing but also further the progress of medical science.

—BRIAN A. FALLON, M.D.,
director of the Lyme Disease Program
at the New York State Psychiatric Institute,
and assistant professor of clinical psychiatry
at Columbia University

NOTES

PART ONE: FOCUSING ON LYME DISEASE
1. June Goodfield, *An Imagined World: A Story of Scientific Discovery* (New York: Harper & Row, 1981), p. 23.

CHAPTER 2: ART AND MEDICINE
1. Hans Zinsser, *Rats, Lice and History* (Boston: Little, Brown & Co., 1935), pp. 21–22.

CHAPTER 3: GOOD TIMES, BAD TIMES
1. Robert Massie, Suzanne Massie, and Robert Massie, Jr., *Journey* (New York: Alfred A. Knopf, 1973), p. 408.

CHAPTER 4: IN THE THROES OF ILLNESS
1. Hans Zinsser, *Rats, Lice and History* (Boston: Little, Brown & Co., 1935), pp. 235–36.

CHAPTER 5: "IT'S ALL IN YOUR HEAD"
1. Norman Cousins, *The Healing Heart* (New York: Norton, 1983), p. 112.

CHAPTER 6: CONFRONTATIONS
1. Henrietta Aladjem, *The Sun Is My Enemy* (Englewood Cliffs, N.J.: Prentice Hall, 1972).
2. Edmund L. Dubois, *Lupus Erythematosus*, 2nd ed. (Los Angeles: University of Southern California Press, 1974).
3. Aladjem, op. cit., p. 127.
4. A. M. Harvey et al., "Systemic Lupus Erythematosus: Review of the Literature and Clinical Analysis of 138 Cases," *Medicine* (December 1954) 33:291–437. (Dubois, op. cit., p. 525. Bibliography, p. 666.)
5. C. L. Thomas (ed.), *Taber's Cyclopedic Medical Dictionary*, 12th ed. (Philadelphia: F. A. Davis Company, 1973), p. T-64.

CHAPTER 7: FINDING AN ALLY
1. René Dubos, *Man Adapting* (New Haven, Conn.: Yale University Press, 1965), p. 409.
2. Henrietta Aladjem, *The Sun Is My Enemy* (Englewood Cliffs, N.J.: Prentice Hall, 1972), pp. 133–34.

CHAPTER 8: CHAOS
1. *The Merck Manual*, 12th ed. (Rahway, N.J.: Merck Sharpe and Dohme Research Laboratories, 1972), p. 1470.

CHAPTER 9: THE TURNING POINT

1. Quoted by Berton Roueché in *Eleven Blue Men and Other Narratives of Medical Detection* (Boston: Little, Brown & Co., 1947), title page.

CHAPTER 10: THE YALE INVESTIGATION

1. Lewis Thomas, *The Lives of a Cell: Notes of a Biology Watcher* (New York: Bantam Books, 1974), p. 96.

CHAPTER 11: MEDIA BLITZ

1. Boyce Rensberger, "A New Type of Arthritis Found in Lyme," *The New York Times,* July 18, 1976, pp. 1, 39.
2. Joel Lang, "Catching the Bug," *Northeast Magazine (The Hartford Courant),* May 11, 1986, pp. 8, 10.
3. Ann Baldelli, "Persistent Mothers Sped Ailment's Discovery," *The Day* (New London, Conn.), Nov. 20, 1994, pp. 1, 12.
4. Judith Mensch, "Lyme Disease," *Maryland Medical Journal,* vol. 34 (July 1985), pp. 691–92.
5. Lang, op. cit., p. 11.
6. Baldelli, op. cit., p. 1.
7. W. E. Mast and W. M. Burrows, "Erythema Chronicum Migrans in the United States," *Journal of the American Medical Association,* vol. 236 (1976), pp. 859–60; W. E. Mast and W. M. Burrows, "Erythema Chronicum Migrans and 'Lyme Arthritis' " (letter to the editor), *Journal of the American Medical Association,* vol. 236 (1976), p. 2392.
8. A. Afzelius, "Report to Verhandlungen der Dermatologischen Gesellschaft zu Stockholm, October 1909," *Archiv fur Dermatologie und Syphilis* 1910; 101:404.
9. R. J. Scrimenti, "Erythema chronicum migrans," *Archives of Dermatology* 1970; 102:104–105.
10. Gerald W. Hazard, Katherine Leland, and Herbert O. Mathewson, "Letter to the Editor," *Journal of the American Medical Association,* vol. 236 (1976), p. 2392.

CHAPTER 12: THE FALL OF 1976

1. Geddes Smith, *Plague on Us* (New York: The Commonwealth Fund; London: Humphrey Milford, Oxford University Press, 1943), p. 77.

CHAPTER 13: EXPLAINING THE RIDDLE: 1977–1983

1. Allen C. Steere, Stephen E. Malawista, David R. Snydman et al., "Lyme Arthritis: An Epidemic of Oligoarthritis in Children and Adults in Three Connecticut Communities," *Arthritis and Rheumatism,* vol. 19 (1977), pp. 7–17.
2. Elisabeth Keiffer, "Women in Action: Mrs. Murray's Mystery Disease," *Good Housekeeping,* March 1977, pp. 80–88.

3. Allen C. Steere and Stephen E. Malawista, "Cases of Lyme Disease in the United States: Locations Correlated with Distribution of *Ixodes dammini,*" *Annals of Internal Medicine,* vol. 91 (1979), p. 730.

4. George E. Ehrlich, "This Is the Decade That Is: Rheumatology," *Journal of the American Medical Association,* vol. 243 (1980), p. 2213.

5. Rachel Carson, *Silent Spring* (Boston: Houghton Mifflin, 1962), p. 189.

6. Gerald Adler, "Current Concepts in Psychiatry: The Physician and the Hypochondriacal Patient," *New England Journal of Medicine,* vol. 304 (June 4, 1981), pp. 1394–96.

7. Polly Murray, "The Hypochondriacal Patient" (letter to the editor), *New England Journal of Medicine,* vol. 305 (Oct. 8, 1981), p. 895.

8. Mary Nelson, "The Doctor of Lyme Disease," *Newsday,* Nov. 9, 1988.

9. Willy Burgdorfer, "Ticks: An Ever Increasing Public Health Menace," *The Connecticut Agricultural Experiment Station Bulletin 822* (December 1984), p. 5.

10. Joel Lang, "Catching the Bug," *Northeast Magazine (The Hartford Courant),* May 11, 1986, p. 15.

11. Willy Burgdorfer et al., "Lyme Disease: A Tick-Borne Spirochetosis?" *Science,* June 18, 1982; 216:1317–19.

12. Alfred Buchwald, "Ein Fall von diffuser idiopathischer Haut-Atrophie," *Arch Dermatol Syph* 1883, vol. 10, pp. 553–56.

13. A. Afzelius, "Report to Verhandlungen der Dermatologischen Gesellschaft zu Stockholm October 1909," *Archives fur Dermatologie und Syphilis,* vol. 101 (1910), p. 404.

14. B. Lipschütz, "Weiterer Beitrag zur Kenntnis des 'Erythema chronicum migrans,' " *Archives fur Dermatologie und Syphilis,* vol. 143 (1923), pp. 365–74.

15. S. Hellerström, "Erythema Chronicum Migrans with Meningitis," *Southern Medical Journal,* vol. 43 (1950), pp. 330–35.

16. E. Hollström, "Successful Treatment of Erythema Chronicum Migrans Afzelius," *Acta Dermato-Venereologica,* vol. 31 (1951), pp. 235–89.

17. E. Binder et al., "Experimentelle Ubertragung des Erythema Chronicum Migrans von Mensch zu Mensch," *Hautarzt,* vol. 6 (1955), pp. 494–96.

18. C. E. Sonck, "Erythema Chronicum Migrans with Multiple Lesions," *Acta Dermato-Venereologica,* vol. 45 (1965), pp. 34–36.

19. Allen C. Steere et al., "The Spirochetal Etiology of Lyme Disease," *New England Journal of Medicine,* vol. 308 (March 31, 1983), pp. 733–40; Jorge Benach et al., "Spirochetes Isolated from the Blood of Two Patients with Lyme Disease," *New England Journal of Medicine,* vol. 308 (March 31, 1983), pp. 740–42.

20. Edward Harris, Jr., "Lyme Disease—Success for Academia and the Community," *New England Journal of Medicine,* vol. 308 (March 31, 1983), pp. 773–75.

PART II: THE SCOPE BROADENS

1. Rudolf Ackermann, Peter Hörstrup, and Roger Schmidt, "Tick-Borne Meningopolyneuritis (Garin-Bujadoux, Bannwarth)," paper delivered at Lyme Disease First International Symposium. Published in *Yale Journal of Biology and Medicine,* 1984, p. 35.

CHAPTER 14: THE 1980S: GETTING THE WORD OUT

1. Arthritis Foundation, Connecticut Chapter, "Know About Lyme Disease" (Wethersfield, Conn., 1986).

2. Jeffrey A. Millstein, Ph.D., "LymeCite: A Database of Citations on Lyme disease, *Borrelia burgdorferi,* and vectors of *B. burgdorferi.*" Unpublished (1994). Belmont Research, 84 Sherman St., Cambridge, Mass. 02140. As of April 1995, Dr. Millstein estimates that over 4,000 papers related to Lyme disease have been written.

3. Paul B. Aronowitz, "A Connecticut Housewife in Francis Bacon's Court: Polly Murray and Lyme Disease," *The Pharos,* vol. 52, no. 4 (fall 1989), pp. 9–12.

4. John Updike, "Wildlife," *Esquire,* August 1987, pp. 62–66.

5. H. Horst, ed., *Einheimische Zeckenborreliose (Lyme-Krankheit) bei Mensch und Tier.* (Lüneburg, West Germany: Perimed Fachbuch-Verl.-Ges., 1991), "A Brief Account of the Mysterious Illness in Lyme, Connecticut, and Neighboring Towns," pp. 11–14; Derrick Brewerton, *All About Arthritis, Past, Present, Future* (Cambridge, Mass.: Harvard University Press, 1992), pp. 65–67, 192.

6. Polly Murray, guest editorial, *Connecticut Medicine,* vol. 53, no. 6 (June 1989), p. 365.

7. C. Lennhoff, "Spirochaetes in Aetiologically Obscure Diseases," *Acta Dermato-Venereologica,* vol. 28 (1948), pp. 295–324.

8. Bonnie Bennett. Personal observations of a group of patients with relapsing fever. Letter written Dec. 28, 1984; personal conversation, Nov. 10, 1984. James H. Katzell, "Case 1: Unexpected Presentations of Lyme Borreliosis (LB) in Northern California," poster presentation at the Fourth International Conference on Lyme Borreliosis, Stockholm, Sweden, June 18–21, 1990. Poster W/TH-P-89, p. 125. (In Katzell's "Case 1," a woman was diagnosed with Graves' disease; she also had positive blood tests for Lyme disease. She refused medication for Graves' disease; however, she did have two weeks of intravenous ceftriaxone followed by three months of doxycycline for her Lyme disease. The therapy cured her Graves' disease. One year later she was still normal. Said Katzell: "This may add endocrinopathies . . . to the amplifying spectrum of problems associated with Lyme borreliosis.")

CHAPTER 15: THE POLITICS OF LYME DISEASE

1. Norman Cousins, *Anatomy of an Illness* (New York: Bantam Books, 1981), pp. 121, 129–30.
2. I would like to thank Gloria Wenk for sending me a copy of the petition.

CHAPTER 16: REPORTING

1. René Dubos, *Mirage of Health: Utopias, Progress, and Biological Change* (New York: Harper & Row, 1959), pp. 203–204.
2. Carl Brenner, "Lyme Disease: Asking the Right Questions," *Science,* vol. 257 (1992), pp. 1845–47.
3. Stephen B. Thacker, Keewhan Choi, and Philip S. Brachman, "The Surveillance of Infectious Diseases," *Journal of the American Medical Association,* vol. 249 (1983), pp. 1181, 1182.
4. "Emerging Infectious Diseases: Lyme Disease—United States, 1991–1992," *CDC Morbidity and Mortality Weekly Report,* vol. 42, no. 18, (May 14, 1993), pp. 345–348.
5. *CDC Morbidity and Mortality Weekly Report* (June 23, 1995), vol. 44, no. 24, pp. 459–62.

CHAPTER 17: THE DIAGNOSIS

1. Thomas S. Kuhn, *The Structure of Scientific Revolutions,* 2nd ed. (Chicago: University of Chicago Press, 1970), p. 68.
2. Sam R. Telford III and Andrew Spielman, "Origins of Lyme Disease in North America," Poster #303, Fifth International Conference on Lyme Borreliosis, Arlington, Virginia, May 30–June 2, 1992.
3. David H. Persing et al., "Detection of *Borrelia burgdorferi* DNA in Museum Specimens of *Peromyscus Leucopus,* "Poster #284, Fifth International Conference on Lyme Borreliosis, Arlington, Virginia, May 30–June 2, 1992.
4. David H. Persing et al., "Addressing the Antiquity of Lyme Disease in the United States: Detection of *B. burgdorferi*–like DNA in Museum Specimens of *Ixodes dammini,* "paper presented at the Fourth International Conference on Lyme Borreliosis, Stockholm, Sweden, June 18–21, 1990.
5. David H. Persing et al., "Detection of *Borrelia burgdorferi* DNA in Museum Specimens of *Ixodes dammini* Ticks," *Science,* vol. 249 (1990), p. 1423.
6. Mary Nelson, "The Doctor of Lyme Disease," *Newsday,* Nov. 9, 1988, p. 5.
7. Ingrid Gamstorp, "Lyme Borreliosis from a Patient's Viewpoint," *Scandinavian Journal of Infectious Diseases,* vol. 77 (1991), suppl. pp. 15–16. This transcription is from my tape recording of Ingrid Gamstorp's lecture at the Fourth International Conference on Lyme Borreliosis, Stockholm, Sweden, June 18–21, 1990.
8. Stuart Beeber, "Lyme Disease: A Pediatrician's Point of View," *New York Medical Quarterly,* vol. 5, no. 3 (1985), p. 99.

9. James H. Oliver et al., "Conspecificity of the Ticks *Ixodes scapularis* and *I. dammini (Acari: Ixodidae)*," *Journal of Medical Entomology*, vol. 30 (1993), pp. 54–63.

10. Edwin J. Masters, "Family Practice Diagnosis and Treatment in a Non-endemic Area," paper delivered at the Lyme Disease 1992 State of the Art Conference, Stamford, Conn., April 11, 1992.

11. Chuck Lay, "The Lyme Bomb," *Today's Farmer*, March 1993, p. 8.

12. Chuck Lay, "As Lyme Disease Debate Rages, More and More People Are Diagnosed," *Today's Farmer*, March 1993, p. 2.

13. Personal communication to Polly Murray, from David Dennis of the Centers for Disease Control, Fort Collins, Col., Dec. 7, 1994.

14. Dorothy Feir et al., "Evidence Supporting the Presence of *Borrelia burgdorferi* in Missouri," *American Journal of Tropical Medicine and Hygiene*, vol. 51, no. 4 (1994), pp. 475–82.

15. Steven W. Luger and E. Krauss, "Serologic Test for Lyme Disease: Interlaboratory Variability," *Archives of Internal Medicine*, vol. 150, no. 4 (1990), pp. 761–63. (lecture, Lyme Public Hall, May 30, 1991.) See also Lori Bakken et al., "The Reproducibility and Accuracy of 45 Laboratories Participating in a Lyme Disease Serological Proficiency Program," Poster #90, Fifth International Conference on Lyme Borreliosis, Arlington, Virginia, May 30–June 2, 1992.

16. James J. Nocton et al., "Detection of *Borrelia burgdorferi* DNA by Polymerase Chain Reaction in Synovial Fluid from Patients with Lyme Arthritis," *New England Journal of Medicine*, vol. 330 (January 27, 1994), pp. 229–34.

17. Allen C. Steere et al., "The Overdiagnosis of Lyme Disease," *Journal of the American Medical Association*, vol. 269 (1993), pp. 1812–16.

18. Joseph J. Burrascano, Jr., "Overdiagnosis of Lyme Disease" (letter to the editor), *Journal of the American Medical Association*, vol. 270 (1993), p. 2682.

19. Martha Kramer, "The Overdiagnosis of Lyme Disease" (letter to the editor), *Journal of the American Medical Association*, vol. 270 (1993), p. 2683.

20. Louis Reik, Willy Burgdorfer, and James O. Donaldson, "Neurologic Abnormalities of Lyme Disease," *Medicine*, vol. 58 (1979), pp. 281–94.

21. Alix Kerr, "The Alarming New Reach of Lyme Disease," *Physician's Weekly*, vol. 2, no. 8 (Dec. 9, 1985).

22. Louis Reik, Willy Burgdorfer, and James O. Donaldson, "Neurologic Abnormalities in Lyme Disease Without Erythema Chronicum Migrans," *American Journal of Medicine*, vol. 81 (1986), pp. 73–78.

23. Alan MacDonald, "*Borrelia* in the Brains of Patients Dying with Dementia" (letter to the editor), *Journal of the American Medical Association*, vol. 256 (1986), p. 2195.

24.   Andrew R. Pachner and Allen C. Steere, "CNS Manifestations of Third Stage Lyme Disease." *Zentralblatt für Bakteriologie, Mikrobiologie und Hygiene* vol. 263 (1986), p. 302.

25.   G. T. Stiernstedt et al., "Clinical Manifestations and Diagnosis of Neuroborreliosis," *Annals of the New York Academy of Science,* vol. 539 (1988), pp. 48–49, 51.

26.   Eric Logigian, Richard F. Kaplan, and Allen Steere, "Chronic Neurologic Manifestations of Lyme Disease," *New England Journal of Medicine,* vol. 323 (1990), pp. 1438–43.

27.   Ilona S. Szer, Elise Taylor, and Allen C. Steere, "The Long-Term Course of Lyme Arthritis in Children," *New England Journal of Medicine,* vol. 325 (1991), p. 159.

28.   Brian A. Fallon, "Psychiatric Presentations of Lyme Borreliosis," paper presented at the Lyme Disease 1992 State of the Art Conference, Stamford, Conn., April 11, 1992.

29.   Brian A. Fallon and Jenifer A. Nields, "Psychiatric Manifestations of Lyme Borreliosis (LB): Part I, A Controlled Study of Major Depression," abstract presented at the Fifth International Conference on Lyme Borreliosis, Arlington, Virginia, May 30–June 2, 1992.

30.   Brian A. Fallon, Jenifer A. Nields, Joseph J. Burrascano, Kenneth Liegner, Donato DelBene, and Michael R. Liebowitz, "The Neuropsychiatric Manifestations of Lyme Borreliosis," *Psychiatric Quarterly,* vol. 63, no. 1 (spring 1998), pp. 95–117.

31.   Alan B. MacDonald, "Human Fetal Borreliosis, Toxemia of Pregnancy and Fetal Death." *Zentralblatt für Bakteriologie, Mikrobiologie und Hygiene: vol.* 263 (1986), pp. 189–200.

32.   P. A. Schlesinger et al., "Maternal–Fetal Transmission of the Lyme Disease Spirochete *Borrelia burgdorferi,"Annals of Internal Medicine,* vol. 103 (1985), pp. 76–78.

33.   L. E. Markowitz et al., "Lyme Disease During Pregnancy," *Journal of the American Medical Association,* vol. 255 (1986), 3394–96.

34.   Steven W. Luger, "Active Lyme Borreliosis in Pregnancy–Outcomes of Six Cases with Stage 1, Stage 2, and Stage 3 Disease," paper delivered at the Fourth International Conference on Lyme Borreliosis (Abstract TU-L-16), Stockholm, Sweden, June 1990. Personal communication, December 1994. See also Klaus Weber et al., *"Borrelia burgdorferi* in a Newborn Despite Oral Penicillin for Lyme Borreliosis During Pregnancy," *Pediatric Infectious Disease Journal,* vol. 7 (1988), pp. 286–89.

35.   C. Meier et al., "Meningoradiculoneuritis Mimicking Vertebral Disc Herniation: A 'Neurosurgical' Complication of Lyme-Borreliosis," *Acta Neurochirurgica,* vol. 98 (1989), pp. 42–46.

36.   Erich Schmutzhard, Iraj Mohsenipour, and Gerold Stanek, "Sciatica

and Antibodies to Borrelia Burgdorferi: A Coincidence?'' Poster #W/TH-P-62, Fourth International Conference on Lyme Borreliosis, Stockholm, Sweden, June 18–21, 1990, p. 98.

37. J. Faller, F. Thompson, and W. Hamilton, "Foot and Ankle Disorders Resulting from Lyme Disease," *Foot and Ankle,* vol. 11 (February 1991), pp. 236–38.

38. Carl Brenner, Statement for the Hearing Before the Committee on Labor and Human Resources, U.S. Senate, Aug. 5, 1993.

39. Paul Lavoie, "Acrodermatitis Chronica Atrophicans with Antecedent Lyme disease in a Californian: Case Report," *Zentralblatt für Bakteriologie, Mikrobiologie und Hygiene,* vol. 263 (1986), pp. 262–65.

40. Oscar Felsenfeld, *Borrelia: Strains, Vectors, Human and Animal Borreliosis* (St. Louis, Mo.: Warren H. Green, 1971), pp. 95, 102.

41. Denise Lang, with Derrick DeSilva, Jr., *Coping with Lyme Disease: A Practical Guide to Dealing with Diagnosis and Treatment* (New York: Henry Holt, 1993), p. 118.

42. Anthony L. Komaroff, " 'Minor' Illness Symptoms: The Magnitude of Their Burden and of Our Ignorance," *Archives of Internal Medicine,* vol. 150 (1990), p. 1587.

43. Burton A. Waisbren et al., *"Borrelia burgdorferi* Antibodies and Amyotrophic Lateral Sclerosis," *The Lancet,* vol. 2 (1987): pp. 332, 333. See also J. J. Halperin et al., "Immunologic Reactivity Against *Borrelia burgdorferi* in Patients with Motor Neuron Disease," *Archives of Neurology,* vol. 47 (1990), pp. 586–94.

44. Louis Reik, Jr., *Lyme Disease and the Nervous System* (New York: Thieme Medical Publishers, 1991), p. 91.

45. Betsy A. Lehman, "For Lupus, a Better Outlook," *The Boston Globe,* August 27, 1990, pp. 25, 29.

46. Suzanne Condon, "Lupus and the Environment," Bureau of Environmental Health Assessment, Mass. Department of Public Health, Boston, *Lupus News,* The Lupus Foundation of America, 1993, vol. 13, no. 3, p. 8.

47. Paul E. Lavoie, Lilly Kong, and Wayne Hogrefe, *"Borrelia burgdorferi* DNA in the Blood of Three SLE Patients," abstract presented at the Fifth International Conference on Lyme Borreliosis, Arlington, Virginia, May 30–June 2, 1992.

48. Edmund L. Dubois, ed., *Lupus Erythematosus,* 2nd ed. (Los Angeles: University of Southern California Press, 1974), pp. 10, 412.

49. *Physicians' Desk Reference,* 49th ed. (Montville, N.J.: Medical Economics Data Production Co., 1995) p. 1879.

50. Bonnie Bennett. Conversation at my home, Nov. 10, 1984.

51. William Boly, "Raggedy Ann Town," *Hippocrates,* July–August 1987, p.

40; Linda Williams, "Stalking a Shadowy Assailant," *Time,* May 14, 1990, p. 66.

52. Dedra Buchwald et al., "A Chronic Illness Characterized by Fatigue, Neurologic and Immunologic Disorders, and Active Human Herpesvirus Type 6 Infection," *Annals of Internal Medicine,* vol. 116 (1992), pp. 103–113.

53. Patricia K. Coyle and Lauren Krupp, *"Borrelia burgdorferi* Infection in the Chronic Fatigue Syndrome," *Annals of Neurology,* vol. 28 (1990), pp. 243–44.

54. Kenneth B. Liegner, "Evidence for Borrelial Etiology and Pathogenesis in a Series of Patients Carrying a Diagnosis of Multiple Sclerosis," abstract of paper presented at the International Northwestern Conference on Diseases in Nature Communicable to Man, Hamilton, Montana, Aug. 12–15, 1990.

CHAPTER 18: TREATMENT, CURRENT CONTROVERSIES

1. Quoted by Oliver Sacks, *A Leg to Stand On* (New York: Simon & Schuster, 1984), p. 203.

2. W. E. Mast and W. M. Burrows, "Erythema Chronicum Migrans and 'Lyme Arthritis' " (letter to the editor), *Journal of the American Medical Association,* vol. 236 (1976), p. 2392.

3. Allen C. Steere et al., "Antibiotic Therapy in Lyme Disease," *Annals of Internal Medicine,* vol. 93 (1980), pp. 1–8.

4. Peter C. Welch, "Lyme Disease in Private Medical Practice," *New York Medical Quarterly,* vol. 5, no. 3 (1985), p. 93.

5. Alix Kerr, "The Alarming New Reach of Lyme Disease," *Physicians' Weekly,* Dec. 9, 1985.

6. V. Preac-Mursic et al., "Survival of *Borrelia burgdorferi* in Antibiotically Treated Patients with Lyme Borreliosis," *Infection,* vol. 17, no. 6 (1989), pp. 355–59.

7. Foreword to Henrietta Aladjem, *The Sun Is My Enemy,* paperback edition (Boston: Beacon Press, 1976), p. x.

8. David B. Bingham, "Lyme Disease," in *When Doctors Get Sick,* Harvey Mandell and Howard Spiro, eds. (New York and London: Plenum Medical Book Co., 1987), pp. 71–77.

9. Steven W. Luger, lecture, Lyme Public Hall, May 30, 1991.

10. Joseph J. Burrascano, Jr. Personal story told at the Lyme Disease 1992 State of the Art Conference, Stamford, Conn.

11. Marcia Barinaga, "Furor at Lyme Disease Conference," *Science,* vol. 256 (1992), p. 1384.

12. Carl Brenner, "Lyme Disease: Asking the Right Questions," *Science,* vol. 257 (1992), pp. 1845–47.

13. *The Lyme Times* (publication of the Lyme Disease Resource Center), vol. 3, no. 2 (fall 1992), p. 49.

14. Carl Brenner, Statement to the U.S. Senate Committee on Labor and Human Resources, U.S. Senate, Aug. 5, 1993.

15. Sen. Howard M. Metzenbaum, D-OH, Hearing, Committee on Labor and Human Resources, U.S. Senate, Aug. 5, 1993.

16. Joseph J. Burrascano, Jr., "Current Problems in the Lyme Disease Field," Statement for the Hearing before the Committee on Labor and Human Resources, U.S. Senate, Aug. 5, 1993.

17. Allen C. Steere, "Statement on the Clinical Features, Diagnosis, and Treatment of Lyme Disease," Hearing before the Committee on Labor and Human Resources, U.S. Senate, Aug. 5, 1993.

18. Joseph J. Burrascano, Jr., Testimony before the Committee on Labor and Human Resources, U.S. Senate, Aug. 5, 1993.

19. Sen. Howard M. Metzenbaum, D.O.H. hearing, Committee on Labor and Human Resources, U.S. Senate, Aug. 5, 1993.

CHAPTER 19: THE MURRAYS

1. Oliver Sacks, *A Leg to Stand On* (New York: Simon & Schuster, 1984), pp. 171–72.

EPILOGUE

1. Norman Cousins, *Human Options* (New York: Norton, 1981), p. 218.

2. Richard J. Baron, "An Introduction to Medical Phenomenology: I Can't Hear You While I'm Listening," *Annals of Internal Medicine,* vol. 103 (1985), p. 609.

3. Gerald Weissmann, "Daumier and the Deer Tick," *Hospital Practice,* May 15, 1989, p. 199.

4. Elisabeth Kieffer, "The Illness You Can't Sleep Off," *Woman's Day,* March 1, 1990, p. 32.

5. Alan G. Barbour and Durland Fish, "The Biological and Social Phenomenon of Lyme Disease," *Science,* vol. 260 (1993), p. 1614.

6. Howard M. Spiro, *Doctors, Patients, and Placebos* (New Haven, Conn., and London: Yale University Press, 1986), pp. 28, 37.

7. Baron, op. cit., p. 610.

8. Eric Cassell, "The Nature of Suffering and the Goals of Medicine," *New England Journal of Medicine,* vol. 306 (1982), p. 639.

9. Oliver Sacks, *The Man Who Mistook His Wife For a Hat and Other Clinical Tales* (New York: Simon & Schuster, 1981, 1983, 1984, 1985, p. viii.

10. Selig Greenberg, *The Troubled Calling* (Toronto: Macmillan, 1965) p. 15.

11. Martina Ziska, (medical director, The Lyme Foundation), "Lyme Disease: State of the Art with an Emphasis on Neurologic Manifestations,"

introductory speech at the 1994 Annual International Lyme Disease
Scientific Conference, Stamford, Conn., April 22 and 23, 1994.

AFTERWORD
1.   William H. McNeill, *Plaques and Peoples* (Garden City, N.Y.: Anchor
Books, 1976), p. 257.

PERMISSIONS AND ACKNOWLEDGMENTS

Grateful acknowledgment is made to the following for permission to reprint previously published material:

Annals of Internal Medicine: Excerpts reproduced with permission from:
1. Dedra Buchwald et al., "A Chronic Illness Characterized by Fatigue, Neurologic and Immunologic Disorders, and Active Human Herpesvirus Type 6 Infection," 1992, 116: 103–13.
2. Allen C. Steere, M.D., et al., "Antibiotic Therapy in Lyme Disease," 1980, 93:1, 1–8.
3. Richard J. Baron, "An Introduction to Medical Phenomenology: I Can't Hear You While I'm Listening," 1985, 103:4, 609.

Annals of Neurology: Excerpt from *"Borrelia burgdorferi* Infection in the Chronic Fatigue Syndrome" by Patricia K. Coyle and Lauren Krupp, 1990, 28:243–44, reprinted with permission from *Annals of Neurology.*

Doubleday, Inc. Excerpt from *Plagues and Peoples* (Doubleday, 1976) by William H. McNeill. Reprinted by permission of Doubleday, a division of Bantam Doubleday Dell Publishing Group, Inc., and by Gerald McCauley Agency, Inc. © 1976 by William H. McNeill.

Foot and Ankle: Excerpt from "Foot and Ankle Disorders Resulting from Lyme Disease" by J. Faller, F. Thomson, and W. Hamilton, 1991, 11:4, 236–38. Reprinted by permission of Williams and Wilkins.

Harper and Row Publishers Inc.: Excerpt from *An Imagined World* by June Goodfield (Harper & Row, 1981). Reprinted by permission of Georges Borchardt, Inc., and A. P. Watt Ltd.

Henry Holt & Co., Inc.: Excerpt from *Coping with Lyme Disease, A Practical Guide to Dealing with Diagnosis and Treatment* by Denise Lang with Derrick DeSilva, Jr. Reprinted by permission of Henry Holt & Co., Inc. All rights reserved. Published in Canada by Fitzhenry & Whiteside Ltd., 91 Granton Drive, Richmond Hill, Ontario L4B 2N5.

Hospital Practice: Excerpt from "Daumier and the Deer Tick" by Gerald Weissmann, M.D., Reprinted by permission of *Hospital Practice* (1989, 24:5,199).

Houghton Mifflin Co.: Excerpt from *Silent Spring* by Rachel Carson. Copyright © 1962 by Rachel L. Carson, renewed 1990 by Roger Christie. Reprinted by permission of Houghton Mifflin Co. and of Frances Collin, Trustee. All rights reserved.

The Journal of the American Medical Association: Permission granted to reprint excerpts of the following articles from *The Journal of the American Medical Association:*
1. Francis Weld Peabody, M.D., "The Care of the Patient," 1927, 88: 877–82.
2. George E. Ehrlich, M.D., "This Is the Decade That Is: Rheumatology," 1980, 243:2213.
3. Stephen B. Thacker et al., "The Surveillance of Infectious Diseases," 1983, 249:1181,1182.
4. Allen C. Steere, M.D., et al., "The Overdiagnosis of Lyme Disease," 1993, 269: 1812–16.
5. Joseph J. Burrascano, Jr., M.D. Letter to the editor re the overdiagnosis of Lyme disease, 1993, 270:2682.
6. Martha Kramer, letter to the editor re the overdiagnosis of Lyme disease, 1993, 270:2683.
7. Alan MacDonald, M.D., letter to the editor, 1986, 256:2195.

Alfred A. Knopf, Inc.: Excerpt from *Journey* by Robert Massie, Suzanne Massie, and Robert

Massie, Jr. Copyright © 1973, 1975. Reprinted by permission of Alfred A. Knopf, Inc.

MacMillan Co.: Excerpt from *The Troubled Calling: Crisis in the Medical Establishment* by Selig Greenberg, M.D. Copyright the MacMillan Co. N.Y. Collier-MacMillan Canada Ltd., Toronto, Ontario. 1965. (All rights reserved).

Maryland Medical Journal: Excerpt from "Lyme Disease" by Judith Mensch. *MD. Med. J.* 1985;34:692. Reprinted by permission.

Medicine: Excerpt from "Neurological Abnormalities of Lyme Disease" by Louis Reik, Jr., M.D. (*Medicine* 58:4, 281–94). Reprinted with permission of Williams and Wilkins.

The Merck Manual: Excerpt from *The Merck Manual of Diagnosis and Therapy,* Edition 12, p. 1470, edited by David N. Holvey. Copyright 1972 by Merck & Co., Inc., Rahway, N.J. Used with permission.

Milwaukee Journal Sentinal: Excerpt from a special report on Lyme disease by Neil D. Rosenberg, July 1, 1990. Reprinted by permission of *The Milwaukee Journal Sentinal.*

The New England Journal of Medicine: Permission granted to excerpt information appearing in the *NEJM:*

1. Eric Cassell. M.D. "The Nature of Suffering and the Goals of Medicine," 306:639. 1982.

2. Edward Harris, Jr. "Lyme Disease—Success for Academia and the Community," 308:740–42. 1983.

3. Eric Logigian et al. "Chronic Neurological Manifestations of Lyme Disease," 323:1438–43. 1990.

4. Ilona S. Szer et al. "The Long-term Course of Lyme Arthritis in Children," 325:159. 1991.

5. Polly Murray. "The Hypochondriacal Patient," 305:895. 1981. Massachusetts Medical Society. Reprinted by permission of the *NEJM.*

The New York Times: Permission to excerpt the following articles:

1. "Mystery of Lyme Disease Is Believed Solved" by Jane Brody. Nov. 18, 1982.

2. "A Road Atlas to Lyme Disease and Other Ills" by Nick Ravo. April 18, 1989.

3. "Name That Disease" by William Safire. June 2, 1991.

4. "Increase in Lyme Cases Creates a Mystery" by Elisabeth Rosenthal. March 21, 1991.

5. "Radical New View of Role of Menstruation" by Natalie Angier. Sept. 21. 1993.

Copyright © 1982/89/91/93 by the New York Times Company. Reprinted by permission.

W. W. Norton & Co.: Excerpts from *Anatomy of an Illness, The Healing Heart,* and *Human Options* by Norman Cousins reprinted with a permission from W. W. Norton & Company, Inc.

Rutgers University Press: Excerpt from *The Mirage of Health* by Rene Dubos. Copyright © 1959 by Rene Dubos. Copyright © 1987 by Rutgers, The State University. Reprinted by permission of Rutgers University Press.

Science: Permission granted to reprint excerpts from the following *Science* articles:

1. "Furor at Lyme Disease Conference" by Marcia Barinaga (256:1384).

2. "The Biological and Social Phenomenon of Lyme Disease" by Alan G. Barbour and Durland Fish (260:1614).

Copyright 1992/93 American Association for the Advancement of Science.

Scribner: Excerpts reprinted with the permission of Scribner, an imprint of Simon & Schuster, Inc., from *In Search of the Sun* by Henrietta Aladjem and Peter H. Schur, M.D. Copyright © 1972 Henrietta Aladjem; copyright © 1988 Henrietta Aladjem and Peter H. Schur.

Simon & Schuster, Inc.:

1. Excerpt from *A Leg to Stand On* by Oliver Sacks. Copyright © 1984 by Oliver Sacks, reprinted by permission of Simon & Schuster, Inc.

2. Excerpt from *The Man Who Mistook His Wife for a Hat* by Oliver Sacks. Copyright 1970, 1981, 1983, 1984, 1985 by Oliver Sacks, reprinted by permission of Simon & Schuster, Inc.

Thieme Medical Publishers Inc.: Excerpt from *Lyme Disease and the Nervous System* by Louis Reik, Jr., M.D. (p. 91, 1991). Reprinted by permission of Thieme Medical Publishers, Inc.

University of Chicago Press: Excerpt from *The Structure of Scientific Revolutions*, Second Edition, by Thomas S. Kuhn reprinted by permission of:
The University of Chicago Press. Chicago 60637.
The University of Chicago Press Ltd., London © 1962, 1970 by the University of Chicago. All rights reserved.

University of Southern California Press: Excerpt from *Lupus Erythematosus*, Second Edition. Edmund L. Dubois, editor. Reprinted with permission of the University of Southern California Press, Los Angeles, Calif. Copyright, University of Southern California, 1974. All rights reserved.

Viking Penguin: Excerpt from "Your Very Good Health" from *The Lives of a Cell* by Lewis Thomas. Used by permission of Viking Penguin, a division of Penguin Books USA Inc.

The Wall Street Journal: Excerpt from "Fate Seemed to Have a Gerstner in Mind for Top Job at IBM" by Michael W. Miller. Reprinted by permission of *The Wall Street Journal*, © 1993 Dow Jones & Company, Inc. All Rights Reserved Worldwide.

Yale University Press: Excerpt from *Man Adapting* by Rene Dubos reprinted with permission of Yale University Press (New Haven and London, 1965).
Excerpt from *Doctors, Patients, and Placebos* by Howard M. Spiro, M.D., reprinted with permission of Yale University Press (New Haven and London, 1986).

INDEX